12/07

REFERENCE

Form 178 rev. 01-07

D1377564

CONTEMPORARY Black Biography

ISSN-1058-1316

CONTEMPORARY

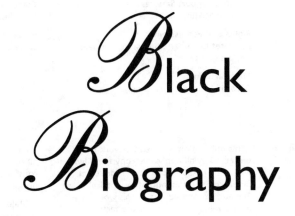

Profiles from the International Black Community

Volume 60

Detroit • New York • San Francisco • New Haven, Conn. • Waterville, Maine • London

Contemporary Black Biography, Volume 60

Sara and Tom Pendergast

Project Editor
Pamela M. Kalte

Image Research and Acquisitions
Leitha Etheridge-Sims

Editorial Support Services
Nataliya Mikheyeva

Rights and Permissions
Margaret Chamberlain-Gaston, Jacqueline Key, Lisa Kincade

Manufacturing
Dorothy Maki, Cynde Bishop

Composition and Prepress
Mary Beth Trimper, Tracey L. Matthews

Imaging
Lezlie Light

ISBN 13: 978-0-7876-7932-3
ISBN 10: 0-7876-7932-1
ISSN 1058-1316

This title is also available as an e-book.
eISBN 13: 978-1-4144-2919-9
eISBN-10: 1-4144-2919-3
Please contact your Thomson Gale sales representative for ordering information.

Printed in the United States of America
10 9 8 7 6 5 4 3 2 1

Advisory Board

Emily M. Belcher
General and Humanities Reference Librarian
Firestone Library, Princeton University

Dr. Alton Hornsby, Jr.
Professor of History
Morehouse College

Ernest Kaiser
Editor, Contributor
Retired Librarian, Schomburg Center for Research in Black
Culture

Dr. Ronald Woods
Director, Afro-American Studies Program
Eastern Michigan University

Contents

Introduction

Contemporary Black Biography provides informative biographical profiles of the important and influential persons of African heritage who form the international black community: men and women who have changed today's world and are shaping tomorrow's. *Contemporary Black Biography* covers persons of various nationalities in a wide variety of fields, including architecture, art, business, dance, education, fashion, film, industry, journalism, law, literature, medicine, music, politics and government, publishing, religion, science and technology, social issues, sports, television, theater, and others. In addition to in-depth coverage of names found in today's headlines, *Contemporary Black Biography* provides coverage of selected individuals from earlier in this century whose influence continues to impact on contemporary life. *Contemporary Black Biography* also provides coverage of important and influential persons who are not yet household names and are therefore likely to be ignored by other biographical reference series. Each volume also includes listee updates on names previously appearing in *CBB*.

Designed for Quick Research and Interesting Reading

- **Attractive page design** incorporates textual subheads, making it easy to find the information you're looking for.

- **Easy-to-locate data sections** provide quick access to vital personal statistics, career information, major awards, and mailing addresses, when available.

- **Informative biographical essays** trace the subject's personal and professional life with the kind of in-depth analysis you need.

- **To further enhance your appreciation** of the subject, most entries include photographic portraits.

- **Sources for additional information** direct the user to selected books, magazines, and newspapers where more information on the individuals can be obtained.

Helpful Indexes Make It Easy to Find the Information You Need

Contemporary Black Biography includes cumulative Nationality, Occupation, Subject, and Name indexes that make it easy to locate entries in a variety of useful ways.

Available in Electronic Formats

Diskette/Magnetic Tape. Contemporary Black Biography is available for licensing on magnetic tape or diskette in a fielded format. Either the complete database or a custom selection of entries may be ordered. The database is available for internal data processing and nonpublishing purposes only. For more information, call (800) 877-GALE.

On-line. Contemporary Black Biography is available on-line through Mead Data Central's NEXIS Service in the NEXIS, PEOPLE and SPORTS Libraries in the GALBIO file and Gale's Biography Resource Center.

Disclaimer

Contemporary Black Biography uses and lists websites as sources and these websites may become obsolete.

We Welcome Your Suggestions

The editors welcome your comments and suggestions for enhancing and improving *Contemporary Black Biography*. If you would like to suggest persons for inclusion in the series, please submit these names to the editors. Mail comments or suggestions to:

The Editor

Contemporary Black Biography

Thomson Gale

27500 Drake Rd.

Farmington Hills, MI 48331-3535

Phone: (800) 347-4253

Jenoyne Adams

(?)—

Author, dancer, literary agent

Jenoyne Adams's first novel—the bestselling *Resurrecting Mingus*—was acclaimed by critics. A poet, journalist, and actress, Adams was also principal dancer with the West African troupe Abalaye, as well as a literary agent for the New York firm of Levine/Greenberg.

Planned to Become a Lawyer

Jenoyne Adams was born and raised in San Bernardino County, California, the daughter of Bertha Dejan and Virgil Adams. She spent her early years in the black projects of San Bernardino, where she was often hospitalized due to complications from her premature birth. Her parents separated when she was quite young. At the age of 11, Adams went to live full time with her father, a construction foreman. Her father kept her supplied with books. Adams was determined to become a lawyer, like the heroine of her first novel, and she had a high-school internship with a corporation. However she began writing and reciting poetry, sharing her poems only with her sister and a few close friends.

At California State University at Fullerton, Adams majored in political science with an emphasis in African-American studies. She achieved fluency in Spanish at University of Malaga in Malaga, Spain, for which she received a certificate. As a journalist, Adams wrote for the *Precinct Reporter*, the major black newspaper in San Bernardino County, and the *Tri-County Bulletin*, an Orange County weekly.

Adams spoke to the Indianapolis *Recorder* about *Resurrecting Mingus* in 2001: "This book came to me in a reoccurring dream, though at the time I thought it was a reoccurring nightmare. I had no intentions of becoming a writer. My goal was to become a corporate lawyer. The dream started occurring in such a heavy rotation, it felt like it was drowning out the rest of my life. I became a freelance journalist to pacify it, but that didn't work. One Saturday morning at 5 a.m. I gave in. I figured if I wrote it down it would go away. It didn't and that morning began the rest of my life."

Published Resurrecting Mingus

While she worked on her novel Adams held a full-time job and sang in her church choir. She met Michael Datcher on a blind date after talking to him on the telephone for a month. They had much in common. Like Adams, Datcher was a journalist and poet; he was also an English professor at Loyola Marymount University. He ran a weekly poetry workshop at the World Stage in Leimert Park in South Los Angeles, and he was writing a book. Datcher proposed to Adams in February of 1997 with a seven-page poem delivered at the World Stage. For a wedding gift, he supported her for a year so she could finish her novel. In the end, it took her another 18 months of writing and revising. The novel was rejected numerous times and she revised again. However in the end Datcher's agent sold it to the highest bidder. Dominick Anfuso, vice president and senior editor at the Free Press, told Lynell George of the *Los Angeles Times*: "She showed signs of real

At a Glance . . .

Born Jenoyne Adams in San Bernardino, CA; married Michael Datcher, 1997. *Education:* California State University, Fullerton, studied political science and African-American studies; University of Malaga, Malaga, Spain, certificate of fluency in Spanish. *Religion:* Christian.

Career: *Precinct Reporter*, San Bernardino County, CA, journalist, 1990s; *TriCounty Bulletin*, Orange County, CA, journalist, 1990s; Los Angeles, CA, freelance journalist, poet, novelist, actress, dancer, 1990s–; writing workshop leader, 2003(?)–; Levine Greenberg Literary Agency, Inc., Los Angeles, CA, associate agent, 2003(?)–; Voices in Harmony, Los Angeles, CA, writing consultant, 2006–.

Memberships: World Stage Anansi Writer's Workshop.

Awards: University of California, Los Angeles, Extension Writing Program Community Access, Scholar; PEN Center USA West Emerging Voices, Fellow, 1998.

Addresses: *Agent*—James Levine, Levine/Greenberg Literary Agency, 307 Seventh Avenue, Suite 2407, New York, NY 10001.

talent. There were just so many powerful themes. A professional black woman who is lost. Plus these sub-issues—biracial identity, alcoholism—it just worked on a variety of levels. Most of us are confused in our skin. I saw an audience for her, and it was broad. And I think she's got a great career ahead of her." Adams and Datcher had their first books published within weeks of each other.

Resurrecting Mingus became a bestseller. The narrator relates the story of Mingus Browning, and her black father and white mother tell their stories in their own voices. Mingus, who has always identified herself as black, finds her loyalties shifting from her father to her mother as her perceptions of the family change. Her father is astonished to find that his wife of 35 years, whom he has left for his secret black family, can go on without him: "maybe I shoulda been happy that she knew how to get along without me. I'da never thought it though. And that's what stole my thunder…All this time I've been knowing that she needed me. How was I supposed to know that I needed her too?…I respected her again. Maybe for the first time. She was standing

up for herself. And even though she was standing up against me, it felt all right." When Mingus makes the painful decision to leave her fiancé, he asks her: "What can't you do with me in your life?" Mingus answers: "Love myself. I've never done that. I've always relied on someone else to do it, even if they did it badly. I'd rather be with you than be with me and something's wrong with that." The *Chicago Defender* called *Resurrecting Mingus* "a stunning debut novel" by an author who has "the skill and courage to write about some of the most controversial issues today in an absorbing and compulsively readable manner."

Adams had trained as a dancer for many years. While she was finishing *Mingus*, she was accepted into the West African dance troupe Abalaye. Soon she had become one of their principle dancers. In 2004 she also began studying martial arts.

Wrote Selah's Bed

Adams told Renee Simms of *Eur Web:* "Whereas *Resurrecting Mingus* came to me in a series of dreams, similarly, *Selah's Bed* came to me during a series of day dreams. I just kept thinking about this couple—how they met young and had so much attraction to each other then real life, pregnancy and change pulls them so far apart that they barely recognize their connection and love for each other anymore." Adams wrote *Selah's Bed* over a two-year period when she was the primary caregiver for her mother who was suffering from a heart attack and adult respiratory distress syndrome. She wrote in the novel's acknowledgments: "I was living pieces of the story as I was writing it."

Selah's Bed is the sexually explicit story of a beautiful middle-aged black woman who has achieved success photographing naked men, but whose marriage to a minister suffers from her unfaithfulness and the demons that haunt her: memories of a rape and an abortion. Selah exudes confidence, which she claims to have learned from her mother, a prostitute whom she barely knew, and she is proud to be a big woman: "Sometimes a big girl with confidence could be too much for some people. They wanted to quiet her down and put her in her place…If anyone stared too hard or too long at her, she'd often go over to them and give them a whisper: 'Big ain't nev-va got betta then this,' and walk off bigger then she came." The story also compassionately confronts her grandmother's addiction to prescription drugs and subsequent Alzheimer's disease. *Selah's Bed* garnered mixed reviews.

Adams's poetry and prose were published in literary journals and anthologies, including books edited by Datcher. Adams was a writing consultant for Voices in Harmony, helping at-risk youth to write and produce socially relevant theater pieces. In 2002 Adams played the title character in Datcher's long one-act play "Silence." Adams and Datcher directed writing workshops together and promoted their books on joint book tours.

In her career as a literary agent, Adams's focused on literary and commercial fiction, narrative nonfiction, and women's issues. Her third book was scheduled for publication by Simon & Schuster in the summer of 2007.

Selected writings

Novels

Resurrecting Mingus: A Novel, Free Press, 2001.
Selah's Bed: A Novel, Free Press, 2003.

Poetry

"Out-of-Body Experience," in *Catch the Fire: A Cross-Generational Anthology of African-American Literature,* edited by Derrick I.M. Gilbert, Riverhead, 1998, p. 109.
"Next Time Take Flesh," in *Brown Sugar 2: Great One Night Stands–A Collection of Erotic Black Fiction,* edited by Carol Taylor, Washington Square, 2003.

Periodicals

"Black Feminist Redux," *Ms.,* Winter 2004/2005, pp. 87-88.

On-line

"Black Sunshine," *Poetry in the Windows,* www. arroyoartscollective.org/archive/poetry/poems3/adams.html (January 24, 2007).

Sources

Books

Datcher, Michael, "The Gift," in *What Makes A Man: 22 Writers Imagine a Future,* edited by Rebecca Walker, Riverhead, 2004, pp. 8-16.
Datcher, Michael, *Raising Fences: A Black Man's Love Story,* Riverhead, 2001.

Periodicals

Chicago Defender, April 16, 2002, p. 11.
Essence, November 2005, p. 152.
Library Journal, February 15, 2001, p. 198.
Los Angeles Times, February 20, 2001, p. E1.
Recorder (Indianapolis, IN), February 2, 2001, p. C1.

On-line

"Black History Month Author Roundtable," *Authors on the Web,* www.authorsontheweb.com/features/0302-bhm/bhm-authors.asp (January 24, 2007).
"A Conversation with Writer Jenoyne Adams," *Eur Web,* www.eurweb.com/printable.cfm?id=9353 (February 21, 2007).
"Interview with Jenoyne Adams," *Bill Thompson's Eye on Books,* www.eyeonbooks.com/cover.php?ISBn=0684873532 (January 24, 2007).
"Jenoyne Adams," *Contemporary Authors Online,* www.galenet.galegroup.com/servlet/BioRC (December 26, 2006).

—Margaret Alic

Lucile L. Adams-Campbell

1953—

Epidemiologist

Dr. Lucile L. Adams-Campbell was the first black American woman to earn a PhD in epidemiology. In 1995 she became director of the Howard University Cancer Center (HUCC), the only black woman to head a cancer institute. Her groundbreaking research focused on racially-based health disparities, women's health issues, and cancer prevention and control among blacks. She published more than 100 peer-reviewed research papers and was a strong advocate for more federal funding for cancer research at minority institutions and for research studies that included blacks and other minorities.

Studied Cardiovascular Disease in Blacks

Lucile Lauren Adams was born on December 30, 1953, in Washington, D.C., the daughter of David Adams, a linguist and accountant, and Florence Adams, a teacher. Lucile knew from an early age that she wanted to be a scientist. She majored in chemical engineering at Drexel University in Philadelphia for four years, including apprenticeships at the Naval Ship Research and Development Center in Annapolis, Maryland, and in Norfolk, Virginia. However she switched to biology, earning her bachelor's degree in 1977 and her master's degree in biomedical sciences in 1979. While teaching undergraduate calculus Adams-Campbell earned her doctorate at the University of Pittsburgh Graduate School of Public Health with a dissertation on behavioral contributions to high blood pressure (hypertension) in blacks. She remained at the University of Pittsburg as a post-doctoral researcher and instructor until 1987, when she became a senior research scientist at the New England Research Institute.

In 1990 Adams-Campbell joined the faculty of Howard University in Washington, D.C. That year she published a report demonstrating that college-age black women were twice as likely as their white counterparts to be overweight. Although her research focused on the relationship between obesity and cardiovascular disease, at Howard she also began collaborating with cancer researchers. A grant from the National Cancer Institute (NCI) enabled her to embark on an epidemiological study of breast-cancer susceptibility genes in blacks.

As director of the HUCC, the only cancer center at a historically black university, Adams-Campbell greatly increased the center's faculty and funding. She focused the center's research on the cancers that most affect blacks–breast, prostate, and gastrointestinal. Adams-Campbell outlined her accomplishments for *Contemporary Black Biography (CBB)*: "We have substantially increased external grant support; constructed important bridges between basic science and bench scientists in cancer research and population science to accomplish our goals; we have made major community outreach efforts, including health screening for underserved populations, in an effort to reduce disparities in medical outcomes."

Born Lucile Lauren Adams on December 30, 1953, in Washington, DC; married Thomas Campbell; children: two. *Education:* Drexel University, BS, 1977, MS, 1979; University of Pittsburgh, PhD, epidemiology, 1983.

Career: University of Pittsburgh, engineering instructor, 1980-84, NIH Cardiovascular Trainee, 1983-85, epidemiology instructor, 1985-87, adjunct professor, 1995–; New England Research Institute, Watertown, MA, senior research scientist, 1987-1990; Howard University, Washington, DC, Department of Physiology and Biophysics, graduate associate professor, 1990-92, psychology professor, 1995–, College of Medicine, Division of Cardiovascular Diseases, associate professor of medicine, 1990-91, Division of Epidemiology and Cancer Control, associate professor of medicine, 1991-94, professor of medicine, 1994–, professor of community health and family practice, 1995-2001, 2005–, HUCC, acting director, 1994-95, director, 1995–; Uniformed Services University of Health Sciences, Bethesda, MD, adjunct clinical assistant professor of medical and clinical psychology, 1997-99; Johns Hopkins University School of Medicine, Baltimore, MD, visiting professor of oncology, 2001–.

Selected memberships: American Association for Cancer Research, committee member and chair, director; American Cancer Society, committee member; American College of Epidemiology, committee member, director; American Heart Association, committee member; NCI, committee member and chair.

Selected awards: Drexel University, Ewaugh Finney Fields Award, 1984; University of Pittsburgh, Distinguished Alumni Award, 1995, Significant Contributor to Public Health, 2000; U.S. Food and Drug Administration, Deputy Commissioner Community Service Award, 1998; Howard University, Distinguished Faculty Author Awards, 2001-06; American Association for Cancer Research, Service Award, 2004.

Addresses: *Office*—Howard University Cancer Center, 2041 Georgia Ave NW, Washington, DC, 20060-0001.

Initiated the Black Women's Health Study

In January of 1995 Adams-Campbell and her co-investigator, Dr. Lynn Rosenberg of Boston University Medical School, mailed 16-page questionnaires to 400,000 black women across the country. This marked the beginning of the largest and most expensive long-term study ever of black American women's health. Adams-Campbell needed the resources and experience of Boston University and the National Institutes of Health (NIH) needed Adams-Campbell to gain the trust of the black community. She told Tamara Jeffries of *Essence* in 2006: "We have to look at Black women's health from a different perspective. It entails a litany of things, and family history, environment and psychological factors are important, including access to fresh fruits and vegetables. You have to look at the whole experience." Adams-Campbell was especially interested in factors responsible for the higher incidence of breast cancer in younger black women as compared with white women of the same age.

Among the Black Women's Health Study (BWHS) findings: women who exercised regularly had less depression and obesity and were at reduced risk for breast and colon cancers; women living in poorer neighborhoods were more likely to have high blood pressure than those living in more affluent neighborhoods; women who had used hormone-replacement therapy for at least five years to combat symptoms of menopause appeared to be at higher risk for breast cancer; severely overweight women were more than 20 times more likely to develop diabetes; earlier onset of menopause in black women was strongly associated with smoking and inversely associated with obesity and the use of oral contraceptives; and the number of black women having mammograms to screen for breast cancer was increasing. The breast-cancer findings were particularly significant. Adams-Campbell told *Essence*: "This used to be viewed as a middle-class White woman's disease. We weren't educated about how breast cancer affected us or what we could do about it. Now we're finally getting the message, but we still need to work on increasing our rates of treatment." In 2004 Adams-Campbell and coworkers demonstrated that the usual model for predicting breast-cancer risk underestimated the risk in black women.

Adams-Campbell told *CBB* that the BWHS "has made major contributions to science in general. It is the first time that this type of study has been undertaken in black women and followed prospectively for valid answers and to look at the factors involved in addressing diseases, such as lupus, sickle-cell disease, and hypertension, that truly impact blacks more than other groups, and to do this across socioeconomic and educational groups." The BWHS was ongoing as of 2007.

Recruited Blacks for Clinical Trials

In 1996, the year her father died from prostate cancer, Adams-Campbell organized a community symposium to promote early screening for the disease. She was involved in a 1999 study that demonstrated that nutrition home-study materials improved cholesterol and blood pressure levels in black adults with widely differing literacy skills. She told the *Washington Informer*: "What we discover in the lab must be applicable to the community we serve. If we do everything behind closed walls, no one will ever know what it is that we do. We must go from the bench to the bedside to the community."

Adams-Campbell was a principal investigator (PI) for the Minority Based Community Clinical Oncology Program, funded by the NCI to recruit blacks into clinical trials. She served as co-PI of a comparative clinical trial of Tamoxifen and Raloxifene for the prevention of breast cancer in postmenopausal women at increased risk of developing the disease. She was also co-PI for a trial of selenium and vitamin E in preventing prostate cancer in older men and a phase III trial comparing a nicotine inhaler and/or Buproprion for smoking cessation and relapse prevention. Adams-Campbell told *CBB:* "I have tried to make certain that Howard University is involved in clinical trials, and from the point-of-views of the community, patients, and physicians, we are making major progress in that area. We have been demystifying clinical trials as a way to strive for having all individuals participate in cancer clinical trials."

Adams-Campbell's involvement in African medical research began in 1992 when, as a board member of the Association of Black Cardiologists, she chaired the American-African International Collaborative Scientist Symposium in Zimbabwe. She maintained research collaborations and partnerships with several African and Jamaican organizations and universities. Her African research focused on hypertension and clinical trials for prostate cancer treatment

Adams-Campbell served on the editorial boards and as a reviewer for scientific journals and on numerous international, national, and local committees. She was an outspoken critic of the NCI, accusing it of failing to recruit minorities for research studies and accusing its grant reviewers of bias against minorities. As of 2007 her research focused on the combination of genetics, behavior, and lifestyle that contributes to the disproportionate numbers of breast cancer cases among blacks.

Selected writings

Periodicals

"The Black Man's Challenge: The Prostate Cancer

Dilemma," *Journal of the National Medical Association,* Vol. 90, No. 11, 1998.
"A New Vision for the 21st Century," *Journal of the National Medical Association,* Vol. 91, 1999, pp. 133-136.
(With others) "Osteoporosis Prevention, Diagnosis, and Therapy," *Journal of the American Medical Association,* February 14, 2001, pp. 785-795.
(With others) "Estrogen Plus Progestin and Colorectal Cancer in Postmenopausal Women," *New England Journal of Medicine,* Vol. 350, 2004 pp. 991-1004.
(With others) "A Prospective Study of Female Hormone Use and Breast Cancer Among Black Women," *Archives of Internal Medicine*, April 10, 2006, p. 760.

On-line

"Office of the Director: Strategic Framework for Action," *Howard University Cancer Center,* www.med.howard.edu/hucc/office_of_director.htm (December 18, 2006).

Sources

Periodicals

Black Issues in Higher Education, March 23, 1995, p. 26; March 18, 1999, p. 30.
Essence, March 2006, pp. 101-103.
New Pittsburgh Courier, April 5-11, 2006, p. B4.
Washington Informer, October 2, 1996, p. 1.

On-line

"Lucile L. Adams-Campbell. Ph.D.," *The African American Women's Institute, Howard University,* http://ora.howard.edu/centers/aawi/campbell.htm (January 20, 2007).
"Lucile L. Adams-Campbell, Ph.D.," *Howard University,* www.howard.edu/newsroom/experts/bio/Adams-Campbell.htm (January 20, 2007).

Other

Additional information for this profile was obtained through an interview with Dr. Lucile L. Adams-Campbell on January 25, 2007.

—Margaret Alic

Mara Brock Akil

1970—

Television producer, screenwriter

Akil, Mara Brock, photograph. Amanda Edwards/Getty Images.

Mara Brock Akil had planned to become a journalist when she was introduced to the theater in the form of a comic skit in a college show. The more she learned about performance and production, the more she became convinced that the kind of work she wanted to do was better suited to the stage and screen than the press. Akil wanted to create work that expressed her own opinions and ideas, and with the confidence and persistence she had learned from her strong-willed mother, she began to pursue a career in television.

Mara Brock was born on May 27, 1970, in Los Angeles, California. When she was eight years old, her mother, Joan Demeter, divorced her husband and took her three children to live in Kansas City, Missouri. Determined to improve her and her children's lives, Demeter took a secretarial job at Morton Labs and began studying computer programming so that she could work her way up to a better job. She eventually became proprietor of her own business, inspiring her daughter Mara to believe that hard work and vision could lead to success.

By the time she was 30, Akil had built a successful career in one of the most competitive businesses in the world. Moreover, she had introduced her own groundbreaking new television series, *Girlfriends.* The show climbed quickly to the top of the ratings, involving an increasingly large audience in the lives of its main characters: four dynamic African-American women friends. However, Akil has never been content simply to entertain. All of her productions have delved into important social issues, from class differences to sexually transmitted disease, drawing audiences in by making her characters real human beings with real problems.

After her graduation from Kansas City's Raytown South High School, Akil entered Northwestern University in Chicago, Illinois, to study journalism. There she had her first theatrical experience when she wrote and performed in a comedy skit for a show at the Black Student Union. Njoki McElroy, a professor in the performance studies department, saw Akil's performance and offered her the lead role in a Northwestern production of a play called *The Colored Museum.*

Akil quickly became more interested in the production side of the theater than in acting. During her senior year, she attended a meeting of the Organization of

At a Glance . . .

Born Mara Brock on May 27, 1970, in Los Angeles, CA; married Salim Akil, 1999; children: Yasin. *Education:* Northwestern University, BA, journalism, 1992.

Career: FOX, *South Central*, writer, 1994-96; UPN, *Moesha*, writer, producer, 1996-99; WB, *The Jamie Foxx Show*, supervising producer, 1996-99; UPN and CW, *Girlfriends*, creator, executive producer, 2000–; CW, *The Game*, creator, writer, executive producer, 2006–.

Selected memberships: Delta Sigma Theta Sorority; Center Theater Group, board member.

Selected awards: The Media Project, Sexual Health in Entertainment (SHINE) Awards, 1999, 2001.

Addresses: *Office*—c/o theOffice, 256 26th Street, Suite 101, Santa Monica, CA 90402-2524.

Black Screenwriters where she met author, screenwriter, and artist Delle Chatman, who taught at Northwestern. Akil soon joined Chatman's screenwriting class, further fueling her determination to be part of the theater.

Upon her graduation from college in 1992, Akil found she had no real wish to look for a job in journalism. She took a job as assistant manager at a Chicago GAP store and looked for a way to begin her career in the entertainment field. Her chance came when a film called *With Honors*, directed by Alek Keshishian, began filming scenes in Chicago. Akil auditioned and was given a speaking part. This experience convinced her that she wanted to work in film and television, and she moved to Los Angeles to build her career.

Once in the center of the entertainment industry, she was aided in her job search by another Northwestern alumni, filmmaker Jerry Zeismer. She soon landed a job as a production assistant, and, within a year, was working as a writer trainee on the FOX network show, *South Central*, a half-hour comedy-drama about a working-class, African-American family in Los Angeles.

The producers of *South Central* appreciated Akil's ideas and talent and hired her as a writer on the UPN network situation comedy, *Moesha*, about an African-American teenager. Akil worked on *Moesha* for four years, eagerly learning as much as she could about

every aspect of television creation and production. She produced some episodes of the show, including one called "Birth Control," which explored issues of teen sexuality, and for which she won a Sexual Health in Entertainment (SHINE) award from The Media Project. While working on *Moesha*, Akil also began to work as supervising producer for a WB sitcom called *The Jamie Foxx Show*, starring Foxx as a would-be actor working in a Los Angeles hotel.

In 1999, when Akil was only 29, she had already impressed network executives so much that they offered her the chance to create her own half-hour comedy show about African-American women. Though she would be the youngest black woman producer in Hollywood, Akil met the challenge with enthusiasm. The result was *Girlfriends*, which debuted on UPN in 2000. The show focuses on the lives of four close women friends: Joan, played by Tracee Ellis Ross; Toni, played by Jill Marie Jones; Lynn, played by Persia White; and Maya, played by Golden Brooks. (After the 2006 season, Jones left the show.) It is, in many ways, a tribute to the strong, caring, and funny black women that Akil herself has known.

She named the show's central character, the driven, successful, and inwardly vulnerable Joan, after her mother, and was determined to present each woman, her life, and her relationships in a complex and nonstereotypical way. She hired a diverse staff of writers and set to work to create a different kind of comedy. "Every artist is a politician inside," she told Jenny Hontz in an interview in *Northwestern Magazine*, "I have an agenda." That agenda was to highlight the social issues that were important to Akil and to show how they affect the lives of real people. While always presented with sharp wit and affectionate humor, *Girlfriends* frequently explored serious subjects, from class to addiction to women's health issues. The show earned Akil another SHINE award for an episode titled about sexually transmitted diseases.

Girlfriends quickly became one of UPN's biggest successes, remaining in production for more than six seasons and going into syndication on other networks as well. However, since television remains a very segregated area of U.S. life, while the show has consistently been among the most-watched programs among black viewers, it has ranked much lower among white viewers. In 2006, the CW network took over UPN, keeping *Girlfriends* in its prime time lineup.

Akil followed her success with *Girlfriends* with a spin-off called *The Game*. *The Game* features a racially mixed cast in a half-hour sitcom about professional athletes and the women in their lives. Though the show has not achieved the audience popularity or critical acclaim of *Girlfriends*, its young producer remains full of energy, optimism, and ideas.

In 1999, as she began work on *Girlfriends*, Akil married another young producer/director named Salim

Akil. In addition to starting a family together, the two also occasionally work together. Salim Akil has directed several episodes of *Girlfriends* and *The Game.*

Sources

Periodicals

Chicago Defender, October 6-October 8, 2006, pp. 10-11.

Essence, April 2001, p. 80; April 2004, p. 138.

Jet, November 1, 2004, p. 32.

Milwaukee Journal Sentinel, December 29, 2002.

New York Beacon, September 24, 2003, p. 27.

Variety, May 27, 2002, pp. S17-18.

On-line

"CW/My TV Stories: She's Got 'Game,'" *TV Barn: Kansas City Star,* http://blogs.kansascity.com/tvbarn/cwmy_tv/index.html (January 26, 2007).

"Dialogue: Mara Brock Akil," *Hollywood Reporter,* www.hollywoodreporter.com/hr/search/article_display.jsp?vnu_content_id=1000708461 (January 26, 2007).

"Girlfriend—with an Agenda, Spring 2004," *Northwestern Magazine,* www.northwestern.edu/magazine/northwestern/spring2004/features/coverstory/sidebar2.htm (January 26, 2007).

"Girlfriends for Life: Mara Brock Akil, Creator of UPN's Girlfriends, Shares with A&U's Chael Needle the Inside Scoop on the Show's HIV Story Lines and the State of Sexual Health on TV," *The Media Project,* www.themediaproject.com/news/itn/040103.htm (January 26, 2007).

—Tina Gianoulis

Mohammed Naseehu Ali

1971—

Writer

The Ghanaian-American writer Mohammed Naseehu Ali has gained wide attention for his short stories, many of them collected in the 2005 book *The Prophet of Zongo Street.* Ali's stories are sharply etched vignettes of urban life in his native Ghana—or of his adopted home, New York City. He has also authored several high-profile nonfiction pieces exploring the complexities of his own background as well as the experiences of Islamic immigrants in the United States in a time of conflict.

Ali was born in Kumasi, Ghana's second-largest city, in 1971. He grew up in a predominantly Islamic neighborhood called Zongo where most male children were given the first name of Mohammed and a middle name describing an attribute of Islam's founder and prophet; Mohammed Naseehu means Mohammed the Sincere One. Zongo, Ali told Eloi Minka of the *AfroToronto* Web site, was "a neighborhood full of characters," and from an early age he wanted to write about them. Ali was creating both music (he was a drummer and singer) and fiction by the time he was nine. When he came to the United States in 1988 to study, however, he began to face choices: his father, an emir, or king, of the members of the Hausa ethnic group in Kumasi, steered him toward the worlds of economics and finance, but the school that he attended, northern Michigan's Interlochen Arts Academy, was focused on creative fields.

Ali's father, Ali wrote in the *New York Times,* "didn't mince words in phone conversations reminding me that, although he had let me attend art school, music and dance were professions for praise singers and storytellers, not for people who had royal blood run-

ning through their veins." But Ali had been entranced by the multiplicity of musical forms that surrounded him at Interlochen—not only classical music but also the jazz of trumpeter Miles Davis and the blues of singer Skip James. During his senior year he had a difficult visit home to Kumasi, where the clash of expectations came into the open. For one thing, he was dressed in casual American hot-weather clothes: light pants and a T-shirt. "You have to stop wearing these rags and dress heavy and nice," Ali's aunt told him (as he recalled in the *Times*), "so people will know you are a true Yankee man."

"But more important," Ali wrote, "I had discovered individualism—the celebration of the self as the most important force of nature. This was in direct contradiction to the culture of the Ghanaian Muslim community, where the determination of an individual to excel was seen as an attempt to 'go beyond where God has placed you.' They were like the proverbial crabs that pull down the ones that seek to climb out of the box." Ali was discouraged by the chaos of Ghanaian life, by his mother's death in childbirth a few years before, by coolness of former friends. He returned to the United States and began to avoid situations that put him in touch with Ghana or with members of his own culture. A two-year stretch went by in which he had no contact with his family.

Ali enrolled at and then graduated from Bennington College in Vermont. He moved to Brooklyn, New York, settling in the Prospect Heights neighborhood, where he continued to work at his writing. His family arranged his marriage to a Hausa woman, but Ali ignored it until

At a Glance . . .

Born 1971 in Kumasi, Ghana; son of a Hausa king; moved to U.S., 1988; married; two children. *Education:* Graduated from Interlochen Arts Academy, Interlochen, MI; Bennington College, Bennington, VT. *Religion:* Islam.

Career: Writer, 2004–; contributor to such periodicals as *Mississippi Review, New Yorker,* and *New York Times.*

Awards: Quills Award nomination, Debut Author of the Year, for *The Prophet of Zongo Street,* 2006.

Addresses: *Home*—Brooklyn, NY. *Publisher*—Author Mail, c/o Amistad Press, 10 E. 53rd St., 7th floor, New York, NY 10022.

2000, when his father told him that he would never speak to him again unless it was face to face. He returned to Ghana, made amends with his family and married the woman to whom his father had engaged him. (The couple has had two children.) Shortly after the visit, his father died. Another trauma occurred on September 11, 2001. Ali was on a New York commuter train under the World Trade Center when a terrorist-piloted plane hit one of the twin towers. He was evacuated from the train and called his wife, but his phone went dead when a second plane hit. He joined the crowds running out of Lower Manhattan.

After these events, he lamented, the "Mohammed Ali" name he used in America began to inspire unease rather than pleased amusement. Strangers left hostile messages on Ali's answering machine. But Ali's writing career began to take a turn upward as his stories began to be published in such journals as the *Mississippi Review.* The appearance of Ali's story "Mallam Sile" in the April 11, 2005 issue of the *New Yorker* magazine marked his breakthrough. Funny and colorful, "Mallam Sile" told the story of a Ghanaian tea shop owner who has given up on the idea of marrying. His shop limps along, struggling financially because of his willingness to extend credit to non-paying customers. His business comes to life, however, when he marries a tough woman, Abeeba, who takes matters into her own hands.

Landing a spot in the *New Yorker,* Ali told Minka, "did more for me than the publication of my book," which followed three months later. That book featured other stories set in Ali's fictional but realistic Zongo Street, all of them tied together by a subtly sketched 14-year-old narrator who is a minor presence in many of them. Both the depiction of the narrator and the technique of introducing varied characters in a neighborhood setting were borrowed, Ali readily acknowledged, from the writing of Indo-Trinidadian writer V.S. Naipaul. "He is a huge part of why I tell stories," Ali explained to Minka. The specific model for Ali's book was a collection of Naipaul stories called *Miguel Street.*

Ali went beyond Naipaul, however, in transferring the settings of some of his stories to his new American homeland. "The True Aryan" describes a young African Web site designer and musician who tries to form a cross-cultural bond with an Armenian-American New York cabdriver. *The Prophet of Zongo Street* won positive reviews from, among others, Pam Houston of *O, The Oprah Magazine,* who called the book "a collection of rich and resonant stories, haunting and ultimately hopeful in their commitment to the truth." As he basked in the attention given his debut book publication, Ali was already looking to new work. He was committed to writing in English (English and French, he argued, belonged to Africans as well as to Europeans) and to representing the experiences of Africans abroad as well as of those in their own countries. One of the two novels on which Ali was at work in 2007 dealt with the subject of polygamy in West Africa. It was a phenomenon he knew well, for his own father had had many wives.

Selected writings

Books

The Prophet of Zongo Street (collected short stories), Amistad, 2005.

Sources

Periodicals

International Herald Tribune, August 20, 2005, p. 7.
New York Times, November 21, 2004, p. 6; September 17, 2005, p. A15.
O, The Oprah Magazine, August 2005, p. 146.

On-line

"Ali, Mohammed Naseehu," *Biography Resource Center,* http://galenet.galegroup.com/servlet/BioRC (February 25, 2007).
"The Prophet of Zongo Street," *AfroToronto,* www.afrotoronto.com/Articles/Nov05/NaseehuAliInterview.html (February 25, 2007).

—James M. Manheim

Wambui Bahati

1950(?)—

Performer, motivational writer and speaker

Wambui Bahati was a rising Broadway star when mental illness eclipsed her career. After a decade as a poverty-stricken single mother struggling with severe depression, Bahati resurrected herself as an inspirational performer. Her one-woman shows used music and humor to present hard facts about mental illness, domestic violence, and other issues to audiences nationwide. Under the title "Miss Inspiration" Bahati utilized Web sites to bring her motivational message to a wider audience.

Became a Successful Actress

Bahati was born John-Ann Washington, named after her father. In her one-woman musical play *Balancing Act,* Bahati recalled her childhood in Greensboro, North Carolina, at the center of the struggle for black civil rights. When she announced that she and her sister were marching with Jesse Jackson, her mother responded: "Before you start marching all over town for freedom, you better march in that kitchen and free those dishes." As a child she was active in community theater. During high school she taught acting workshops and directed children's plays for the Greensboro Parks and Recreation Department. However by the age of eight she was already experiencing both the highs and lows of bipolar disorder, sometimes called manic-depression. She told Brenda Alesii of *bp* magazine: "I was always uncomfortable, crying at the drop of a hat, experiencing severe depression. Then I would have laughing attacks. I was a loner, but good at camouflaging it. I was often the life of the party—

singing, dancing, and yet I'd go home and feel such sadness."

After graduating from high school in 1968 John-Ann Washington studied acting at New York University School of the Arts. One day she was walking the two blocks from her apartment to her dance class and found herself in Los Angeles with no recollection of how she got there. For four months she supported herself by babysitting before returning to New York, pretending as if nothing had happened.

At age 21 Washington made her professional theater debut in *Godspell* at Ford's Theater in Washington, D.C. She performed on Broadway in *Godspell* and *Jesus Christ Superstar* and in the national Broadway touring companies of *Two Gentlemen of Verona, Jesus Christ Superstar, The Wiz,* and *Don't Bother Me, I Can't Cope.* She also appeared in regional and stock productions of *The Magic Show, Godspell, Little Ham, Nunsense, Crowns,* and a musical version of *Gone With the Wind,* as well as various children's theater productions. In 1970s show business, Washington's often erratic behavior was barely noticeable. She was under treatment for depression, but didn't recognize that her highs—the feelings of floating and invincibility—were part of her disease.

Spiraled Downward

Washington's touring days ended with *The Wiz* in San Francisco in 1984 when her second daughter was born prematurely. She and her husband at the time settled

At a Glance . . .

Born John-Ann Washington in 1950(?), in Greens-boro, NC; changed her name to Wambui Bahati, 1995; divorced; daughters: Marie and Julie Blondina. *Education:* New York University School of the Arts, BMI Lehman Engel Musical Theatre, Clark Center of Performing Arts. *Religion:* Ordained non-denominational minister.

Career: Touring the United States, actress and singer, 1971-84; touring conference and college circuit, writer, producer, and performer of one-woman shows, 1998–; Miss Inspiration Productions, principal, 2001(?)–; "Beautiful Energies" Emotional Freedom Tech-niques practitioner, 2005(?)–.

Memberships: Actors Equity Association; Dramatist Guild; Greensboro Playwrights Forum; International Natural Healers Association.

Awards: North Carolina, President's Award; Toledo, Ohio, mayor's proclamation; Bennett College, Belle Ringer Image Award, 1998; Greensboro Commission on the Status of Women, Woman of Achievement Award, 1998; National Alliance for the Mentally Ill, Lionel Aldridge Award, 1999.

Addresses: *Web*—www.wambui-bahati.com.

with their children in San Rafael, California, but Wash-ington's mental state deteriorated. Following a divorce she moved back to New York with her children. Washington found work as a theater manager and as an assistant to Avery Brooks who was performing a one-man show about Paul Robeson. However she told Alesii, "I couldn't get myself together to go on audi-tions, I was dealing with two young children, everything was so difficult. We ended up on welfare." After several hospitalizations and a period of homelessness, Wash-ington and her daughters moved back to Greensboro in 1989, deciding it was better to be poor there than in New York. Doctors told her that she would spend the rest of her life in and out of institutions for the mentally ill.

Washington tried to work while her mother cared for the girls. However as she told Mark Burger of the *Winston-Salem Journal*, "It got to the point where I couldn't function. Just taking a shower became an event. My children were literally taking care of me."

The girls went to live with their father in New Jersey. In 1994 Washington was hospitalized following a suicide attempt. Her first day there, she was doing the other patients' hair and makeup, giving dance lessons, and, according to Penelope Green of the *New York Times*, "counseling the counselors." It was then that she was finally diagnosed with bipolar disorder.

Bahati told Green: "I hated my life, rotting in public housing, taking medications for my medications, and so I decide that I want to die. I've got the television on, 24/7, and in the background, getting on my very last nerve, is a Tony Robbins infomercial. The gall of him, I think, to take people's money and tell them he can fix their lives with some tapes—in four easy payments. I decide that before I go out, I'm going to prove this guy's a phony." She bought the tapes. "The main thing I heard from this guy is this: 'Whatever they say you have, that's not who you are.'"

Reinvented Herself as Wambui Bahati

Gradually Washington's life began to change. She returned to school, became a vegetarian, took up meditation, and attended group-therapy sessions. In 1995 she changed her name to Wambui Bahati, which means "singer of songs" and "my fortune is good" in Swahili. She began writing. She told Burger: "I've always heard people say, 'Write what you know.' I figured I knew me and I knew this illness…once I started talking about it, I started feeling good about it. People came up to me, sharing their stories and thanking me."

At the suggestion of her first black female therapist, Bahati wrote *Balancing Act*. It premiered in 1998 at the Greensboro Cultural Center. With a $15,000 grant from the A.J. Fletcher Foundation, Bahati took it on a 10-city tour for the North Carolina affiliate of the National Alliance for the Mentally Ill. Bahati told Cathy Gant-Hill of the Piedmont *News & Record:* "This is the only illness I know, where you're blamed for having the illness which then perpetuates the illness. I think people would rather say my relative has cancer or diabetes, than to say, 'Oh, my daughter has a mental illness.' That's sort of the reason I wrote the play." The show's success led to performances at conventions, confer-ences, and other events nationwide. Bahati had a new career.

Bahati created her second one-woman musical "I Am Domestic Violence" for a one-time performance at a YWCA in 1998. Word of the 35-minute program spread and over the following years she performed it many times. Bahati wrote the play "The Welfare Blues" for the Greensboro chapter of the National Organiza-tion for Women, whose members turned it into a traveling show. In 2002 she created "Who Cares?" for the Mental Health Partnership Steering Council Annual Meeting, to dramatize the relationship between mental illness and homelessness.

Formed Miss Inspiration Productions

In 2001 Bahati and her daughters moved into a Habitat for Humanity condominium in New York City, donating many hours of "sweat equity" in exchange for their home.

Through her company, Miss Inspiration Productions, Bahati wrote and produced custom songs, presentations, and performances on topical issues. These included "Live and In Person—It's Racial Injustice," "Didn't You See My Show: My Journey Through Manic Depression—and Back," "Don't Let a Breakdown Keep You Down," and "Reminding Your of Your Magnificence." Her on-line "Self-Power Store" sold self-improvement books and products. She became a practitioner of Gary Craig's Emotional Freedom Techniques to help clients with pain relief and overcoming fear of public speaking. On her Web sites Bahati published articles on a variety of motivational and self-help topics. In 2006 she began publishing an e-zine entitled *You Are Magnificent!*

In 2007 Bahati released a CD, *Crazy for Me*, describing her experiences with bipolar disorder. She also began facilitating "Celebration and Joy" workshops and seminars. These would last from an hour to a day and take place live, on-line, and via the telephone. Bahati was in the process of creating a series of new self-help tools for those living with bipolar disorder and their families and friends. She planned to relocate to Sedona, Arizona.

Selected works

Nonfiction

"Be the Star That You Are," *Inspiration-Motivation-Celebration,* www.inspiration-motivation-celebration.com/Be-the-Star-That-You-Are.html (February 7, 2007).
"Domestic Violence is Alive and Well," *Wambui Bahati,* www.wambui-bahati.com/Domestic-Violence-Article.html (February 7, 2007).
"Fear Be Gone," *Articles Factory,* www.articlesfactory.com/articles/self-help/fear-be-gone.html (February 7, 2007).
"How to Have a Great Day Every Day—Create an Attitude of Gratitude," *Inspiration-Motivation-Celebration,* www.inspiration-motivation-celebration.com/How-to-Have-a-Great-Day-Every-Day.html (February 7, 2007).
"9 Steps Toward Nontoxic Health and Beauty," *Inspiration-Motivation-Celebration,* www.inspiration-motivation-celebration.com/nontoxic-health-and-beauty.html (February 7, 2007).

"Miss Inspiration's 10 Tips for Relieving Depression," *Inspiration-Motivation-Celebration,* www.inspiration-motivation-celebration.com/Inspiration-Depression.html (February 7, 2007).
"Television Fast," *Inspiration-Motivation-Celebration,*www.inspiration-motivation-celebration.com/Television-Fast.html (January 26, 2007).

One-Woman Shows

Balancing Act—The Musical, 1998–.
I Am the Domestic Violence, 1998–.
Who Cares?, 1998–.

Plays

Godspell, touring Broadway production, 1971-84.
Jesus Christ Superstar, touring Broadway production, 1971-84.
The Wiz, American Theater Productions, 1977-79, 1983-84.

Recordings

Crazy for Me—How I Got Over Bipolar Disorder and Other Life Stuff, 2007.

Sources

Periodicals

bp, Winter 2005.
More, May 2005, pp. 114-115.
News & Record (Piedmont, NC), October 3, 1998, p. B1.
New York Times, April 4, 2004, p. 6.
Winston-Salem Journal (NC), May 16, 1999, p. E1.

On-line

"About Wambui Bahati," *Inspiration-Motivation-Celebration,* www.inspiration-motivation-celebration.com/WambuiBahati.html (February 7, 2007).
Crazy for Me, www.crazy-for-me.info/index.html (January 26, 2007).
"Custom Presentations," *Wambui Bahati,* www.wambui-bahati.com/Custom-Presentations.html (February 7, 2007).
"Emotional Freedom Techniques," *Inspiration-Motivation-Celebration,* www.inspiration-motivation-celebration.com/Emotional-Freedom-Techniques.html (February 7, 2007).
"Wambui Bahati 'Miss Inspiration,'" *Wambui Bahati,* www.wambui-bahati.com (January 26, 2007).

—Margaret Alic

Mary J. Blige

1971—

Singer, songwriter

Blige, Mary J., photograph. AP Images.

"Mary J. Blige has been called the inventor of New Jill Swing," Ron Givens wrote in *Stereo Review* in 1993. When the vocalist came to the public's attention the previous year, she became a magnet for the kind of superlatives music critics love to create. In an interview for the *Source*, Adario Strange described his subject as a "delicate ghetto-princess songstress," "the flower of the ghetto," and "the real momma of hip-hop R&B." In his *Washington Post* review of Blige's second album, Geoffrey Himes called her "the premier soul diva of the hip-hop generation." She rose in esteem over the years to be crowned by the music media as the Queen of Hip Hop Soul.

Grew Up in the Ghetto

Part of the fuel for Blige's rocket to hip-hop stardom was her "street cred." She was born on January 11, 1971, in the Bronx, and raised in Savannah, Georgia, before moving to the Schlobohm Housing Projects—or "Slow Bomb" projects, as its residents called it, in Yonkers, New York. Blige's coming of age on the mean streets of the Bronx provided her with the "credentials"

demanded by audiences who also grew up on city streets. Blige described the setting for *Essence*'s Deborah Gregory, recalling that there "was always some sh** going on. Every day I would be getting into fights over whatever. You always had to prove yourself to keep from getting robbed or jumped. Growing up in the projects is like living in a barrel of crabs. If you try to get out, one of the other crabs tries to pull you down." The family, including Blige's older sister and two younger brothers, subsisted on her mother Cora's earnings as a nurse after her father left the family in the mid-1970s. "My mother made me strong," Blige told Strange. "Watching my mother struggle to raise us and feed us made me want to be a stronger woman," she continued.

Blige's environment also provided the sound and encouragement that first shaped her musical identity. A professional jazz musician, her father left his mark on Blige's ability to harmonize during the brief time he was present. Block parties in the Bronx taught her the rhythms and sampling styles created by the early hip-hop deejays. At home, her mother played a steady stream of R&B, soul, and funk, including Sam Cooke, Aretha Franklin, Stevie Wonder, Chaka Khan, and

At a Glance . . .

Born Mary Jane Blige on January 11, 1971, in Bronx, NY; raised in Savannah, GA, and Yonkers, NY; daughter of Cora (a nurse) and a jazz musician; married Kendu Isaacs (a music producer), 2003. *Education:* GED.

Career: Singer, 1992–; actress, 1998–.

Awards: Soul Train Music Award, 1993; New York Music Award; NAACP Image Award; double-platinum album award for *What's the 411?*; Grammy Award, for Best Rap Performance by a Duo or Group (with Method Man), 1995; American Music Award, 1998; Soul Train Lady of Soul awards, 1997, 1998; celebrity spokesperson, MAC AIDS Fund, 2001, 2002; Grammy Award, for Best Female R&B Vocal Performance, 2002; Grammy Award, for Best Pop Collaboration with Vocals (with Sting), 2003; Grammy Award, for Best R&B Album, for Best R&B Song, and for Best R&B Female Vocal Performance, all 2006.

Addresses: *Web*—www.mjblige.com.

Gladys Knight. Blige sang regularly with her mother and sister in the choir at the House of Prayer Pentecostal Church, honing vocal skills and imbibing gospel. "We used to go to church all night. Everybody would be real good to us," Blige told Emil Wilbekin in a *Vibe* interview. She expanded on the experience for *Essence*'s Gregory, remembering that she "felt so much better going to church every Sunday, just being there, testifying and just being kids. It was a lot of fun." By the time Blige was a teenager, she had solo spots in the choir and she made the rounds of local talent shows. Though she attended Lincoln High School—a school that specialized in the performing arts—studied music and participated in school sponsored talent shows, she dropped out of high school in the eleventh grade.

While she enjoyed singing, Blige did not expect to make her living at it and, like most teenagers in her position, helped bring in money with several part-time jobs. She told Allison Samuels of *Newsweek*, "People in church would say 'You should do something with your voice.' And I'd be like 'What? I am living in the projects in Yonkers. What am I going to do with my voice?'" Her first "demo" tape was, in fact, just a karaoke style recording made one night at a mall to entertain friends when she was 17. Before too long, however, the cover of Anita Baker's "Caught Up In The Rapture" found its way to Andre Harrell, an executive

with Uptown Records: Blige's mother gave it to her boyfriend, who gave it to a friend, who gave it to R&B vocalist Jeff Redd. Redd passed it on, enthusiastically, to Harrell. On Harrell's initiative, Blige was brought onto Uptown's growing roster of young R&B talents. Sean "Puffy" Combs (later known as P. Diddy) became the young singer's mentor when the company began preparing her album.

Invented the New Jill Swing

In 1992, *What's the 411?* introduced Blige's voice to audiences with a growing interest in the New Jack Swing take on R&B. The album not only fit neatly into that R&B revival, but also began to define it. Driven primarily by the single "Real Love," *411* reached double-platinum status after it sold more than two million copies in a short time. Its appeal crossed over from the R&B charts and entered the Top Ten on *Billboard*'s pop chart. When Havelock Nelson gave the album an "A" in his *Entertainment Weekly* review in August of 1992, he began with the news everyone would soon know—that Blige was "the first diva to deliver frisky, fly-girl funk" and that she "conquers everything she tackles." He concluded that the album was "one of the most accomplished fusions of soul values and hip-hop to date."

Nelson described, in particular, how Blige took the then male-defined domain of New Jack Swing and remade it in her own image, kicking off the rage for New Jill Swing. She became known as the initiator of a new female incarnation of hip-hop. "Mary has become an icon of today's young Black nation," wrote the *Source*'s Strange, "representing the feminine yet strong-willed woman that many young girls hope to be, and the sexy yet not too cute for a ruffneck girlfriend that many brothers from the hood long for." In April of 1993, *Rolling Stone* reviewer Steve Hochman noted that Blige had "become the role model for the new breed of strong hip-hop women." Strange dubbed her the "first true feminine hero of R&B lovin' ghetto residents." The singer commented on the phenomenon herself, telling Hochman, "I think I'm creating a style for women—a more feminine version of the way a lot of hip-hop guys dress now." As Strange noted, the impact of *411* showed up soon on other performers, as "baseball caps and boots suddenly became in vogue for female singers" and "divas everywhere demanded hip-hop tracks to back up their cubic zirconian efforts."

The accolades were marred, however, by some bad publicity. It seemed to begin at the 1993 Soul Train Music Awards, where Blige accepted her award not in the expected glittering evening gown, but in standard street gear: jeans and a shirt. The public expressed its disapproval instantly: as the *Source*'s Strange reported, "radio stations everywhere were flooded with phone calls from disgruntled fans." That incident occurred in the midst of other, less public, reports of bad behavior. Wilbekin recounted the history for *Vibe*, recalling that the "stories of tardiness, cancellations, and general lack of professionalism are endless. Mary was eight hours late to one magazine photo shoot, and threw a fit and walked out of at least one more. She conducted interviews where she did as much drinking as talking and acted like a zombie on national television. Then there was the concert in London where she was so out of it the crowd booed her off the stage."

Worked on Image

It was only after the release of her second album that Blige was able to reflect on what might have fed her behavior at the time. She speculated that the attention had disconcerted her—that she had not been prepared, socially or professionally, for the kind of intense spotlight music celebrity creates. Harrell suggested to Wilbekin in *Vibe* that "the whole experience was overwhelming for her. She wasn't ready to be put under the microscope in that fashion." Friend and manager Steve Lucas told Gregory that "Mary got an undeserved bad rap because of what was going on around her—the confusion, the lack of organization. When you communicate honestly with Mary, there aren't any problems. She's willing to cooperate and do whatever it takes to be successful. She's basically a very sweet, humble person." The difficulty of the situation was magnified, Blige admitted to *Rolling Stone*'s Hochman, by her basic shyness. "I'm just not a very open person," she told him. "The most open I am is when I sing. I've always been kind of shy." On a more concrete note, she also felt there were problems with her management, which she changed before recording the second album. Combs was fired at Uptown and in 1993 started his own company, Bad Boy Entertainment, where Blige took her management business while still recording with Uptown.

Blige also pursued practical measures to prepare herself for the fresh onslaught of publicity that would accompany the second album: she enrolled with a public relations firm, Double XXposure, that trained artists to deal with the demands of public reputation. She worked extensively with the company's president, Angelo Ellerbee, whom she later credited with not just polishing her interview style, but changing her life more broadly. She told Wilbekin in *Vibe* that Ellerbee "gave me a totally new kind of life. There was a time when I wouldn't read nothin'," but Ellerbee sparked her interest in books her for the first time, introducing her, for example, to a novel by Zora Neale Hurston called *Their Eyes Were Watching God.*

When Uptown released *My Life* in 1994, it marked many changes for Blige, including the personal refining that turned around her public image. The vocalist also contributed lyrics for most of the songs; she had been writing before the debut album, but had little confidence in her skill as a lyricist. The sound of the music shifted also, due in part to the use of live horns and strings in place of the standard sampling, moving Blige deeper into the fusion of hip-hop and soul. Ultimately, all of the changes added up successfully for Blige and her producers: *My Life* debuted in December in the top position on *Billboard*'s R&B album chart.

In 1996, Blige released another album, *Share My World*. Along with the album, she sported a new attitude: self-love. She parted company from people who she felt were negative influences, including her producer and mentor, Combs, Deathrow Records president Suge Knight, and K-Ci of Jodeci fame, her on-again, off-again boyfriend. Her new attitude can also be traced to her renewed commitment to God. Blige spoke to Christopher John Farley of *Time*, "God comes first. If I don't love him, I can't love anybody. And if I can't love me, I can't love nobody."

Share My World also broadened Blige's horizons. She worked with producers Jimmy Jam and Terry Lewis, TrackMasters, and R Kelly. Though known for songs with strong hip hop beats, *Share My World*'s songs were more mellow and showed Blige headed for mainstream R&B and pop. Amy Linden of *People* exclaimed, "Some might gripe that the overall sound is more polished than on her two previous multi-platinum CDs—and it is." The album also included the Babyface-produced and written song, "Not Gon' Cry," from the *Waiting To Exhale* soundtrack. The song became the jilted black woman's anthem.

Continued to Transform Herself

Blige also continued to work on her image. In the beginning she did not care about her career or herself. During her interviews, Blige opened up and spoke about her lifestyle, which included using hard drugs. She told Kevin Chappell of *Ebony*, "I did a lot of stuff, things that a lot of girls wouldn't do, because of a lack of self-love. I did drugs, I did a lot. I did things, not just weed, but beyond…." Her finances also were not in order. She made both management and personal changes. "I'm a young lady now; with growing up comes a lot of responsibilities. So there are a lot of things that I have to do, and there are a lot of things that I can't do anymore…. I want to challenge myself more to see what comes out of it. Patience is a virtue to me," she was quoted as saying in *Ebony*.

In 1998 Blige headlined her own tour, and that summer she released a live album, called *The Tour*. "It was a great energy. And it's really at the concert; there are no studio tricks. I'm not afraid for the audience to hear my voice crack," she told Anita Samuels of *Billboard*. The album featured a medley of previous hits and two new covers. Blige also started her own label, Mary Jane Entertainment. She toured again as a headliner in The Mary Show in 2000 and appeared with Aretha Franklin on the annual *VH1 Divas Live* broadcast in 2001. With seemingly bottomless energy, Blige made her television acting debut on *The Jamie Foxx Show* in 1998.

Blige's next album, simply entitled *Mary* found Blige teaming up with legends such as Elton John, Stevie Wonder, and Aretha Franklin. Critics described the album as more mature, toning down the raunchier elements of her persona that had been evident since her debut and repositioning herself as a true soul singer. *Mary* was Blige's first attempt to truly shape her new image and the results were spectacular. The single "All That I Can Say" with Lauryn Hill hit the *Billboard* top ten charts and the album was nominated for both a Grammy and a *Billboard* Music Award.

Starting in 1999 and continuing on into 2000 and 2001, Blige has been very open and vocal about the path that her career and personal life took throughout the 1990s and how hard she has worked to turn those around into something that she can be proud of. Blige talked of an abusive relationship that she finally realized she had to get out of before something serious happened to her. In an interview with *Essence* she says of the relationship, "When I looked back I knew I did the right thing, because if I didn't break out I was going to die. Somebody wanted me dead and subliminally it must have been me, because I drew someone to me who wanted to kill me." Blige has spoken at length about her newfound faith in religion. Blige has openly said that it is God that has allowed her to make the changes that she has made in her life. In a *Jet* interview with Calerence Waldron, Blige said, "I'm trying to build my foundation on the wisdom, the Word, so that I will be able to pass on the right information to the universe. Because you get exactly what you put out there. I'm just happy with that."

One of the main regrets that Mary J. Blige has made public was the fact that she dropped out of high school before getting her diploma. Blige has repeatedly told interviewers that part of the reason that she was so careless with her money and her fame during her early career was due to the fact that she didn't have the proper education and didn't know how to properly invest her money or who she should trust. Blige studied with tutors and gained her Graduate Equivalence Degree (GED). Starting in 2000, Blige began touring schools, trying to convey the message that education was the most important thing and that students needed to stay in school. She told *Jet*, she emphasized to teens to "… stay in school. Just be patient and pray. Finish school, finish high school. Don't drop out."

Made Further Strides

Blige continued to further her career and image with her 2001 release of her album *No More Drama*. This much-developed album with songs such as "Love," "Family Affair," and "No More Drama" earned her another Grammy nomination and secured Blige's place in the soul diva category. Blige attributed the popularity of the album to the fact that she herself is continuing on her in journey of self discovery and that her fans have turned the corner with her. In a *Jet* magazine interview, Blige says of *No More Drama*, "This album is a continuation of a turnaround. The *Mary* album was a

cleanup. It was about cleaning up me. And this album? It's about solidifying and moving even further with the things I've learned and the strides I've made."

The positive reviews on Blige are endless. Music critic Geoffrey Himes, among others, paid particular tribute to Blige: "Blige may be a gospel-trained siren like older soul divas," he remarked in the *Washington Times*, "but these arrangements sound like no record ever made by Aretha Franklin, Diana Ross or Patti LaBelle. All the gooey orchestrations that have sugarcoated romantic crooners from Dinah Washington to Anita Baker are gone, leaving a skeletal rhythm track and a spectacular voice freed from all superfluous sentiment and ornamentation." J.D. Considine, of Baltimore's *Evening Sun*, noted that "Blige has more than surpassed expectations" and argued that as "good as the grooves are, it's her vocal work that ultimately drives these songs." Similarly, Himes declared her a "major voice of her generation."

She reunited with Diddy for *Love and Life*, in 2003. Also that year, she married music producer Kendu Isaacs. Blige won a Grammy award in 2004, with Sting, for Best Pop Collaboration with Vocals for their work, "Whenever I Say Your Name." In addition to making hit after hit, Blige continued to act. She has appeared in *Prison Song*, but it may be her last film as she explained in *People*, "I didn't like being on the set all day and doing scenes over and over…. I like performing more than getting up in the morning." Nevertheless, Blige did continue to act, appearing on the CBS series *Ghost Whisperer* in 2007. Blige has lent her name and celebrity to support causes she believed in. She has appeared in ads for cosmetic company MAC's Viva Glam lipstick, which raised money for the MAC AIDS fund. Blige has performed at three VH1's *Divas Live* concerts that helped raise money for the cable channel's Save the Music Foundation. Blige was also featured on Carson hair company's Dark & Lovely's permanent hair color box, named Red Hot Mary, after the singer.

Achieved a Breakthrough

As Sean Combs explained to Strange in the *Source*, Blige "represents all the honeys in the urban communities in Detroit, Harlem, Chicago, and Los Angeles [who are] growing up and going through regular every day things that are a part of hip-hop culture." Blige sums up herself the best. Though gifted with a beautiful voice, she lacked confidence in herself. Mary J. Blige has come through her growing pains into a mature young lady who cares about herself. She stated in *Time*, "You better believe that I give a damn now."

Her newfound confidence showed in her later recordings. In *The Breakthrough*, Blige included song that showcased her past, such as "Enough Cryin" and "Baggage," as well as her calmer present sense of self, as in "Be Without You." Blige explained her different approach to this album to Richard Harrington of the *Washington* Post: "I remember when I was a woman that was solely about pain—everything was pain, pain, pain. Now we're selling triumph over tragedy, and that's what [the album] was all about—being a victor instead of a victim. I put a lot of work into trying to get myself together, to get to the point where I could have the strength to show people my weaknesses like that." The album was a triumph itself, selling more copies in its first week than any other R&B album for a female solo artist. Blige was also honored in 2006 with eight Grammy nominations for her music—more than any other artist that year. For her efforts, she won three Grammy Awards, for Best R&B Album, for Best R&B Song, and for Best R&B Female Vocal Performance.

Blige continued her personal healing and next revisited her past as a way of moving on. She offered listeners her own take on her 15-year career with her 2006 album, *Reflections—A Retrospective*. The album featured re-recordings of some of her biggest hits as well as four new songs, including "We Ride (I See the Future)." "I'm just taking a look back before I move forward again," Blige told Jessica Herndon of *People* about the album. Blige's transformation from an unfocused young woman to a poised, principled R&B diva without missing a beat proves the Queen still reigns.

Selected discography

Albums

What's the 411?, Uptown/MCA, 1992.
My Life, Uptown/MCA, 1994.
Share My World, MCA, 1996.
The Tour, MCA, 1998.
Mary, MCA, 1999.
No More Drama, MCA, 2001.
Dance for Me, MCA, 2002.
Love & Life, Geffen, 2003.
Not Today, Geffen, 2003.
Love Is All We Need, Geffen, 2004.
The Breakthrough, Geffen, 2005.
Reflections—A Retrospective, Geffen, 2006.

Sources

Books

Brown, Terrell, *Mary J. Blige*, Mason Crest, 2007.
Torres, Jennifer, *Mary J. Blige*, Mitchell Lane, 2007.

Periodicals

Atlanta Journal, November 29, 1994.
Billboard, January 16, 1993; July 25, 1998.
Boston Globe, December 15, 1994.
Dallas Morning News, April 4, 2002.
Ebony, January 1998; January 1999; June 2000.
Entertainment Weekly, August 7, 1992; November 20, 1992; December 3, 1993; November 25, 1994.
Essence, March 1995; November 2001.
Evening Sun, (Baltimore, MD), December 2, 1994.
Jet, November 29, 1999; August 28, 2000; September 18, 2000; October 1, 2001; January 29, 2007, p.60.
Newsweek, May 5, 1997.
People, December 5, 1994; May 19, 1997; July 17, 2000; January 8, 2007, p. 42.
Philadelphia Tribune, August 6, 2006, p. 18.
Rolling Stone, April 15, 1993; January 25, 2007; February 8, 2007.
Source, January 1995.
Stereo Review, April 1993.
Time, April 28, 1997.
Us Weekly, February 12, 2007, p. 48.
Vibe, February 1995.
Washington Post, November 27, 1994; February 11, 2007, p. Y5.

On-line

All Music Guide, www.allmusic.com (January 5, 2005).
"Mary J. Blige," *MTV.com*, www.mtv.com/bands/az/blige_mary_j/bio.jhtml (January 7, 2005).
Mary J. Blige, www.mjblige.com (January 5, 2005).
"Mary J. Blige, Making 'The Breakthrough,'" *National Public Radio*, www.npr.org/templates/story/story.php?storyId=5165863 (April 3, 2007).
Rock On The Net, www.rockonthenet.com (January 5, 2005).

Other

Additional information for this sketch was obtained from Uptown Records.

—Ondine E. LeBlanc, Ashyia N. Henderson, Ralph Zerbonia, and Sara Pendergast

Lawrence D. Bobo

1958—

Sociologist

Lawrence D. Bobo is an eminent American sociologist whose work, though not widely known outside of academic circles, examines issues that have significant impact on the lives of millions of Americans. Since 2005 he has been the Martin Luther King Jr. Centennial professor of sociology at Stanford University in California, where he continues to conduct a long-term survey project involving public opinion on contemporary race relations in America. A few months after Hurricane Katrina devastated the city of New Orleans, Louisiana, Bobo addressed an audience at Emory University in Atlanta, Georgia, and asserted that the natural disaster had brought to light some painful truths that he and others in his field had long known. "Katrina forced a recognition that an illness diagnosed many years ago still requires treatment," he said, "That illness in the heart of American democracy is an enduring racial divide."

Bobo was born on February 18, 1958, in Nashville, Tennessee, the son of a physician, Joseph, and a teacher, Joyce Cooper Bobo. By the age of six, he had settled on his own career direction in law, and became a skilled debater during his high school years in preparation. But at Loyola Marymount University in Los Angeles, he grew uneasy with the pre-law school curriculum he had followed, and was drawn to the ideas presented in his sociology courses. As he explained in an interview that appeared on the National Academy of Sciences Web site, the persistent need to present both sides of an argument in a debate had wearied him. "You were mostly concerned with advancing a winning argument in the moment, rather than finding something that was lasting," he reflected.

Bobo first became intrigued by a sociology course in deviant behavior and criminology. Yet Bobo's switch to a social-science major was not altogether out of the ordinary: in Atlanta, his mother's family were longtime friends of Dr. Edward Franklin Frazier, a leading black sociologist whose 1939 book, *The Negro Family in the United States,* is considered a landmark in the field of African-American studies. Frazier, in fact, was his mother's godfather, and though he died in 1962, Frazier's ideas and professional renown were an influence on Bobo in his decision to pursue a degree in sociology.

After graduating with top honors from Loyola Marymount in 1979, Bobo went on to the University of Michigan, where two sociologists whose work intrigued him, Mary Jackman and Howard Schuman, were teaching at the time. He earned his master's degree in 1981 and a doctorate four years later, and was hired by the University of Wisconsin at Madison as an assistant professor of sociology. He co-authored his first book, *Racial Attitudes in America: Trends and Interpretations,* with Schuman and Charlotte Steeh, during this period. In 1990, Bobo moved on to the University of California at Los Angeles as a full professor and program director for survey research, and spent the next seven years there.

Bobo joined the faculty of Harvard University in 1997 as a professor of Afro-American studies and sociology. He was recruited by the scholar Henry Louis Gates Jr.,

in African-American studies and race relations, including Cornell West, author of *Race Matters,* and sociologist William Julius Wilson.

In addition to his teaching duties and research work, Bobo also became a member of the executive committee of the W. E. B. DuBois Institute, the first research center at a major American university dedicated to the study of the history, culture, and social institutions of Africans and African Americans. In 2004, Bobo served as one of the founding editors of its *Du Bois Review: Social Science Research on Race,* a journal dedicated to publishing new research and criticism from sociologists and other scholars on the issue of race in America.

Bobo has authored dozens of professional papers himself, as well as contributed to or edited several scholarly tomes. Of the latter category, he has co-edited *Prismatic Metropolis: Inequality in Los Angeles,* a 2000 work, and *Urban Inequality: Evidence from Four Cities,* published in 2001. Not long after setting up the *Du Bois Review,* Bobo announced his decision to leave Harvard for a position at Stanford University in Palo Alto, California, which had offered his wife, Marcyliena Morgan, a teaching position as well. Morgan specializes in language, culture, and identity issues in the realm of African-American studies, and created the Hip-Hop Archive while at Harvard. This on-line portal is a leading source for research on contemporary black music and its place in contemporary culture.

At Stanford, Bobo became the Martin Luther King Jr. Centennial professor of sociology and was named program chair for the department of African and African American Studies. He also serves as director of Stanford's Center for Comparative Study of Race and Ethnicity. For a number of years he has been involved in a long-range, ongoing study called the Race, Crime, and Public Opinion project. Its survey questions attempt to gauge current public opinion on matters of race, crime, poverty, and political enfranchisement in America.

One series of questions in Bobo's Race, Crime, and Public Opinion project focused on the fairness of the criminal justice system, and the effect that the federal government's ongoing War on Drugs has had on black families since the 1980s. In a 2006 article Bobo penned for the journal *Social Research,* he and co-author Victor Thompson wrote that the latest findings from the survey tended to confirm that "we do not have a criminal justice system free of the taint of race bias. Indeed, we believe our evidence on public opinion makes it clear that, in the eyes of most African Americans, the system continues to be seen as essentially unfair by design." In the same article, he and Thompson went on to assert that in the first years of the twenty-first century, U.S. "social policy would seem

the literary critic who headed Harvard's Afro-American studies department at the time and was leading a major effort to make it one of the foremost programs in its field in the United States. Bobo's colleagues were among some of the best-known contemporary scholars

to be driven mainly by a punitive and retributive logic. Our results suggest that this is a sure path to deepening racial polarization and a further weakening of the legal system's claim to fairness and legitimacy."

Selected writings

Books

(With Howard Schuman and Charlotte Steeh) *Racial Attitudes in America: Trends and Interpretations,* Harvard University, 1985.

(Editor, with David O. Sears and Jim Sidanius) *Racialized Politics: The Debate about Racism in America,* University of Chicago Press, 2000.

(Editor, with others) *Prismatic Metropolis: Inequality in Los Angeles,* Russell Sage Foundation, 2000.

(Editor, with Alice O'Connor and Chris Tilly) *Urban Inequality: Evidence from Four Cities,* Russell Sage Foundation, 2001.

Prejudice in Politics: Public Opinion, Group Position, and the Wisconsin Treaty Rights Dispute, Harvard University Press, 2006.

Sources

Periodicals

American Journal of Sociology, September 2003, p. 496.

Social Research, Summer 2006, p. 445.

On-line

"Lawrence D. Bobo," *Stanford University,* www. stanford.edu/dept/soc/people/faculty/bobo/bobo. html (February 20, 2007).

"Interview: Lawrence Bobo," *National Academy of Sciences,* www.nasonline.org/site/PageServer? pagename=INTERVIEWS_Lawrence_Bobo (February 20, 2007).

"Unity Month Keynote: Katrina Exposed Racial Divide," *Emory Wheel,* http://media.www.emory-wheel.com/media/storage/paper919/news/2005/ 11/18/News/Unity.Month.Keynote.Katrina. Exposed.Racial.Divide-1648399.shtml (April 2, 2007).

—Carol Brennan

James Brown

1933-2006

Singer, songwriter, keyboardist

Brown, James, photograph. Donald Kravitz/Getty Images.

If a famous person's nicknames tell a lot about them, James Brown's nicknames must say a mouthful. He was known at one time as Soul Brother Number One, the Hardest Working Man in Show Business, Mr. Dynamite, and Mr. Sex Machine and went on to be named the Godfather of Soul. But then there is plenty to know about James Brown. He had the highest number of singles to reach the top 20, and the second-highest number of singles to reach the top 100 after Elvis Presley; he reinvented soul music at least twice; and it is impossible to know what soul music, funk, disco, or rap would sound like if not for his musical influence. He also attracted his share of both admirers and detractors among blacks and whites, Democrats and Republicans, as a political figure. Moreover, Brown made an impact on American culture, black and otherwise, that few others could equal.

Overcame Early Obstacles to Success

James Joe Brown, Jr., was born on May 3, 1933, although various other dates have been ascribed to him over the years, near Barnwell, South Carolina, and Augusta, Georgia. He was stillborn in his family's one-room shack, and the family had given him up for dead, but he was resuscitated by his great-aunt Minnie. His father, Joe Brown, worked the area to get sap from trees, which he sold to turpentine manufacturers. The four of them lived in the area until James's mother, Susan (Behlings) Brown, left when James was four years old. In his 1986 autobiography, *James Brown, The Godfather of Soul,* Brown expressed his regret at not being raised by both his parents.

When Brown was six, Joe moved him and his aunt to Augusta in a search for more work. They moved in with another aunt, Honey, who ran a bordello on U.S. Highway 1. It was, to say the least, an unusual environment for a young child to grow up in, as Brown wrote in his autobiography, reprinted in *Current Biography*: "I guess I saw and heard just about everything in the world in that house, when the soldiers were there with the women." The family did not have much money, and James was embarrassed that he had to attend school in ragged clothes. One day Joe brought home an old pump organ, though, and James discovered that he had a natural knack for playing music.

At a Glance . . .

Born James Joe Brown Jr. on May 3, 1933, near Barnwell, South Carolina, and Augusta, GA; died on December 25, 2006, in Atlanta, GA; son of Joe Brown, a turpentine worker, and Susan Behlings; married Velma Warren 1953 (divorced 1969); Deidre Jenkins 1970 (divorced 1981), Adrienne Lois Rodriguez 1984 (died 1996); and Tomi Rae Hynie, 2001; children: six.

Career: Recording and performing artist, mid-1950s-2006.

Awards: 44 Gold Records; Grammy Awards, 1965, 1986; Rock and Roll Hall of Fame, charter member, 1986; Grammy Lifetime Achievement Award, 1992; Rhythm & Blues Foundation Pioneer Awards, Lifetime Achievement Award, 1993.

Until he could begin his career, however, young Brown shined shoes, picked cotton and peanuts, and delivered groceries to earn money.

Brown found many diversions to pique his interest during childhood. Music was one, and he learned to play the drums, piano, guitar, and to sing gospel. He also particularly enjoyed the jump blues music played by Louis Jordan and was impressed by circuses and traveling minstrel shows, the something-for-everybody philosophy of which later helped inspire his James Brown Revue. He found some early success as a boxer, using his left-handed style to confuse his young opponents. An unfortunate diversion ended his childhood freedom prematurely at age 15. To get money to buy decent clothes for school, Brown sometimes stole objects from unlocked cars. He was caught and received a sentence of eight to 16 years at the Georgia Juvenile Training Institute.

Developed Signature Sound

While in jail Brown got a leg up on his music career, forming a gospel quartet which included Johnny Terry, who would later become an original member of Brown's Famous Flames vocal group. Brown impressed the warden with his commitment to gospel music while in the facility, and when he received a promise of a job upon his release, he was paroled in 1952 after serving only three years of his sentence. Immediately upon his release Brown formed a gospel group with Terry and Bobby Byrd called The 3 Swanees. The group soon moved to Macon, Georgia—which Little Richard and The Five Royals had made

into a bit of a local music mecca—began playing more rhythm and blues-oriented material and changed its name to the Flames.

Once in Macon the group hired as its manager Clint Brantly, Little Richard's manager, and he convinced the Flames to add the "Famous" adjective to their name. Early in 1956 the group cut a record, "Please, Please, Please," for King records, which released it on its Federal subsidiary. The song became a hit, peaking at number six on the rhythm and blues charts, and Brown's career was underway. The name of the group was soon changed to James Brown and the Famous Flames, although at the time Brown had yet to refine any of the distinctive styles which would later make him a legend. "Please, Please, Please," and its follow-up hit, "Try Me," from 1958, were fairly ordinary rhythm and blues songs which could have been recorded by any number of artists at the time. More distinctive during the 1950s was Brown's live act, which included a 20-piece band, four warm-up soloists, two vocal groups, a comedian and a troupe of dancers. As for Brown himself, he put forth an energy in his performances which was second to none and exceeded most. As Rolling Stone Bill Wyman would later tell *Rolling Stone* magazine: "You could put Jerry Lee Lewis, Little Richard, Chuck Berry and Bo Diddley on one side of the stage and James Brown on the other, and you wouldn't even notice the others were up there!"

In the early 1960s, Brown found his trademark sound with such hits as "I'll Go Crazy," and "Think." The characteristics of the James Brown "sound" were staccato horn bursts, a scratchy guitar, and a prominent bass guitar, all coming together to provide a kind of rhythmic excitement which contrasted sharply with the era's more traditional musical tools of verse-chorus-verse song construction and melody. It began a string of hits that would be the greatest of Brown's career, running until the end of the decade.

Brown felt he faced a problem in 1962, however. Although he had a string of hits on the rhythm and blues charts, including "Baby, You're Right," and "Lost Someone," both of which peaked at number two, and his singles had also fared respectably on the pop charts, he felt his best work was being done in concert. The energy and excitement of his live performances were not coming through on his records. Brown was convinced that in order to communicate his style to the record-buying public he needed to record a live album, an unusual step in rock music at that time and one King found expensive and impractical. Brown decided to take matters into his own hands, rented the Apollo Theater in Harlem, miked the band and the audience, produced the album himself and even put the theater's ushers in tuxedos, all of which cost him $5,700. The gamble paid off, as the album, recorded in November 1962, at the height of the Cuban Missile Crisis, became a huge phenomenon which is to this day regarded as one of the finest live rock and roll albums ever recorded. Brown's stage style found him segueing immediately from one song to another, a practice which would ordinarily cause problems for radio stations wanting to cue up a single song. It did not matter in the end, as black radio stations took the then-unheard-of step of playing the record a side at a time, as if the two sides were 20-minute songs.

Brown's sound was now known to the public, and his tireless touring schedule, which included as many as 350 dates in a year (hence the nickname, The Hardest Working Man in Show Business), began to draw even larger audiences. Brown's dancing also became legendary: His trademark move was to grab the microphone stand, slide down into the splits, pop back up out of them and erupt into a pirouette, a move few other mortals dared attempt for fear of any number of injuries. During the mid-1960s Brown hit upon another bit of on-stage mania which became his show-stopping, show-closing trademark for several years, in which he would sing the song "Please, Please, Please," until collapsing in mock anguish and exhaustion in a heap on stage, whereupon his backup singers would drape his lifeless form with a cape, help him to his feet, and lead him toward the wings, only to have him throw the cape off, return to front-stage center, resume the song and start the whole process over again. The act was a great crowd-pleaser wherever Brown performed.

Troubles with Famous Flames Lead to Funk

While Brown's stage show was a hit with audiences everywhere, the members of his backing group differed among themselves on his qualities as a boss. While some of his band members, such as Terry and Byrd, stayed with him for many years, many found his leadership style tyrannical and unbearably egotistical. Brown levied fines for a number of offenses he found intolerable, including lateness, wrinkled uniforms, scuffed shoes, and even missed steps and notes on stage. Other accusations which band members have accused Brown of over the years included denying writing credits and record royalties, leaving musicians stranded on the road, threatening them with guns, stealing their girlfriends, and exhibiting erratic behavior due to drug abuse.

Brown kept the Flames together through 1970, though, and the group had some huge hit records, including "Papa's Got a Brand New Bag—Part 1," "I Got You (I Feel Good)," "It's a Man's Man's Man's World," "Cold Sweat—Part 1," "I Got the Feelin'," "Say It Loud—I'm Black and I'm Proud—Part 1," "Give It Up or Turnit a Loose," and "Mother Popcorn— Part 1," all of which reached Number One on the rhythm and blues charts and most of which reached the top ten on the pop charts. Brown also became a fairly prominent voice in the black community during the most crucial days of the civil rights movement in the late 1960s, appearing on television to help quell riots in the streets of Boston and Washington, D.C. after the assassination of Martin Luther King Jr., and was once recruited by H. Rap Brown to assist with his Black Power movement. Many blacks did not approve of Brown's public appearances with politicians such as Hubert Humphrey and Richard Nixon—whom Brown endorsed for president—and one of the ironies of Brown's career in this era was that he was simultaneously distrusted by both whites (for songs such as "Say It Loud—I'm Black and I'm Proud," which some found uncomfortably militant), and blacks (for endorsing Nixon, disavowing violence and proclaiming himself a Republican).

During the late 1960s the Famous Flames underwent numerous personnel changes as the fallout from Brown's tough discipline found members leaving the band more frequently. Brown finally decided to disband the group, and in 1971 his new group, the JBs, made its debut with a song called "Hot Pants." The new band had a sound markedly different from the old band, a sound that would come to be called funk. It was a sound he had been gradually moving toward over the late 1960s, but with the JBs the style was realized in full. In his autobiography Brown explained, "I had discovered that my strength was not in the horns, it was in the rhythm. I was hearing everything, even the guitars, like they were drums. I had found out how to make it happen." The JBs would go on to have about five more years' worth of hits before the disco era began to see their popularity wane.

During this period, however, Brown's music began to feel the scorn of rock critics, who called it repetitive and monotonous. A typical Brown album of this period would feature a handful of songs, each consisting of a single riff which would be sustained for several minutes, while Brown spoke his mind about any number of topics over top of the music. Robert Palmer, writing in *The Rolling Stone Illustrated History of Rock and Roll*, was one who argued against this verdict. "Attacking him for being repetitive is like attacking Africans for being overly fond of drumming," he wrote.

Experienced Personal and Professional Difficulties

Things in Brown's personal life began to take a turn for the worse in the mid 1970s. In 1973 his son, Teddy, was killed in an auto accident, and Bobby Byrd quit the band to pursue a solo career. Also that year, the Internal Revenue Service stepped up its attempts to collect back taxes from Brown. In 1968 the IRS claimed he owed nearly $2 million; now they added another $4.5 million to the tab. A few years later his second wife Deirdre left him (his first marriage, to the former Velma Warren, fell apart in 1968). All the while his relationship with his record company since 1971, Polydor, steadily deteriorated, as Brown felt the label did not understand his music or his market.

Brown had built himself a formidable business empire over the first two decades of his career. He had a large house, a fleet of cars, several radio stations (including one in Augusta in front of which he had shined shoes as a youngster), a booking agency, 17 publishing companies, a record label, a production company and a Lear jet. But with his tax problems mounting, the government began taking bites out of his empire. The radio stations, which were also having union problems, became the target of a government investigation, and the government also took possession of many of Brown's properties, including his jet and his home. In 1978 he was arrested on stage at the Apollo for defying a government order not to leave the country during the investigation of the radio stations.

The late 1970s and early 1980s were a sort of rebuilding period for Brown's career. He severed his ties with Polydor, hired well-known lawyer William Kunstler to handle his legal affairs, renewed his religious faith, and hit the rock club circuit around New York. He also found a vehicle for his music on celluloid, appearing in *The Blues Brothers* and *Doctor Detroit*, and singing the theme song for *Rocky IV*, "Living in America." That song hit number four on the pop charts in 1985, his first top ten pop hit in 17 years.

In 1984 Brown embarked on a union that dramatically shaped the next decade of his life when he married Adrienne Modell Rodriguez, a hairstylist on the syndicated music television program "Solid Gold." The pair would go on to have a stormy relationship, as Brown had with many of the women in his life. At one time Adrienne appeared beaten and bruised in the National Enquirer, allegedly from a Brown beating; she would later claim it was a publicity stunt, but beating women was an activity Brown had already garnered a reputation for in the past. Drug use, particularly PCP, was also reportedly a major factor in the marriage, although both parties would vociferously deny it. On a happier note during this decade, Brown became a charter member of the Rock and Roll Hall of Fame at induction ceremonies in 1986. "That night, while I was being inducted," he recalled in *Current Biography*, "I think I felt for the first time that the struggle was over."

Brown, though, sank deeper and deeper into his drug use until, according to an April 1989 article in *Rolling Stone*, his band members feared he would die. His rendezvous with rock bottom began October 24, 1988. There has been some disagreement about exactly what happened that day, but this much seems to have been confirmed: Brown, high on PCP, burst into an insurance seminar in the building next to his office in Augusta. He carried a shotgun that did not work and complained that people from the seminar had been using his private bathroom. The police were called, and Brown fled in his truck. The police chased him into South Carolina, shooting out his tires. Brown circled back, and the police chased him back to Augusta, before he drove the truck into a ditch. Police claimed that Brown was incoherent and attempted to sing and

dance while being given a sobriety test, but he was later acquitted of driving under the influence of PCP. Brown claimed that he had actually pulled over at one point during the chase, but police had riddled his truck with bullets, and he drove off on the rims in fear for his life when they stopped to reload. He claimed his truck had 23 bullet holes when the incident was over. At any rate, Brown was released on bail, and the very next day was again pulled over and arrested for driving under the influence of PCP.

The legal trial that followed the police chase was a source of almost as much disagreement as the chase itself. Apparently, the judge and Brown's lawyer advised him to plead guilty and accept a 90-day jail term, but Brown insisted upon his innocence and went through with the trial. He was convicted of aggravated assault and failing to stop for a police car with its blue lights on, and received concurrent six-year sentences from Georgia and South Carolina. Some, including Brown, have claimed that racial bias had much to do with the severity of the sentences.

Experienced Career Resurgence

Brown's time in prison was a very bad time for him in some ways, very good in others. He was shocked to discover that many of the young black inmates at the prison had no idea who he was, and was disappointed that some of his powerful friends did not attempt to gain his release or even visit him. Having had several friends in presidential administrations, Brown did not think he would do much time of his six-year sentence, but it took about two years for him to finally be paroled. However, Brown heard much of his own music in prison, although it took some doing to convince his fellow inmates that it was his music. He heard it in the samples on the rap and hip-hop records the prisoners listened to. Brown did not like his music being used on so many records he did not approve of, but hearing how much his music was being used—he is universally acknowledged as the most-sampled performer of all time—renewed his determination that his music was still as immediate and fresh as ever and convinced him his career would take off again upon his release.

Indeed, Brown's career did experience a resurgence upon his release. There were several factors as to why James Brown was so "hot" upon his release from prison. One was certainly the publicity he had received for his legal troubles. Another was the popularity of hip-hop and the obvious lineage leading back to Brown's music. Another was that Brown's music was known by the white community more than ever before, as in his heyday his American audience was almost exclusively black. Also, Brown's music had undergone a sort of critical reappraisal in the late 1980s, as rock writers reconsidered the criticisms they had made in the 1970s and concluded that his music had been groundbreaking and extremely influential, after all. Yet another reason was the release of *Star Time!*, the boxed set retrospective of Brown's career, and *Love Over-Due*, his new studio album, both of which were released in 1991. Amazingly, considering the decade-long slump that preceded his incarceration, James Brown had come back as hot as ever.

Tragedy struck Brown's life again in 1996, however, when Adrienne died from taking PCP while using prescription medicine. She also had a bad heart and was weak from having undergone liposuction surgery. But it was clear that Adrienne's death would not prevent Brown from doing what tax problems, imprisonment, controversy, and even disco already had failed to prevent him from doing: performing. Brown maintained a rigorous touring schedule over the next decade, and eventually remarried.

While on tour in 2006, Brown was diagnosed with pneumonia on December 23. The illness brought his musical career to a stop; he was hospitalized and died of heart failure on Christmas Day. Augustus, Georgia, honored him with a seven-foot-tall bronze statue. As in life, Brown experienced controversy in death. A legal battle over his estate ensued, delaying his burial and the construction of a Graceland-like mausoleum in his honor. Yet it is Brown's "music that really matters," wrote Michael Kohlenberger of *Take Pride! Community Magazine*, adding "The music is what makes the man and what makes the legend." As the 1992 edition of the *Rolling Stone Album Guide* said, "James Brown may never have captured the zeitgeist as Elvis Presley or the Beatles did, nor can he be said to have dominated the charts like Stevie Wonder or the Rolling Stones, but by any real measure of musical greatness—endurance, originality, versatility, breadth of influence—he towers over them all."

Selected works

Albums

Please, Please, Please, King, 1959.
Thing, King, 1960.
James Brown Presents His Band, King, 1961.
Excitement Mr. Dynamite, King, 1962.
Live at the Apollo, King, 1963.
Prisoner of Love, King, 1963.
Pure Dynamite! King, 1964.
Papa's Got a Brand New Bag, King, 1965.
I Got You (I Feel Good), King, 1966.
Mighty Instrumentals, Smash, 1966.
James Brown Plays New Breed (The Boo-Ga-Loo), Smash, 1966.
It's a Man's Man's Man's World, King, 1966.
Handful of Soul, Smash, 1966.
James Brown Sings Raw Soul, King, 1967.
James Brown Plays the Real Thing, Smash, 1967.
Live at the Garden, King, 1967.
Cold Sweat, King, 1967.

I Can't Stand Myself (When You Touch Me), King 1968.
I Got the Feelin', King, 1968.
James Brown Plays Nothing But Soul, King, 1968.
Live at the Apollo, Vol., II, 1968.
Thinking About Little Willie John and a Few Nice Things, King, 1968.
Say It Loud, I'm Black and I'm Proud, King, 1969.
The Popcorn, King, 1969.
It's a Mother, King, 1969.
It's a New Day—Let a Man Come In, King, 1970.
Sex Machine, King, 1970.
Super Bad, King, 1971.
Hot Pants, Polydor, 1971.
Revolution of the Mind (Live at the Apollo Theater, Vol. III), Polydor, 1971.
There It Is, Polydor, 1972.
Get on the Good Foot, Polydor, 1972.
The Payback, Polydor, 1974.
Hell, Polydor, 1974.
Hot, Polydor, 1976.
Get Up Offa That Thing, Polydor, 1976.
Solid Gold, Polydor UK, 1977.
Take a Look at Those Cakes, Polydor, 1979.
The Original Disco Man, Polydor, 1979.
People, Polydor, 1980.
Hot on the One, Polydor, 1980.
Soul Syndrome, Polydor, 1980.
Nonstop! Polydor, 1981.
Bring It On! Churchill/Augusta, 1983.
The Federal Years, Part One, Solid Smoke, 1984.
The Federal Years, Part Two, Solid Smoke, 1984.
Ain't That a Groove, Polydor, 1984.
Doing It to Death, Polydor, 1984.
The CD of JB (Sex Machine and Other Soul Classics), Polydor, 1985.
Gravity, Scotti Bros., 1986.
James Brown's Funky People, Polydor, 1986.
In the Jungle Groove, Polydor, 1986.
The CD of JB II (Cold Sweat and Other Soul Classics), Polydor, 1987.
I'm Real, Scotti Bros., 1988.
James Brown's Funky People (Part 2), Polydor, 1988.
Motherlode, Polydor, 1988.
Soul Session Live, Scotti Bros., 1989.
Roots of a Revolution, Polydor, 1989.
Messing With the Blues, Polydor, 1990.
Star Time, Polydor, 1991.
Love Over-Due, Scotti Bros., 1991.
20 All-Time Greatest Hits, Polydor, 1991.
The Greatest Hits of the Fourth Decade, Scotti Bros., 1992.
Living in America, Scotti Bros., 1995.
Funk Power 1970: A Brand New Thang, Polydor, 1996.
Dead on the Heavy Funk, Polydor, 1998.

James Brown's Funky People (Part 3), Polydor, 2000.
James Brown The Next Step, Fome, 2002.

Books

I Feel Good, New American Library, 2005.
(With Bruce Tucker) *James Brown, The Godfather of Soul,* Macmillan, 1986.

Sources

Books

Danielsen, Anne, *Presence and Pleasure: The Funk Grooves of James Brown and Parliament,* Wesleyan University Press, 2006.
Encyclopedia of African-American Culture and History, Macmillan.
(With Bruce Tucker) *James Brown, The Godfather of Soul,* Macmillan, 1986.
Rolling Stone Album Guide, Random House, 1992.

Rolling Stone Illustrated History of Rock and Roll, Random House, 1992.
Who's Who in Soul Music, Weidenfeld and Nicolson, 1991.

Periodicals

Atlanta Journal-Constitution, December 31, 2006, p. A14.
Augusta Chronicle (GA), December 31, 2006, p. A6.
Current Biography, March 1992, p. 18.
Jet, October 15, 1984, p. 38; February 26, 1996, p. 18.
Rolling Stone, April 6, 1989, p. 36; August 23, 1990, p. 98; June 27, 1991, p. 60.
Take Pride! Community Magazine, February 2007, p. 14.

Other

James Brown: The Man, The Music, and the Message (documentary), re-release 2007.
Soul Survivor: The James Brown Story (film), 2004.

—Mike Eggert and Sara Pendergast

Ursula M. Burns

1958—

Corporate executive

Starting at Xerox Corporation as an engineering intern, Ursula M. Burns climbed the corporate ladder to become the first woman president of Business Group Operations (BGO), Xerox's largest unit. Burns and Xerox chief executive officer (CEO) Anne Mulcahy steered the company from near-bankruptcy to financial stability.

Studied Engineering

Ursula M. Burns was born on September 20, 1958, in New York City. She was the middle child of three raised by their single mother Olga in the low-income projects of Manhattan's Delancey Street. Her mother took in ironing and ran a home-based daycare to enable her children to attend private Catholic schools. Burns told Claudia Deutsch of the *New York Times*: "She felt it was the only way to get us good educations, and keep us safe." An excellent mathematics student, Burns earned her bachelor's degree from the Polytechnic Institute of New York in 1980. She wanted a well-paying career. Through a graduate engineering program for minorities, Xerox helped pay the tuition for her master's degree program in mechanical engineering at Columbia University. The program included a summer internship with the company.

From 1981 on Burns held several engineering positions at Xerox, in the areas of product planning and development. By 1987 she had entered management, heading up various engineering teams. However Burns was convinced that she would never rise to the highest managerial levels as an engineer. In 1990 she became

executive assistant to the vice president of marketing and customer operations. The following year she was named executive assistant to Xerox chairman and CEO Paul A. Allaire. About 40 percent of her time was spent traveling with Allaire in the United States and abroad. In August of 1997 Burns told Cassandra Hayes of *Black Enterprise* that these positions provided her with "16 years of education in a year."

There was no doubt within the company that Burns was an extraordinarily intelligent and savvy woman. David A. Nadler, a Xerox consultant, told Deutsch: "Even in her 30's, she was a smart, unconventional thinker who'd embrace new ideas even while older executives at the table were rejecting them."

Climbed the Corporate Ladder

Between 1992 and 1997 Burns headed several Xerox business units. She spent two years in London as vice president and general manager of the Workgroup Copier Business. By 1997 she was back in Connecticut as vice president and general manager of the $3 billion Departmental Copier Business, overseeing the design, development, manufacturing, sales, and service of workgroup digital and light-lens copiers. That year she was named a corporate vice president. Some people grumbled as this young black woman was rapidly promoted to upper executive positions. Burns told Hayes in February of 1998: "When I first entered the organization, I was viewed as a novelty and drew a lot of attention without even trying. But the awe that people have over my achievements translates either

At a Glance . . .

Born Ursula M. Burns on September 20, 1958, in New York City; married Lloyd F. Bean, 1988; children: Malcolm, Melissa. *Education:* Polytechnic Institute of New York, BS, engineering, 1980; Columbia University, MS, mechanical engineering, 1981.

Career: Xerox Corporation, Stamford, CT, summer intern, 1980, various engineering positions in planning and product development, 1981-90, executive assistant to vice president of marketing and customer operations, 1990-91, executive assistant to chairman and CEO, 1991-92, vice president and general manager of various business units, 1992-95, London, UK, vice president and general manager of Workgroup Copier Business, 1995-97, Stamford, CT, vice president and general manager of departmental copier business, 1997-00, vice president for Worldwide Business Services, 1999, senior vice president of Corporate Strategic Services, 2000, senior corporate vice president, 2000–, president of Document Systems Solutions Group, 2001-02, president of Business Group Operations, 2002-2007; president, Xerox Corporation, 2007–.

Selected memberships: Boards of Directors: American Express; FIRST - For Inspiration and Recognition of Science and Technology; National Association of Manufacturers; National Center on Addiction and Substance Abuse at Columbia University; University of Rochester.

Selected awards: Rochester Business Alliance Women's Council, Athena Award; *Time*/CNN Annual List of Global Business Influentials, 2003; *U.S. Black Engineering & Information Technology,* 50 Most Important Blacks in Technology, 2003-05; *Fortune,* 50 Most Powerful Women in American Business, 2003-06; *Black Enterprise,* 75 Most Powerful African-Americans in Corporate America, 2005, 50 Most Powerful Black Women in Business, 2006.

Addresses: *Office*—Xerox Corporation, 800 Long Ridge Road, Stamford, CT 06904.

control that. But being the youngest person to pass through all the gates is what I did have control over. The fact that I did it faster than others has nothing to do with my race and gender. It was my performance."

In May of 2000 Burns was named senior vice president for Corporate Strategic Services in the Worldwide Business Services group, in charge of the company's worldwide manufacturing, integrated supply chain, and environment, health, and safety operations. In 2001 she became president of the Document Systems and Solutions Group, Xerox's largest global enterprise, generating as much as 40 percent of the company's revenues.

Burns became BGO president in December of 2002, with responsibility for more than 80 percent of the company's sales, about $14 billion annually, as well as some 14,000 employees worldwide. Burns oversaw six major business groups: production, office, information management, the Xerox Innovation Group, the Xerox Engineering Center, and paper, supplies, and supply-chain operations.

Helped Turn Xerox Around

Xerox was nearly bankrupt in 2002 and accounting irregularities had led to a $10 million fine for fraud. While Mulcahy reassured employees and stockholders and formulated a plan to save the company, Burns began implementing their plans for a major restructuring. At home, recovering from an emergency hysterectomy, she negotiated a contract with the company's unionized workers in Rochester, New York. Meanwhile she looked for ways to outsource their jobs. By convincing Xerox to outsource the manufacture of many of its products, Burns reportedly saved the company $2 billion in 2003. In a February 2006 *Fortune* magazine profile, Mulcahy called Burns "the ultimate straight-shooter." Burns led the company's rebound in the field of digital copiers and printers, introducing 21 new products and cutting prices on many older products. She told Deutsch in 2003: "Essentially, I'm the Ms. Inside for the operational side of the business." However by then Burns was becoming more of a public figure, talking to the media, investors, and customers and serving on numerous corporate and nonprofit boards. Mulcahy told Deutsch: "Ursula is articulate, she has deep knowledge, she's credible—and, yes, we are developing her externally."

Burns began dating Lloyd F. Bean, a Xerox scientist, in 1981. They married in 1988 and Bean retired in 2001. In the meantime Xerox provided financial support for the couple to maintain two households. In 1992 Burns told Joan Harrell Carter of *Black Enterprise:* "I see my husband two, maybe three times a month. We've been married for three years, but we've

into 'I'm super brilliant' or 'I must have floated through.' I can't just be a regular employee, and that is an insult. Being a black woman is who I am and I can't

only had the same home base for one year. He lives in our official home in Rochester, and I live in a town-house in Stamford." Despite her rapid corporate ascent, with the advent of their children Burns insisted that her weekends remain free. She told Carol Hymowitz of the *Wall Street Journal* in 2006: "We have to let go of external expectations of what it means to be a successful mother, wife and business person, and each define that for ourselves. No one will die if you don't show up at every business meeting or every school play." She told Gail Sheehy of *Glamour* in 2006: "I wasn't home almost all last week, but Tuesday night I had to be there for my son's volleyball game; he told me this was a big deal…on Saturday night when we were sitting around, everyone was happy, because I'd covered the things that were really important."

As of 2007 some viewed Burns as a potential successor to Mulcahy. However Burns had her critics. Some accused her of both micromanaging and under-managing. Others criticized her listening skills and said she sometimes moved too quickly. However Mulcahy told the *New York Times*, "Every weakness is one she can easily fix." Burns lacked no confidence in herself. Burns told Deutsch, "My perspective comes in part from being a New York black lady, in part from being an engineer. I know that I'm smart and have opinions that are worth being heard." Her confident outlook continued to work in her favor; in April 2007, it was announced that Burns would lead Xerox as president. Whether or not Burns chooses to lead Xerox in the future as CEO, it is clear that her leadership abilities are recognized by her organization and respected throughout the business world.

Sources

Books

International Directory of Business Biographies, St. James Press, 2005.

Periodicals

Black Enterprise, February 1992, pp. 246-249; August 1997, p. 62; February 1998, pp. 107-111.
Ebony, September 2003; March 2004, pp. 44-48.
Fortune, February 6, 2006, p. 54.
Glamour, September 2006, p. 272.
Jet, July 7, 2003, p. 31.
New York Times, June 1, 2003, p. 3.2.
Time, December 1, 2003, p. 78.
Wall Street Journal, November 20, 2006, p. B.1.

On-line

"Executive Biographies: Ursula M. Burns," *Xerox Newsroom*, www.xerox.com/go/xrx/template/inv_rel_newsroom.jsp?ed_name=Ursula_Burns&app=Newsroom&format=biography&view=ExecutiveBiography&Xcntry=USA&Xlang=en_US (February 15, 2007).
"Xerox Turns To Burns For Growth," *Forbes*, http://www.forbes.com/business/businesstech/2007/04/04/xerox-burns-faces-markets-equity-cx_rs_0404autfacescan01.html (April 5, 2007).

—Margaret Alic

Earl Caldwell

1941(?)—

Journalist

Earl Caldwell was a pioneering journalist who covered several significant events of the civil rights era and its aftermath. He was the sole journalist present at the scene when Martin Luther King Jr. was assassinated in 1968, and later found himself on the wrong side of the law when he covered the Black Panthers for the *New York Times* in the early 1970s. Between 1979 and 1994 he was a columnist for the *New York Daily News,* but moved away from daily journalism when he grew weary of the increasingly commercialized world of daily print journalism. Not long after leaving that job, he lamented the end of the golden era for journalists, who had been seen as crusading heroes just 20 years before. "The lines are drawn now in a way that pits people against each other," he told *New York Times* writer William Glaberson.

Born in the early 1940s, Caldwell grew up in central Pennsylvania, in a small town where his was one of just a handful of black families. As a teenager, he began working for Clearfield's local newspaper, *The Progress,* and moved on to a job with the *Intelligencer-Journal* of Lancaster, Pennsylvania. It was an era when college journalism programs had not yet become mandatory for cub reporters, and Caldwell's career was also indirectly boosted by the civil rights movement, for some civil rights leaders would, when approached by the media, agree to a story only if a black journalist was assigned to interview them.

Hired by New York Times

Caldwell worked for a Rochester, New York, newspa-per before landing a job at a prestigious daily, the *Herald Tribune,* in New York City in 1965. He went on to a brief stint with the *New York Post* before the *New York Times* offered him a position as a national correspondent, and he became the first African American ever to hold that title at the newspaper. His byline began appearing in March of 1967, and he covered an extensive range of issues that were shaking black and urban America in the years immediately following the ostensible end of the civil rights movement.

Though federal legislation had been enacted to secure equal protection for African Americans earlier that decade, poverty and social injustice still dominated parts of U.S. cities with large black populations, and a new political awareness as well as anger began to rise. Some of Caldwell's earliest stories for the *Times* focused on the campaigns of black political candidates, a walkout by teachers in a Harlem school because the building was drastically underheated, and a strike in Boston by an organized group of women welfare recipients that erupted into a minor riot. Over the next year, that last incident would be followed by increasingly longer, and far deadlier, clashes in largely African-American neighborhoods in Cincinnati, Ohio, Newark, New Jersey, and Detroit, Michigan, and Caldwell was sent to cover all of them for the *Times.*

Just after his first anniversary with the newspaper, Caldwell traveled to Memphis, Tennessee, to write about a visit there by Dr. Martin Luther King Jr., who planned to lead a march in support of striking munici-pal sanitation workers. Caldwell checked in a room at the black-owned Lorraine Motel, where King and his entourage were also staying, and interviewed the civil rights leader on April 3. He returned to his room, wrote the story, and went to bed. The following day, unable to meet with King again for a planned second interview, Caldwell stayed in his room and wrote a briefer story about city officials' attempts to stop the march from taking place. Later that afternoon, he heard a loud blast and rushed outside, where he saw people ducking for cover; he also noticed a man near a thicket of bushes across from the motel. Realizing King had just been shot, he called his editor in New York to deliver the news, and immediately began interviewing eyewitnesses for his next story.

Never Questioned by Investigators

Journalists cultivate an eye and an ear for detail that help them fill in or uncover a story, and though Caldwell was the sole reporter on the scene that day, he was not questioned by authorities until 31 years later. He spent the hours following the tragedy meeting with others instead, and found that he was not the only one who had spotted someone running away from the bushes; the thicket was inexplicably cut down a few

days later. At its onset, the official investigation seemed to focus on a white loner, James Earl Ray, who was believed to have fired the fatal shot from a flophouse across the street—a conclusion that was immediately viewed as suspicious. Many thought the government was responsible for King's death, and conspiracy theories abounded in the immediate aftermath and lingered on four decades later. Even the first sentence of Caldwell's story about the assassination for the *Times* noted that the civil rights leader was felled by a shot from "a distant gunman who then raced away and escaped."

Other elements of Caldwell's story became the template for suspicions about who had murdered King. Just before he was shot, King was standing on his motel-room balcony and speaking with the Reverend Jesse Jackson—at the time, a young aide of King's—and Caldwell's article quoted Jackson as saying, "when I turned around, I saw police coming from everywhere. They said, 'Where did it come from?' And I said, 'Behind you.' The police were coming from where the shot came…. We didn't need to call the police. They were here all over the place."

The rest of Caldwell's career in journalism would prove equally as tumultuous as that first year with the *Times.* He covered the murder trial of Angela Davis, an African-American scholar and activist linked to a notorious prison escape by some members of the Black Panther organization in which a California judge was killed. The Panthers, a militant group, were regularly in the headlines for their increasingly provocative acts and statements, and Caldwell was sent to cover the group during the heated months of the trial in northern California. "I had incredible access, it was an exciting group to be on the inside with," he told journalist Rebecca Neal in an article that appeared on America's Intelligence Wire. "They were geniuses with using the media to sell their story." But Caldwell soon found himself on the other side of the law: his belongings were searched at the courthouse, and a film canister containing marijuana was discovered. Caldwell was arrested, but acquitted on the charge, with a judge agreeing that his bag and belongings were often left open and unguarded in the room used by the press at the Davis trial's courthouse.

Asserted Reportorial Privilege

Caldwell's troubles soon deepened, however: the U.S. Department of Justice contacted him and asked him to work as a secret informer for the Panthers, and he refused. Then he was asked to provide information anyway via grand-jury testimony, but Caldwell refused to appear. For that, he was charged with contempt of court, and the *New York Times* supported his case, on the grounds that journalists should not be compelled to name their sources. There were two similar contempt charges against other reporters at U.S. newspapers, and a legal defense team joined the three cases together for trial and took it all the way to the U.S.

Supreme Court. In their final decision, the High Court justices reversed a lower court's ruling in the *United States v. Caldwell* which agreed with Caldwell that he was protected by the First Amendment from having to divulge his sources to the government. In response, states began to enact "shield" laws that granted journalists the right to protect their sources, but the issue remained a controversial one; in 2004, journalists for the *New York Times* and *Time* magazine were jailed for several weeks when they refused to disclose their sources.

Caldwell continued to write for the *New York Times* until mid-1974, and went on to a job with the *New York Daily News*. In 1979, he achieved another career first, this time as the first black journalist to write a regular column in a major daily newspaper in New York City. He held the job for the next 15 years, but resigned in early 1994 after a clash with his bosses at the paper. He had written a column about a hushed-up New York City police department investigation into charges that one of its white officers had sexually assaulted five black men in separate incidents. His editor asked him to change some of the wording, he refused, the column never ran, and Caldwell left the paper.

A collection of Caldwell's *Daily News* columns, *Black American Witness: Reports from the Front,* was published in 1995. He has been a professor of journalism at Hampton University, and host of a radio show the Pacifica network, "The Caldwell Chronicle." He is also associated with the Robert C. Maynard Institute for Journalism Education in Oakland, California, which seeks to increase diversity in U.S. newsrooms, and serves as director of its History Project. In the interview with Neal that appeared on America's Intelligence Wire, Caldwell conceded that while black journalists had made incredible strides since his generation first appeared on the scene, times had changed for the worse, too. Most major media outlets were part of large corporations, and the focus was on profit, not prestige. "If I was just starting out," he admitted, "I don't know if I see anything that would attract me to this business."

Selected writings

Books

Black American Witness: Reports from the Front, Lion House Publishing, 1995.

Sources

Periodicals

America's Intelligence Wire, April 6, 2004.
Broward Times (Coral Springs, FL), April 8, 2004, p. 1; April 15, 2004, p. 2.
Editor & Publisher, May 14, 1994, p. 17; August 13, 1994, p. 15.
New York Times, April 5, 1968, p. 1; June 8, 1972, p. 57; July 18, 1994.
San Francisco Chronicle, November 19, 1999, p. 6.
Virginian Pilot, April 6, 2004, p. E1.

On-line

"Earl Caldwell Biography," *Robert C. Maynard Institute for Journalism Education,* www.maynardije.org/news/features/caldwell/Biography-EarlCaldwell/ (February 20, 2007).
"The Caldwell Journals," *Robert C. Maynard Institute for Journalism Education,* www.maynardije.org/news/features/caldwell/ (April 3, 2007).

—Carol Brennan

Cedric the Entertainer

1964—

Comedian, actor

A major television star of the late 1990s and a member of the phenomenally successful Original Kings of Comedy tour, the man known as Cedric the Entertainer had built the beginnings of his own comedic industry by the early 2000s. A commercial aired during the Super Bowl in 2001 and a host of film projects launched him on a trajectory toward superstardom. The key to his success was that he combined the cultural strengths of the 1990s black renaissance in comedy with an Everyman quality, shared by only a few comedians, that induced audiences of all kinds to identify with him.

Cedric the Entertainer has often refused to divulge his last name, but he was born Cedric Kyles in St. Louis, Missouri, on April 14, 1964. His mother, a school reading specialist, encouraged his talents as a performer—but not, at first, as a comedian. "He was very bent on entertaining with singing and dancing," she told *Jet*. "He was always singing and dancing in plays. I couldn't nail down the comedic part because that didn't come until later." Despite his large, somewhat rotund physique, Cedric remained a talented dancer with an unexpected gracefulness that some have compared to that of the classic film comedian Jackie Gleason.

Enjoyed Performing

Attending Southeast Missouri State University, Cedric pursued his interest in performing with a television major and a theater minor. After graduating, however, he took a job as an insurance claims representative with a State Farm agency in Normal, Illinois. Still a performer at heart, Cedric entered a stand-up comedy competition in Chicago and walked away with a $500 prize. After that, most weekends saw him making the two-hour drive back to his hometown for appearances in comedy clubs. At some time during this period, he took the name "Cedric the Entertainer;" he intended it as a reference to his all-around abilities as a performer.

Another first prize, this one in the Miller Genuine Draft Comedy Search, led to wider tours and a realization that life as a comedian was within his reach. Cedric's breakthrough came in Dallas in 1989, when he was in the audience at a Dallas comedy club in which fellow African-American comedian Steve Harvey was a principal player. As the mirthless audience endured an unsuccessful act from a visiting headliner, Cedric decided to ask the house management if he could perform a five-minute set at no charge. His miniature set brought the house down, and Harvey, impressed, brought Cedric back to Dallas to headline his own show.

As a comedian, Cedric was notable for his almost total avoidance of profanity—in stark contrast to the vast majority of other touring comedians, black and white. "If I use a curse word it's because of the character I'm portraying," he explained to *Jet*. "I use curse words like a Lawry's seasoning salt. It's hidden somewhere inside the joke. I use it as a tenderizer." His humor was in the observational vein popular among other comedians, but his act was distinctive in its use of dance and physical motion and in its gentle spirit, usually devoid of the anger that so often seems to seethe behind the

At a Glance . . .

Born Cedric Kyles on April 14, 1964, in St. Louis, MO; son of Rosetta Kyles; married Lorna Wells, a stage-set costumer, 1999; children: Tiara (from previous relationship) and Croix Alexander (with Wells). *Education*: Southeast Missouri State University.

Career: Comedian, starting in St. Louis, MO, 1980s–; State Farm Insurance, Normal, IL, claims adjuster, mid-1980s; Miller Genuine Draft Comedy Search competition, late 1980s; Original Kings of Comedy, tour member, 1998-99; A Bird and A Bear Entertainment, production company, founder, 2002–.

Awards: Four NAACP Image Awards, for Best Supporting Actor in a Comedy Series, for the *Steve Harvey Show*; BET, Richard Pryor Comic of the Year Award, 1994; AFTRA Award.

Addresses: *Web*—www.ceddybear.com.

comedian's smile. "I'm a little bit cuddly," he told *USA Today*. "I'm a Cedi-bear."

That's not to say that Cedric was incapable of comedy with an edge. Perhaps one of his funniest sequences, captured on film in the *Original Kings of Comedy* concert tour documentary directed by filmmaker Spike Lee, originated while then-President Bill Clinton was beleaguered by questions about his relationship with White House intern Monica Lewinsky. Cedric's routine depicted how a black president might respond to similar questioning. "You gonna ask me about that in front of my wife?" he asks, according to the *New York Times*, and lunges toward an imaginary reporter.

Landed Television Gig

Cedric first appeared on television in 1992 in a stand-up segment on the *It's Showtime at the Apollo* program, and later performed on the *Def Comedy Jam* on cable TV's HBO network. 1994 brought his first ongoing gig when he became the host of Black Entertainment Television's *Comic View*, succeeding his future *Original Kings of Comedy* tour-mate, D.L. Hughley. *Comic View* featured a segment of his own, entitled "Ced's Comedy Crockpot." That year Cedric won the Richard Pryor Comic of the Year Award. Harvey emerged as something of a mentor to Cedric, which led to Cedric's receiving a continuing role on the hit situation comedy the *Steve Harvey Show*. Cedric played a high school coach named Cedric Jackie

Robinson. The role brought Cedric an unprecedented four consecutive NAACP Image awards for outstanding actor in a comedy series.

It was the *Original Kings of Comedy* tour itself that really cemented Cedric's status as a star in urban America. That tour, which became the top-grossing comedy program of all time and pointed to a pent-up demand for high-quality entertainment among black audiences, featured Hughley, Harvey, and Bernie Mac along with Cedric. Running from 1998 into 1999, the program spawned first a recording, which won a 1999 Grammy nomination for Best Spoken Comedy Album, and then Lee's acclaimed film.

The tour and film also put Cedric on the radar screens of Hollywood talent spotters in a big way. He landed parts in a string of films released in 2001, including *Kingdom Come*, *Serving Sara*, directed by Reginald Hudlin, and *Dr. Doolittle 2*, in which he was heard as the voice of a bear in a zoo. Cedric also wrote and developed the film *Preaching Ain't Easy*, which also featured Harvey and Bernie Mac. In 2001 Cedric developed a pilot episode for a series of his own on the WB network in which he would star, as he told the *Los Angeles Times*, as the coach of "the losingest team in the NBA." He also planned a stage revue that would nurture the careers of young comedians.

National celebrity came to Cedric, not as a result of any of these endeavors, however, but rather from a television commercial broadcast during the Super Bowl in January of 2001. Superbly tailored to Cedric's talents as a physical comedian and to his likeable Everyman persona, the commercial featured Cedric bringing an attractive date home to his apartment. Offering her something to drink, he goes to the kitchen for two bottles of Bud Light beer. Once he is safely out of her sight, he erupts into an enthusiastic dance—but forgets that by so doing he is shaking the still-closed beer bottles. Thus his date is drenched when her bottle is opened.

Won National Attention

The commercial ranked Number One out of 57 ads broadcast during the Super Bowl according to viewer polls. Cedric's performance inspired *USA Today* to dub him Madison Avenue's MVP. "I definitely noticed a difference in how people respond to me after the Super Bowl when I was out and about," Cedric told the *Los Angeles Times*. The following year Cedric appeared in another Bud Light ad that reached Number Three in the Super Bowl ranking. The exposure boded well indeed for Cedric's growing career. He was featured on his own variety show, *Cedric the Entertainer Presents*, on the Fox network in 2002. But his film career, that started with supporting roles in such films as *Serving Sara*, *Big Momma's House*, and *Barbershop* and its sequel, soon eclipsed his television work.

His *Barbershop* role garnered the most attention. As Eddie, a curmudgeonly barber, Cedric spouted off color jokes about some of the civil rights movement's greatest heroes. "Rosa Parks didn't do nothing but sit her Black ass down," Cedric's character, Eddie, grumbles in *Barbershop.* The role drew the ire of some in the black community, and Rosa Parks herself refused to attend the NAACP Image Awards that Cedric hosted in 2003. Cedric stood up to the negative attention in stride. "The point of the barbershop was that, while in there, people could speak their truth even if it wasn't the truth," he explained to Davina Morris of the *Voice.* His character Eddie, he continued, was "an antagonist.... He'd say things to get people fired up so they could give their own opinions. Not only did that work inside the film, but the controversy it sparked outside the film inspired people to talk about these heroes and research their stories to find out why Eddie said the things he did." The sequel was less controversial and in the end, Cedric's congenial personality and warmth overshadowed the outcries. Although he found himself explaining his character Eddie on CNN, Cedric told Kam Williams of the *Afro-American* that he "never experienced any personal attacks. I talked with Jesse Jackson and Rosa Parks, afterwards, and the King family, and we all arrived at an understanding about it with one another. Nobody ever blamed me, personally." The attention, however, had firmly put Cedric in the national spotlight. His celebrity made him a headliner.

To make the leap to leading roles in feature films, Cedric and his longtime manager Eric C. Rhone founded the production company, A Bird and A Bear Entertainment in 2002. The company's first film, *The Johnson Family Vacation,* released in 2004 and grossed over $30 million dollars. More than a vehicle for profits, his own company, Cedric explained to Alan Hughes of *Black Enterprise,* was about control. "We can control the style of the movie and its content and its characteristics," he asserted. "Often, especially as African Americans, [we're] accused of doing things on-screen that [are] considered buffoonery or something to that nature. Well, that's really determined by the writers and the powers–the people writing the check." With the power firmly in his hands, Cedric hoped to develop projects with "a certain Cedric The Entertainer kind of energy to them." Critics agreed that though the overall film lacked certain qualities, Cedric was a capable leading man. He followed that film with a full slate of others, including *The Honeymooners* and *Code Name: The Cleaner.*

With endorsement deals with McDonalds and Budweiser and a multimillion-dollar film deal with MGM, Cedric had a business acumen that he could leverage to create a long-lasting, profitable career worthy of his comedic talent. As he explained to Hughes, Cedric believed that comedians were "their own industry." His not only included career making deals, but also charitable efforts. Cedric started Cedric the Entertainer Charitable Foundation to offer scholarships and outreach programs to inner-city youth and their families in St. Louis, with plans to expand the programming nationally. Cedric vision, business sense, generosity, and talent gave him strong foundations for building his industry.

Selected works

Films

Big Momma's House, 2000.
Serving Sara, 2001.
Barbershop, 2002.
Intolerable Cruelty, 2003.
Barbershop 2: Back in Business, 2004.
Johnson Family Vacation, 2004.
Lemony Snicket's a Series of Unfortunate Events, 2004.
Man of the House, 2005.
Be Cool, 2005.
The Honeymooners, 2005.
Charlotte's Web, 2006.
Code Name: The Cleaner, 2007.
Talk to Me, 2007.

Television

It's Showtime at the Apollo, 1992.
Comic View, host, BET, 1994.
Steve Harvey Show, 1996–.
Cedric the Entertainer Presents, 2002.

Sources

Periodicals

Afro-American, March 15-21, 2003, p. 7; October 24, 2003, p. B1.
Black Enterprise, July 2001, p. 64; December 2004, p. 130.
Chicago Sun-Times, February 5, 2001, p. 51.
Essence, April 2001, p. 80.
Interview, August 2000, p. 57.
Jet, September 20, 1999, p. 58; March 12, 2001, p. 58.
Los Angeles Times, February 6, 2001, p. F1; June 20, 2003, p. E32.
New York Times, August 18, 2000, p. E12.
USA Today, January 30, 2001, p. B3.
Voice, October 19, 2003, p. 4.
Washington Informer, January 4-10, 2007, p. 29.

On-line

"In the Spotlight: Cedric," *Webster University,* www.webster.edu/depts/business/notabene/06fall/cedric.htm (April 4, 2007).

—Ashyia Henderson, James Manheim, and Sara Pendergast

Janet Langhart Cohen

1941—

Media consultant, Television personality

As wife of the U.S. Secretary of Defense, Janet Langhart Cohen was one of the most prominent spouses in Washington from 1997 to 2001. The former beauty pageant winner, Boston television personality, media consultant—and longtime Democrat—wed a Republican senator in 1996, and their union has been celebrated more as a triumph over multicultural issues in America than political ones. Though there had been other high-profile interracial couples in Washington power circles, including Supreme Court Justice Clarence Thomas and his wife, Janet and her husband William S. Cohen—appointed to his cabinet post in the Clinton Administration in late 1996—were the country's highest-ranking such pair on the official protocol lists. *Washington Post* writer Kevin Merida called them "the best advertisement for the kind of dialogue and interpersonal racial progress President Clinton is now pushing, the kind of progress that can't be legislated." After Cohen's tenure ended, the couple remained prominent social commentators. Janet penned her personal memoir, *From Rage to Reason* in 2004. And in 2007, the couple co-authored *Love in Black and White: A Memoir of Race, Religion, and Romance*, the story of their life together.

Developed Passion for Civil Rights

Cohen was born Janet Floyd on December 22, 1941, and grew up in public housing in racially segregated Indianapolis. She was raised by her mother, who worked as a hospital ward secretary. After spending two years at Indianapolis's Butler University, Cohen found success as a model in the 1960s, winning several beauty pageants, including "Miss Sepia" of 1966 and "Miss International Auto Show" two years later. It was a different era, and one that ignited in her a sense of injustice over racial attitudes in America. She recalled that on one occasion, she arrived at an audition for an appliance commercial and caused somewhat of a stir; an African-American woman pitching products in a nationwide ad campaign was still a rarity at the time.

Cohen married her first husband, Tony Langhart in 1968, just as her career was taking off. She was working at a Chicago television station (she eventually became a weathercaster there), and the couple married just weeks after the tragic assassination of Martin Luther King Jr. Both were ardent civil-rights supporters, and "it was a kind of sentimental reaction to that loss," Cohen told the *Washington Post*'s Merida in a 1997 interview. They divorced later that year.

As a result of her ratings success in Chicago, Cohen was hired by a Boston television station in 1974 as the co-host of *Good Day*, a local news program. She arrived in the city while a vicious battle over school busing was raging, a crisis whose worst moments were captured in news footage of residents of one neighborhood throwing stones at yellow schoolbuses full of children. The racially charged atmosphere lingered in sections of Boston for years afterward. Cohen was overwhelmed. "I felt betrayed because I had a notion of Boston as the cradle of liberty," she told *Boston Globe* writer John Powers. "Boston was our beacon of fairness and justice and in many ways, it is. I didn't get those ideas from romance. So I would go on the air and

At a Glance . . .

Born Janet Floyd, December 22, 1941, in Indianapolis, IN; daughter of a hospital ward secretary; married Tony Langhart, 1968 (divorced, 1968);
married Robert Kistner, 1978 (a physician and researcher; divorced, 1989); married William Cohen
(politician and U.S. cabinet secretary), February 14,
1996. *Education*: Attended Butler University, 1960-62.
Politics: Democrat.

Career: Began as Ebony Fashion Fair model; affiliated
with WISH-TV, Indianapolis, IN; WBBM-TV, Chicago,
television weathercaster in Chicago, late 1960s;
WCVB-TV (Channel 5), Boston, MA, co-host of "Good
Day," 1974-78; affiliated with NBC network, 1978 and
the America Alive show; served as assistant press
secretary in the 1988 presidential campaign of Michael
Dukakis; co-host of New England Today, 1993(?);
co-anchored America's Black Forum with Julian Bond
on Black Entertainment Television (BET), 1996(?);
Langhart Communications, an image-consulting firm,
founder, 1996–; author, 2004–.

Memberships: United Negro College Fund, former
board member; U.S. National Arboretum, former
board member; Global Citizens Circle.

Awards: VFW Award, 2000; Zack Fischer Award,
2001.

Addresses: *Office*—Langhart Communications, 5335
Wisconsin Avenue, NW, Suite 440, Washington, DC
20015. *Web*—www.langhartcommunications.com.

say: 'Why are you doing this? Why are you stoning
black children? How do you reconcile this? Where is
the cardinal?'" In response, a local civil rights leader
invited Cohen to her home, and gently reminded the
newscaster to direct her words not to groups of viewers, but rather "to the good people of Boston. They'll
know who they are," Cohen recalled in the *Boston
Globe* interview.

Cohen's combination of frankness, affability, and glamour earned her a devoted following. On the streets of
Boston, she was a celebrity, a favorite with both black
and white viewers. Boston Globe reporter Jack Thomas offered praise years later, saying, "Cohen is known
for surprises, and for style, passion and ambition." In
1978, NBC hired her to co-host America Alive, and

that same year she married another prominent Bosto-
nian, gynecologist Dr. Robert Kistner. Several years her
senior, the physician had been part of the team of
research scientists responsible for the birth control pill.
As his wife, Cohen never needed to work again; they
lived a lavish lifestyle that included a condominium at
the city's posh Ritz Hotel. Yet Cohen was loathe to
abandon her career for good. She returned to television in Boston for a time, but was released from her
contract in a notorious 1987 incident when she refused
to draw lottery numbers, declaring to the press that she
had no ambition to become "Vanna Black."

Employed Energies toward Politics

Cohen's skills soon found a more appropriate outlet
when she became assistant press secretary for the
1988 presidential campaign of Massachusetts governor Michael Dukakis. The Democratic Party nominee
lost the election to George Bush, but her involvement
in the high-stakes world of media and politics injected
added ambition into Cohen's career plans. By then,
Kistner had retired, and was enjoying a more relaxed
life in Palm Beach; their marriage failed when the pair
realized they had far different goals. They split amicably
in 1989, but Kistner tragically committed suicide a year
later. In time, Cohen renewed an acquaintance with a
politician she had once interviewed in the 1970s, a
senator from Maine named William S. Cohen.

Cohen had been raised Jewish but rejected the religion
at the age of 12 when he was told he could not have a
bar mitzvah unless his Protestant mother converted. A
moderate Republican who had served in Congress
since 1972, Cohen was often at odds with more
conservative elements in the party and was known as
one of the few Republicans who still supported
affirmative-action programs. He also wrote poetry and
novels. When he and Janet started dating, a well-
connected New England family wrote him and asserted
that dating an African American woman would ruin his
political career. The family had donated large sums of
money to his campaigns over the years, and Cohen
decisively informed them that their funds and opinions
were no longer welcome.

In the early 1990s, Cohen was hired by the cable
network Black Entertainment Television (BET) and
co-anchored *America's Black Forum*, a talk show,
with civil-rights activist Julian Bond. She also founded
Langhart Communications, a consulting company that
helps corporate executives and government officials
improve their on-camera demeanor. After a courtship
of several years, Janet Langhart and William Cohen
married on Valentine's Day in 1996 in a formal room
of the U.S. Capitol building. The ceremony was attended by several prominent political figures, including
Republican Congressmen Alfonse D'Amato and Trent
Lott, as well as journalists such as Andrea Mitchell and
Dan Rather.

Became First Lady of the Pentagon

By this point in his career, Cohen had decided not to run for re-election in the 1996 campaigns. In his farewell speech, he told his colleagues in Congress that bipartisan politics—primarily, the bitter struggle between the Democratic White House and Republican-controlled Congress—was the main reason for his leaving office. He reminded them in his address that "we are all on the same side," the *Washington Post* reported. In a surprise announcement a few months later, Cohen was named Defense Secretary after Clinton won a second Oval Office term. As a member of the Senate Armed Services Committee during his tenure in Congress, Cohen had often locked horns with Clinton's first Defense Secretary, William Perry, but when Perry stepped down, he recommended Cohen to take his place.

Janet suddenly became one-half of one of the most prominent interracial couples in the United States. In her role as the wife of the man who oversees all of the country's armed forces, she traveled often with her husband to visit American troops stationed around the globe—including to some of the harsher, troubled regions of the world—and tried to use her position to call attention to the plight of military families far from home. She was popular with troops and enjoyed speaking with them one-on-one. Janet Langhart's marriage to Cohen also provided inspiration to the more than 1.4 million active-duty servicemen and women, many of whom are non-Caucasian. Furthermore, many military personnel marry someone of another background. "It's a military of volunteers and G.I. Janes and whites and blacks and Latinos and Asians who look at [Cohen] and his spouse and see the America of the millennium," wrote the *Boston Globe*'s Powers.

Cohen often queried soldiers and servicepeople about conditions on American bases overseas, conspiratorially telling them, "You can level with me," as she explained in the *Boston Globe* interview with Powers. "Maybe I can't do anything about it, but I can hear you, and I can take it back to my husband." Cohen also was sensitive to the plight of those who are not sheltered by the benefits of an American passport. In Sofia, Bulgaria, for a NATO summit with Cohen, the wives of American embassy officials told Cohen how abysmal the hospital conditions were in the city for its residents; she returned home, marshalled support from pharmaceutical companies for supplies and had them flown over. During her tenure as First Lady of the Pentagon, Cohen, as her husband described to Lynn Norment of *Ebony,* was "perhaps the most actively engaged first lady of the Pentagon, ever." From 1997-2001, Cohen produced and hosted a weekly television program called *Special Assignment,* that was broadcast to troops around the globe; organized Pentagon Pops, a musical tribute to the military; arranged a military family forum for spouses to voice their concerns to Pentagon officials; and started the Citizen Patriot Organization. She also served as First Lady of the USO

until 2001 when Cohen was replaced by Donald Rumsfeld as Secretary of Defense.

The high profile of Janet Langhart Cohen and William Cohen in American culture shone a spotlight on their interracial marriage. They have remarked that as an interracial couple, they have never experienced overt discrimination, although some people feel the need to bring up African-American subjects. But she remained nonplused by the attitudes of others. "Look at me," she told the *Globe*'s Powers. "I grew up in the ghetto in a single-parent family. I went to a private college on a scholarship. And here I am on Pennsylvania Avenue with the Secretary of Defense. If that isn't a reflection on how great this country is." Determined to tell her story, Cohen published her memoir *From Rage to Reason: My Life in Two Americas* in 2004. In it she traced her rise from charity hospital to college scholarship to beauty pageants to high-profile journalist to national attention. Then in 2007, the Cohens shared their story of how they came from such different backgrounds to find romance in their joint memoir *Love in Black and White: A Memoir of Race, Religion, and Romance.* The details of Janet's early life and her marriage to Cohen offer hope for America as a melting pot.

Selected works

Books

From Rage to Reason: My Life in Two Americas, Dafina Books/Kensington, 2004.
(With William S. Cohen) *Love in Black and White: A Memoir of Race, Religion, and Romance,* Rowman and Littlefield, 2007.

Sources

Periodicals

Boston Globe, March 9, 1989, p. 77; September 16, 1997, p. E1.
Ebony, November 2000, p. 154.
Jet, October 10, 1988, p. 33; February 12, 1996, p. 32; March 4, 1996, p. 16; May 24, 2004, p. 33.
Washington Post, December 6, 1996, p. A26; December 14, 1997, p. F1.

On-line

"On Faith: Guest Voices: Love Is a Force That Pulls Hearts Together," *Newsweek* and *Washingtonpost. com,* http://newsweek.washingtonpost.com/on faith/guestvoices/2007/02/love_is_a_force_that _pulls_hea.html#more (April 3, 2007).
"Tavis Smiley Archives: Janet Langhart Cohen, March 1, 2007," *Tavis Smiley Group,* www.pbs.org/kcet/ tavissmiley/archive/200703/20070301_cohen. html (April 3, 2007).

—Carol Brennan and Sara Pendergast

Natalie Cole

1950—

Singer, songwriter, actress

Inheriting a beautiful voice from her famous father, Natalie Cole has sold millions of records worldwide. During the 1970s she sang on six major albums and collected several Grammy Awards. In the midst of this successful recording career she became addicted to drugs. After a long battle, she again rose to the top of the charts in 1991 with her hugely successful album, *Unforgettable... With Love* It became "the most significant album of the decade," according to Earl Calloway of the *Chicago Defender,* and made Cole a superstar in her own right. She continued to develop as an artist; she even broke free of the jazz standards that made her famous, with her 2006 album *Leavin'* on which she explored classic rhythm and blues and pop favorites.

Born to Famous Singers

Natalie Cole was born to singers Maria Hawkins Cole and Nat King Cole on February 6, 1950 in Los Angeles, California. She was one of five children and although Mr. and Mrs. Cole had already adopted a niece, Carol (Cookie), Natalie was their first biological child. She was first called Stephanie, but the couple soon changed her name to Natalie. The Coles later adopted a son, Kelly, and in 1961 their twin girls, Casey and Timolin, were born. Nat Cole began calling Natalie "Sweetie," a name she is still known by among family and close friends.

Even though her parents hoped she would not go into show business, Cole developed an interest in music. Not only was her father a famous singer, her mother

had been a successful singer with the bands of leaders Benny Carter, Duke Ellington, and Fletcher Henderson. Maria Cole also sang and recorded duets with her husband. Natalie's uncle, Eddie Coles, was a successful musician as well.

Cole's early life could be described as that of a princess in a musical world. Shortly before she was born, her parents had bought a house in the elite Hancock Park section of Los Angeles. They were the first black family to do so in the still-discriminatory 1950s, causing a considerable stir in the exclusive neighborhood. When Cole was growing up her parents experienced racial discrimination and her father received threats. He sometimes performed with police officers on stage. Young Natalie was unaware of the difficulties; Maria and Nat Cole successfully shielded their children from these problems.

Visitors to the Hancock Park house frequently included singers, musicians, songwriters, and other people related to music and show business. Pearl Bailey, Aretha Franklin, Billie Holiday, Sarah Vaughan, Ella Fitzgerald, Nancy Wilson, Carmen McRae, Duke Ellington, and Count Basie were just a few. Natalie recalled to *Jet*, "Not only did I meet and get to know some of these great singers and musicians, but I fondly recall addressing them as 'aunt' and 'uncle.'"

When Cole was as young as three-and-a-half her father would take her and Cookie to the studio when he worked. One day he announced his intention to have her and Cookie record. But he told reporters that young Natalie often yawned while singing so he did not

At a Glance . . .

Born on February 6, 1950, in Los Angeles, CA, daughter of Nat King Cole and Marie Hawkins Ellington Cole; married Marvin Yancy 1976 (divorced); married Andre Fischer 1989 (divorced); children: Robert Adam Yancy. *Education*: University of Massachusetts, BA 1972.

Career: "I'm With You," Greek Theater, Los Angeles (debut performance), singer, 1961; solo artist 1973; Capitol Records, singer, 1975-1987; Elektra, singer 1987-1990s; Verve Records, singer, 2000(?)–.

Awards: 2 Grammy Awards, 1975; Grand Prix Award 5th Tokyo Music Festival, 1976; 1 Grammy Award 1976; Soul Train Best Single (Female) Award, 1987; Soul Train Best Single (Female) Award, 1992; NARAS MusiCares Person of the Year, 1992; 3 Grammy Awards, 1992; 3 NAACP Image Awards, 1992; 2 American Music Awards, 1992; Grammy Award, 1993; Honorary degree from Berklee College of Music, 1995; Grammy Award, 1996; Urban League , Whitney M. Young, Jr. Award, 2000.

Addresses: *Web*—www.nataliecole.com.

know if they would be successful in recording a song. Cole was six when she sang on a Christmas album, and a year later both she and Cookie sang with their father on "Ain't She Sweet."

Even though she had been singing informally since she was three Cole told David Wild in *Rolling Stone*, "I had a really horrid voice early on." But when she was 11 she began to practice singing and recording popular songs on a tape recorder her father had given her. She proved her ability to Nat Cole when at the age of 11 she sang Ella Fitzgerald's hit, "Undecided." Not only was her father delighted with her voice, he was also surprised that she had chosen a jazz song over what seemed to be her greatest interest, rock 'n' roll.

Cole's interest in music had not been restricted to her father's crooning ballads and jazz. Like many kids of the 1960s she had developed a taste for rock 'n' roll. Even though her father did not care for it, he brought home the records she requested, slipping jazz titles in the stack with the Beatles. Ironically, when the Beatles' "I Want To Hold Your Hand" topped the pop charts, her father's "That Sunday That Summer" was also there.

In 1961 Cole made her professional singing debut with her father in "I'm With You" at the Greek Theater in Los Angeles. Despite her famous father she had to audition for the part. Cole enjoyed her stage experience and as an adolescent formed and sang in a jazz group, the Malibu Music Men. Even though she had made her debut she did not turn to professional singing. She attended boarding school in the East until age 15 when her father passed away. Cole and her father had enjoyed a special closeness and she took his death from lung cancer very hard. She returned home from school to be with her family. Her father had tried to steer her into medicine or law and his death served as the stimulus she needed to seriously consider medicine as a career.

Developed Her Own Musical Taste

Cole later moved to Massachusetts when her mother remarried and relocated the family. Cole worked as a receptionist and pursued her interest in rock 'n' roll by attending rock concerts. She enrolled in the University of Massachusetts at Amherst in 1968. Typical of young people during the sixties she became involved in partying and drug experimentation. Cole worked as a waitress during the summer of 1971, but found herself singing with the house band before long. She performed with Black Magic at small local clubs and although she did not like it, the club owners insisted on using "Nat King Cole's daughter" as a draw.

Cole graduated from the University of Massachusetts in 1972 with a bachelor degree in child psychology. Instead of pursuing a related professional career, she had found that performing was her first love. She worked at developing her own style as a solo singer, singing only a few of her father's songs, and aiming more for a combination of rock, jazz, and soul. In 1973 she debuted in New York, singing at Shepheard's, and then later at Madison Square Garden.

A turning point came in 1974 when Cole connected with two songwriters and producers from Chicago— Chuck Jackson and Marvin Yancy. They had seen her perform at a nightclub there and sent some of their songs to Cole. After having her make a demo tape they tried to get her a recording contract, but their efforts were unsuccessful until Capitol Records made an offer. She wished to avoid comparisons to her father by signing with a label other than his. However, in 1975 she recorded her first album, *Inseparable*, with Capitol. It was the start of a rapid rise to stardom for Cole when it went gold, selling over 500,000 copies. Two songs from that LP, "Inseparable" and "This Will Be" were hits that reached both the pop and rhythm-and-blues charts with "This Will Be" reaching the Top 10. She received two Grammys at the 1976 awards ceremony for New Artist of the Year and for Best Female Rhythm and Blues Vocal Performance. She performed "This Will Be" for the audience.

Career Blossomed

In 1976 Cole released *Natalie*, which had a hit single, "Sophisticated Lady." She co-wrote the rhythm-and-blues song with Jackson and Yancy, and for it she won her second Grammy for Best Female Rhythm-and-Blues Vocal Performance in 1977. It can be difficult for an artist in any genre to top a previous hit, and even though *Natalie* also went gold it did not receive the acclaim of *Inseparable*.

Cole had been raised in her mother's Episcopalian tradition, but during this time she made the decision to embrace the Baptist denomination. Cole was drawn to the church-oriented lifestyle of an aunt, Evelyn Coles, during a visit to Chicago. While there she also became better acquainted with Marvin Yancy, who was a Baptist minister, in addition to being a songwriter and producer. They married in 1976. Yancy divided his time between his congregation at the Fountain of Life Baptist Church in Chicago and his work in New York. For the most part, he did not accompany Cole when she toured. Their son Robert Adam Yancy was born in 1978.

Cole's third album, *Thankful*, was released in 1977. It was a resounding success and went platinum, selling over a million copies. The single from that album, "Our Love," was a hit that reached the top five of both the pop and soul charts. Cole recorded *Unpredictable* later that year, which also went platinum, as did her hit single, "I've Got Love On My Mind."

Natalie Cole's star continued to rise, and in 1978 she hosted an hour-long special on CBS. She also released her fifth album, *Natalie Live*, a two-record set that went gold. In the fall she gave a sold-out concert at the Metropolitan Opera House in New York. Cole had worked hard to perfect her rhythm and blues style and was successful in both the pop and blues arenas. She was often compared to Aretha Franklin, who had been considered the Queen of Soul by the music industry and fans since the 1960s. Cole was influenced by Franklin's gospel-flavored style. When she began to forge her way in the music industry she first concentrated on rock 'n' roll, inspired by Janis Joplin, the Beatles, Jefferson Airplane, and Stevie Wonder, but she found herself drawn to Franklin's music. However, Franklin did not have the corner on soul—Cole had grown up surrounded by great black song stylists like Billie Holiday, Carmen McRae, Sarah Vaughan, and Ella Fitzgerald, all of whom influenced her music tastes and eventual style. Despite comparisons many critics and writers acknowledged voice and stylistic differences as well. It was said those comparisons did not sit well with Aretha Franklin and even caused a feud between the two singers.

In 1979, Cole explored another facet of recording by collaborating with soul singer Peabo Bryson. The resulting duet album *We're the Best of Friends* went gold. She also released *I Love You So* that year and it went gold. Natalie Cole seemed headed for the legendary fame her father had achieved but those very demands her parents had referred to were taking a toll on her personal life and career. Despite her achievements she was plagued by self doubt. This coupled with her intense recording and touring schedule had led to a dependence on drugs. Just as other performance artists have found through the years, chemical dependency led to self-destruction as well as the destruction of live performances. Cole had basked in fan adoration and yet she felt she was not worthy of their praise and of her success. She told Richard Harrington of the *Washington Post*, "As my success escalated, so did the drug problem." During this time Cole had bitter fights with her record company, and her relationships with her manager and other music professionals became strained. She remembered to *Essence* Her world crashed around her as album sales dropped, her performances were highly criticized, and her marriage disintegrated. She and Yancy separated in 1979, but he continued to produce her records.

Drug Addiction Nearly Ruined Her Career

By 1983 Cole's career was in ruins and she was unable to go on. She made several unsuccessful attempts to overcome her drug addiction and her mother had been put in charge of her estate by the court. Maria Cole was also caring for Natalie's son. In November of 1983 Cole entered the Hazelden drug-treatment center in Minnesota. It took her six months to recover. Later, she told Alan Carter in *Redbook*, "I will never get to that point again."

An album Cole had recorded during this difficult period and right before entering Hazelden, *I'm Ready*, was released in 1983 despite her protests over the title. She felt it was at great odds with her physical and mental condition of the time. The album sales were disappointing at only 40,000 copies sold. After her release from the clinic she set about reestablishing her career, and regaining the approval of her fans. Her next release, *Dangerous*, was also disappointing although it had sales of almost 150,000 copies.

It was not until 1987 that Cole's career reached the heights of success again. She had signed with a new label, and her LP *Everlasting* yielded three hit singles with "Jump Start," "I Live For Your Love," and "Pink Cadillac." "Pink Cadillac" was rocker Bruce Springsteen's song; Cole's rhythm-and-blues treatment sent it into the top five of the charts in the United States and England.

On another positive note, Cole married record producer Andre Fischer in 1989 and became a stepmother to his three children. Cole also hosted a talent show, "Big Break," helping new performers to break into the business.

Recorded Her Father's Music

While Cole had done a few of her father's songs in her performances, she had avoided focusing on them and his style. But later, she performed more of his songs, comfortable that she had finally established her own style and identity. Audience acceptance and favorable comparison to her father encouraged her, and in the early nineties she revealed a desire that she had had for some time—to record an entire album of her father's songs. Her desired project was met with skepticism, but the resulting album in 1991, *Unforgettable... With Love*, was a huge crossover success that went platinum many times over. Not only did Cole sing her father's songs, but "Unforgettable" was done with the help of technology with the original recording and Natalie's singing and orchestra accompaniment blended together to sound as if father and daughter actually sang a duet. The album and song earned Cole three Grammy awards, including Best Traditional Pop Performance, Album of the Year, and Record of the Year. It also brought Cole two American Music Awards. The album was recorded in the same Capitol studio that her father used. She toured much of 1992 promoting the album and giving performances. When she could she spent time with her family and worked with charities, including the Children's Diabetes Foundation, the Rainforests Foundation, the American Red Cross, the Minority AIDS Project, and the Permanent Charities Committee, an entertainment industry effort.

Her schedule was equally full in 1993. Early in the year Cole made her television dramatic acting debut in "I'll Fly Away," an NBC series. In March of that year, she sang at the Academy Awards show and by spring she had released a recording in the same vein of *Unforgettable... With Love*, except this album, *Take A Look*, held a collection of songs her father's friends and acquaintances had made famous. She told *Jet*, "This album actually is the album that I've always wanted to do and that is an album of jazz standards with great stuff that my dad turned me on to when I was about 10 or 11 years old." *Take A Look*, with its jazz-oriented sound sold just under 500,000 copies and appealed to a smaller consumer base than *Unforgettable... With Love,* which had become a multiplatinum album with more than 14 million copies sold.

Enjoyed Newfound Success

Cole branched into new performance venues in 1994. In January she sang the national anthem, accompanied by the Atlanta University Center chorus, at the Super Bowl and received much acclaim. In February she traveled to Sun City, South Africa, to perform in her own show. She was the first African American to perform since the country was desegregated.

Her jazz-flavored Christmas album, *Holly and Ivy*, was also released in 1994. Although she had not been planning to do a holiday album, she received a song from a friend that started the process. She told *Jet*, "Michael [Masser] called and said, 'I've got this beautiful Christmas song I wrote just for you.' He played it for me, and it was beautiful and then we thought, why not put out a whole album....then I was running around in April, looking for Christmas songs." The album received favorable reviews, and Cole performed songs from it when she starred on an episode of PBS TV's "Great Performances." Also in 1994 Natalie played the title role in the USA cable network movie, *Lily In Winter*. It was her television movie-acting debut. Of the experience Cole revealed to *Jet*, "Acting is probably one of the least glamorous jobs in Hollywood."

Seeking the huge success of *Unforgettable... With Love*, Cole released *Stardust* in the fall of 1996. Once again and with the help of technology, Cole sang with her late father on "When I Fall In Love." (The song won Cole another Grammy Award for best pop collaboration.) Not wanting the album to be another version of *Unforgettable... With Love*, Cole and her producers Phil Ramone, David Foster, and George Duke chose songs recorded by various artists, and not just her father. Of the songs, Cole told J.R. Reynolds of *Billboard*, "The songs are more sculpted than those on *Unforgettable*, and vocally, they have more drama." Her label, Elektra, sought to not only reach the massive audience appeal of *Unforgettable... With Love*, but to also appeal to international consumers and broaden her fan base. Selected tracks on the album were recorded in several different languages, including Portuguese, Italian, and French. Cole told Reynolds, "I'm just lucky that I pick up foreign languages fairly easily." Several television guest shots, and an international tour schedule in 1997 followed the album's release.

Searched for New Direction

By the late 1990s Cole had found herself pigeonholed as a performer. "People seem to always think of me as a jazz performer," Cole told the Seattle publication, the *Skanner*. "But I've always said I sing jazz, but I'm not a jazz singer." She explained that with *Unforgettable...* she had been attempting "to make a transition to jazz there, not stay in it for the rest of my life." While she acknowledged that the success of *Unforgettable...* had given her "the kind of opportunities that few artists ever get to have," as she told Rita Charleston of the *Philadelphia Tribune,* Cole wanted to "keep reinventing myself." To try to break out of the pigeonhole in which she had found herself, Cole recorded "the kind of pop and R&B I did when I was starting out" for her 1999 album *Snowfall on the Sahara,* as she told the *Skanner*. The album included renditions of songs from such different artists a Roberta Flack and Taj Mahal.

Cole published her autobiography, *An Angel on my Shoulder,* in 2000. The book was a long time in coming. Before writing it, Cole had to gain a perspective on her life that only time could give. Written after

15 years of sobriety and recovering from her second failed marriage, Cole offered readers a candid look at her life. Yet the writing was not easy. "Even after all these years, I had many moments of anxiety, anger and grief when I recalled certain things. It's almost like you're back to the day it happened," Cole explained to Melba Newsome of *HealthQuest*.

But Cole had clearly moved on, and with her personal life in order, she continued to nurture her career. She released a jazz album in 2002 called *Ask a Woman Who Knows*, with covers of music by Dinah Washington and Sarah Vaughan, among others. She also branched into acting, appearing episodes of *Grey's Anatomy, Touched by an Angel,* and *Studio 60.*

For her 2006 album, *Leavin'*, Cole again signaled her interest in moving on. Again moving away from the jazz that made her famous, Cole worked to put her own stamp on others' pop and rhythm-and-blues songs. She also involved herself in all aspects of production—"up to my hairline," as she said on her Web site—making critical decisions to create an album that introduced her new direction. For the album Cole covered such disparate artists as Fiona Apple, Etta James, Neil Simon, and Sting. She also covered Aretha Franklin's "Day Dreaming," the first of Franklin's songs that Cole had ever recorded. Citing Franklin as her "musical mentor," Cole expressed hope that Franklin approved of her rendition of the song, which earned Cole a Grammy nomination. Cole's intentional approach to *Leavin'* seemed to signal that she knew exactly where she was going and that her fans might want to join her.

Selected works

Books

An Angel on my Shoulder, 2000. Recordings *Inseparable,* (includes "Inseparable" and "This Will Be"), Capitol, 1975.
Natalie, (includes "Sophisticated Lady"), Capitol, 1976.
Unpredictable, Capitol, 1977.
Thankful, (includes "Our Love"), Capitol, 1977.
Natalie...Live!, Capitol, 1978.
I Love You So, Capitol, 1979.
We're The Best Of Friends (with Peabo Bryson), Capitol, 1979.
Don't Look Back, Capitol, 1980.

Happy Love, Capitol, 1981.
I'm Ready, Capitol, 1983.
Everlasting, (includes "Jump Start," "I Live For Your Love," and "Pink Cadillac"), Elektra, 1987.
Good To Be Back, Elektra, 1989.
Unforgettable... With Love, (includes "Unforgettable"), Elektra, 1991.
Take a Look, Elektra, 1993.
Holly and Ivy, Elektra, 1994.
Stardust, Elektra, 1996.
Snowfall on the Sahara, Elektra, 1999.
Ask a Woman Who Knows, Verve, 2002.
Leavin', Verve, 2006.

Sources

Books

Gourse, Leslie, *Unforgettable: The Life and Mystique of Nat King Cole,* St. Martin's Press, 1991.
Press, Skip, *Natalie & Nat King Cole,* Skip Press, Crestwood House, 1995.

Periodicals

Billboard, August 31, 1996, p. 9.
Chicago Defender, April 7, 2001, p. 17.
Ebony, December 1999, p. 190.
HealthQuest, January 31, 2001, p. 12.
Jet, July 5, 1993, p. 57; November 22, 1993; December 19, 1994, pp. 38, 40.
Philadelphia Tribune, October 13, 2006, p. E4.
Redbook, October 1993, p. 153.
Rolling Stone, September 19, 1991, p. 19.
Washington Post, April 30, 1986, p. C1.

On-line

Natalie Cole: Official Website, www.nataliecole.com (March 28, 2007).

Other

Additional information for this profile was obtained from the liner notes for the *Unforgettable... With Love* CD.

—Sandy J. Stiefer, Allison M. Marion, and Sara Pendergast

Marcia Cooke

1954—

Federal judge

In 2004 Marcia Cooke became Florida's first black female federal judge. She ruled on a number of high-profile cases, including one of the first terrorist cases to be heard in a civilian court. Her decisions broke new legal ground.

Became a Federal Prosecutor

Marcia Gail Cooke was born on October 16, 1954, in Sumter, South Carolina, the daughter of Heyward and Ella Randolph Cooke. She earned her bachelor's degree from Georgetown University in Washington, D.C. in 1975 and her law degree from Wayne State University in Detroit in 1977. She was admitted to the Michigan Bar Association and to the U.S. District Court (Eastern District) in Michigan in 1978. In 1983 she was admitted to the 6th Circuit U.S. Court of Appeals.

Cooke began her career defending indigent clients, first as a Legal Aid attorney and then as a public defender in Detroit. Moving to the other side of the courtroom, she then spent three years as a federal prosecutor. After a short period with a law firm, Cooke was named to the U.S. District Court in 1984. For the next eight years she served as a federal magistrate judge in Detroit.

In 1992 Cooke moved to Miami, Florida, where she held several positions in the U.S. Attorney's office. She was admitted to the Florida Bar in 2001. Cooke first garnered public attention in 1999 when Florida Governor Jeb Bush appointed her as his chief inspector general with oversight over the state's administrative

agencies. When hiring scandals erupted in Florida's Department of Business and Professional Regulation, Cooke was called in to investigate. She issued a controversial report that, although critical of the department head, placed the blame for the misdeeds on the departmental staff. Cooke went to work for Miami-Dade County as an assistant county attorney in 2002.

Appointed to the Federal Bench

President George W. Bush appointed Cooke to a lifetime position on the federal court as U.S. District Court Judge for the Southern District of Florida, replacing the pioneering black judge, the late Wilkie D. Ferguson, in November of 2003. However her appointment required confirmation by the U.S. Senate and Senate Democrats had been blocking the president's judicial nominations. Cooke had been interviewed and recommended by Florida's bipartisan judicial selection commission; she had the endorsement of Florida's two Democratic senators; and she was a Democrat with apparently liberal credentials. Nevertheless Senate Democrats were suspicious of her association with Jeb Bush, the president's brother. Finally Republicans and Democrats reached an election-year compromise: the Bush administration agreed to not make recess appointments in exchange for the confirmation of its non-controversial judicial nominees. The Democrats agreed to the deal to avoid the appearance of opposing the appointment of a black, female, Democratic judge. In a unanimous vote in May of 2004, Marcia Cooke became the first judicial nominee

At a Glance . . .

Born Marcia Gail Cooke on October 16, 1954, in Sumter, SC. *Education:* Georgetown University, BS, 1975; Wayne State University, JD, 1977. *Religion:* Roman Catholic. *Politics:* Democrat.

Career: Wayne County Legal Services, Detroit, MI, staff attorney, 1978-79; Detroit Defender's Office, assistant defender, 1979-80; U.S. Attorney's Office, Detroit, MI, assistant attorney, 1980-83; Miro, Miro & Weiner, Bloomfield Hills, MI, associate, 1983-84; U.S. District Court, Eastern District, Detroit, magistrate judge, 1984-92; U.S. Attorney's Office, Southern District, Miami, FL, director of professional development and training, 1992, 1994-99, executive assistant U.S. attorney, 1992-94, acting administrative attorney, 1996-97; Executive Office of the Governor, FL, chief inspector general, 1999-02; Miami-Dade County, FL, assistant county attorney, 2002-04; U.S. District Court, Southern District, Miami, FL, judge, 2004–.

Selected memberships: American Bar Association; Federal Bar Association, board of directors; National Bar Association, Miami-Dade County Chapter, Women Lawyers Division; Order of Barristers; Women's Economic Club.

Awards: The National Conference for Community and Justice, Pathfinder Award, 1986.

Addresses: *Office*—U.S. District Court, Southern Division of Florida, 301 N. Miami Ave, Miami, FL, 33128.

reach Florida. Over the strong objections of the boy's Florida relatives and the Cuban-exile community, Gonzalez was eventually returned to his father in Cuba. Cooke ruled that the federal agents who returned Gonzalez had immunity and that there were no violations of the constitution. In another controversial case in October of 2006, Cooke declined to rule on a request to terminate the parole of cult leader and convicted murderer Yahweh Ben Yahweh who was dying of cancer.

Presided Over Terrorism Case

Beginning in 2005 Cooke presided over one of the first terrorism cases to be heard in U.S. District Court. Jose Padilla, Kifah Jayyousi, and Adham Amin Hassoun were charged with being members of the Islamic terrorist group Al Qaeda and sending money, supplies, and recruits to violent Islamic groups in Bosnia and Chechnya. Padilla, an American citizen, had been held by the Navy as an enemy combatant for nearly four years, sparking one of the biggest controversies of the Bush administration's war on terror. In a surprise move in January of 2006, Cooke granted bail to Jayyousi, a former Detroit assistant school superintendent, while denying bail for Padilla. Cooke expressed her concern that Jayyousi would not be able to fully participate in his defense given the difficult conditions under which he was being held. Cooke further ordered: that the defendants not be shackled while appearing in her court; that federal prosecutors turn over critical evidence to the defense; and that a conference room be provided for the defense lawyers and their clients. Cooke was quoted in the *Miami Herald:* "I don't want to run a prison. What I want to do is make sure that prisoners in administrative detention have access to their lawyers."

Cooke was repeatedly critical of the prosecution's case and twice ordered prosecutors to provide additional information. She was quoted in the *South Florida Sun-Sentinel* of June 21, 2006, as calling the government's indictment "light on facts." However Cooke had to walk a fine line between the defendants' right to a fair trial and the government's need to protect classified information. On July 5 Cooke ruled that Padilla could see classified documents and videotapes of statements made during his detention.

In August of 2006 Cooke ruled that there were overlapping charges against the defendants and she dismissed the most serious charge, which carried a life sentence. Cooke wrote, as quoted in the *Miami Daily Business Review* that month as saying: "There can be no question that the government has charged a single conspiracy count multiple times, in separate counts, when in law and fact, only one crime has been committed." Cooke's decision was overturned on appeal and the charge reinstated.

Cooke proceeded with the case in the same careful, considered manner. She expanded the jury-selection

to be confirmed by the U.S. Senate following the compromise.

In a statement quoted in the *Miami Times* Cooke said: "I would be remiss if I let this moment pass without noting the privilege, honor and responsibility that I feel today as a result of...becoming the first Black female appointed to the bench in Florida." At her swearing-in, Cooke's parents helped her into her judicial robe.

Soon after ascending the bench Cooke was presiding over high-profile, controversial cases. One her first rulings was to dismiss a lawsuit that charged federal agents with using excessive force to seize Elian Gonzalez from his relatives' Miami home. Gonzalez was a six-year-old Cuban refugee who was rescued after his mother and companions drowned while attempting to

pool for the trial to 3,000 Miami-area residents in October of 2006. She was quoted in the *Los Angeles Times* in October: "we are now talking about a trial on a global scale."

On January 12, 2007, following defense claims that Padilla suffered from severe psychiatric problems resulting from his treatment while in military custody, Cooke ordered a three-month delay in the trial to allow for a full examination of Padilla's mental competency. Cooke's ruling was seen as one of the most important legal developments in the war on terror. Neal Sonnett, a Miami attorney and chair of an American Bar Association task force on enemy combatants, told the *Los Angeles Times* on December 17, 2006, that Cooke "is a very fair judge. She's very bright. She knows the law very well. And I think this is the kind of case in which the court understands that the world is watching."

Sources

Periodicals

Florida Times Union, May 18, 2004, p. B6.

Los Angeles Times, October 27, 2006, p. A.19; December 17, 2006, p. A.18.
Miami Daily Business Review, February 21, 2006; August 22, 2006.
Miami Herald, February 3, 2006.
Miami Times, May 26-June 1, 2004, p. 1A.
New York Times, August 26, 2004, p. 18.
Palm Beach Daily Business Review, January 10, 2006.
Palm Beach Post, May 19, 2004, p. 17A.
South Florida Sun-Sentinel (Fort Lauderdale), March 28, 2006; June 21, 2006; September 15, 2006.
Tampa Tribune, November 14, 1999, p. 2.
Washington Post, July 14, 2006, p. A.12; August 22, 2006, p. A.2; November 22, 2006, p. A.11; December 8, 2006, p. A.4; December 19, 2006, p. A.12; January 13, 2007, p. A.9.

On-line

"Jose Padilla," *Jurist Legal News & Research,* http://jurist.law.pitt.edu/currentawareness/padilla.php (January 22, 2007).

—Margaret Alic

Michael Datcher

1967—

Writer

Poet and journalist Michael Datcher recounted his journey of personal enlightenment and effort to build stable, committed relationships in his life in a 2001 memoir, *Raising Fences: A Black Man's Love Story.* In it, he recounted his own difficult youth and his struggle to become a responsible, emotionally available partner. Discussing the book with Tyrone Beason of the *Seattle Times,* Datcher noted that African-American men seem to find themselves trapped in a pop-culture-cemented reputation as tough or hard, but "what's hard is being vulnerable," he asserted. "What's hard is telling the truth. What's hard is not running away."

Datcher was born in 1967 in Chicago to a teenage mother who had been the victim of a sexual assault. She decided to give him up for adoption and was able to choose his adoptive parent, Gladys Datcher, who raised him in Long Beach, California. Datcher's earliest years were spent in a rough part of the city, but his mother's financial status grew, and she moved them to a succession of increasingly safer neighborhoods. Nevertheless, Datcher did come of age in a community marked by a near-total absence of positive male role models. "Of the thirty families that lived in our east-side Long Beach, California, apartment building during the mid-seventies, I never saw a father living in a household," he wrote in *Raising Fences.* "I never even saw one visit." The interactions he did see between adults were perhaps even more perilous to an impressionable mind: in a 1998 article he wrote that appeared on *Salon.com,* he recalled an episode between his aunt and her boyfriend after "she said something he didn't

like. He reached back and slapped my aunt in the face so hard she flew out of her chair and onto the floor. The kids stood there, frozen. We were completely captivated. It was like a movie."

Datcher was a gifted student, and in the sixth grade was offered a chance to attend a magnet school. Every morning he boarded a bus that took him and other students cross-town to the new school, which was located in a neighborhood vastly different from his own. "The homes looked like houses on TV. They were big and brand new," he wrote in his memoir. "They had large, grassy front yards with basketballs, Big Wheels, bats, and bikes just lying out there. . . . I realized it wasn't just me who was excited about the whole scene. The bus was filled with mostly black kids who'd never seen an environment like this."

Despite the educational opportunities he enjoyed, Datcher was still pulled down by negative forces in his own neighborhood. As a teen, he committed acts of petty crime and endured some harrowing encounters with the police. He returned to a less self-destructive path as a young man, however, and graduated from the University of California at Berkeley in 1992; from there, he went on to the Los Angeles campus of the U.C. system to pursue a graduate degree in African-American studies. During this period, he learned his girlfriend was pregnant, and he was crushed by the idea that he would now join the ranks of single black men who were fathers of children raised in a household other than their own. "My dream is dead," he recalled thinking to himself, he told Beason in the *Seattle Times* interview. "A woman I do not love is having my

At a Glance . . .

Born in 1967, in Chicago, IL; son of Gladys Datcher; married Jenoyne Adams (a writer), 1997(?). *Education:* University of California, Berkeley, BA, 1992; University of California, Los Angeles, MA.

Career: *Los Angeles Times, Los Angeles Magazine, Washington Post, Vibe, Essence,* and *Baltimore Sun,* journalist; *Image* magazine, editor in chief; Loyola Marymount University, visiting assistant professor of creative writing; poet; World Stage Anansi Writer's Workshop, Los Angeles, CA, director of literary programs, 1993–.

Memberships: PEN Center USA West (member of board of directors).

Addresses: *Office*—Loyola Marymount University, University Hall 3854, 1 LMU Dr., Los Angeles, CA 90045-2659.

baby," and he realized that he had unwittingly become part of "a stereotype, making black babies out of wedlock."

Datcher even dropped out of school for a time and began drinking. But in 1995, a year after the child was born, a blood test revealed that he was not the father after all. Revitalized, he returned to school and continued his involvement in a weekly poetry workshop at the World Stage, a jazz club in a southwestern Los Angeles neighborhood called Leimert Park. There, he met a fellow poet, Jenoyne Adams, and the two began dating. In a *Los Angeles Magazine* article he wrote a few years later, he described Adams as "such a fierce woman that she aroused in me a desire to be a more complete man." In February of 1997, he took the stage during the weekly poetry series and delivered a poem that was a marriage proposal, which Adams accepted.

In addition to *Salon.com* and the *Los Angeles Magazine,* Datcher has also written for *Vibe,* the *Washington Post,* and the *Los Angeles Times,* and served as editor-in-chief for *Image* magazine before taking a position on the creative-writing faculty of Loyola Marymount University in Los Angeles. His first published book, *Tough Love: Cultural Criticism and Familial Observations on the Life and Death of Tupac Shakur,* was co-edited with Kwame Alexander and appeared in 1997. His next work was the memoir *Raising Fences,* which earned a raft of critical acco-

lades when it was published in 2001. A reviewer for *Publishers Weekly* asserted that "Datcher's memoir combines attitude, honesty and romance.... This triumphant tale is a stunning tribute to perseverance, courage and the power of positive thinking." Doug Jones, writing in *Black Issues Book Review,* also commended its candor, noting that many of those "caught on the pages of *Fences* are recognizable, human and encumbered by insecurities and fears that make them behave in cruel, selfish ways (Datcher included)."

The title of Datcher's memoir was a play on the phrase "white picket fence," a signifier for the homes he saw on that cross-town bus ride as an adolescent, where children were raised by two-parent families in crime-free neighborhoods. It was also a pun on the idea of "razing," or tearing down fences—by his generation of African-American men who were disinclined to build a family life that mimicked the white, middle-class world, but also by those who hoped to erase such the barriers between black and white America. In an interview with Val Zavala of KCET, a Los Angeles-area public radio station, Datcher argued that a desire for a stable home life was a universal one. "You raised the question . . . 'Do black people really want to have families?' That is typical of how black people are perceived," he reflected. "You know, black people are human as well. It's the demonizing of black people or the lack of an honest reflection of what black people are like."

Selected writings

Books

(Editor with Kwame Alexander) *Tough Love: Cultural Criticism and Familial Observations on the Life and Death of Tupac Shakur,* Alexander, 1997.
Raising Fences: A Black Man's Love Story, Riverhead Books, 2001.

Sources

Periodicals

Black Issues Book Review, May 2001, p. 56.
Dallas Morning News, April 9, 2001.
Los Angeles Magazine, December 2000, p. 146.
Publishers Weekly, January 8, 2001, p. 56.
Seattle Times, March 24, 2001, p. C1.

On-line

"Beat It," *Salon.com,* www.salon.com/news/1998/01/28news.html (February 20, 2007).
"Life & Times Tonight Transcripts: 3/28/01," *KCET Online,* www.kcet.org/lifeandtimes/archives/2001 03/20010328.php (April 6, 2007).

—Carol Brennan

Debra J. Dickerson

1959—

Writer

Debra Dickerson is the living embodiment of the American Dream. Born and raised in the ghetto, her life was distinguished by lacks—lack of money, lack of role models, lack of hope. Despite these odds, Dickerson not only survived, but thrived—at the Pentagon, in Harvard Law School, and as a prominent writer and thinker. Though she reached the top through hard work, luck, and a lot of pluck, she never forgot where she came from. "There was no way I could turn my back on my birth class," she wrote on her *Debra Dickerson* Web site. "My unique perspective keeps me from straying too far into self-congratulation and never lets me forget that though my belly is full, that even though society treats me with respect, my bus driver and my doorman face daily dehumanization."

Escaped Brutal Childhood through Books

Born in 1959, Debra J. Dickerson was raised in a family of six siblings in the all-black ghettoes of northern St. Louis. Her parents were ex-sharecroppers who had migrated to Missouri to escape the racial oppression of their native South. Her father, an ex-Marine and junk salesman, and her mother, a domestic worker and waitress, raised their children in a household run by the convictions of the Southern Baptist church. Discipline, cleanliness, and godliness were the driving values. Her father, however, took the tenet of "spare the rod, spoil the child" too far and Dickerson suffered severe beatings at his hands. When she was 12, her mother found the courage to take the children and move away.

Dickerson held up her mother as "the most powerful [example] I know of a dignified life righteously, courageously, unflinchingly lived under horrendous circumstances," as she wrote on her Web site.

Dickerson found solace from her chaotic life in books. "I just read everything, anything I could get my hands on," she noted on her Web site. "The only time I wasn't reading was when I was asleep but even then I slept with books the way other girls slept with dolls." Her literary appetite nourished her intellect and earned her admission to a privileged school for talented children. Nonetheless, she suffered from her family's deeply entrenched belief that no black child could amount to much. "Moving up North was their entire plan for us," she recalled to *Frontpage Magazine*. "Just not picking cotton. Just not having to step off the sidewalk when whites passed. They had no conception that their children really could be anything they desired and worked hard enough for." When she told her father that she wanted to become a lawyer, he laughed in her face.

After graduating in the top of her class and acing college entrance exams, Dickerson was inundated with scholarship offers from colleges including Duke and Bryn Mawr but, because of what she has called her family's "philosophy of insignificance," Dickerson was too intimidated to even speak with the admissions counselors. Instead she began working as a waitress and enrolled in community college. Six weeks before graduating with a 3.9 G.P.A., Dickerson dropped out. "I suppose I don't think I deserved official recognition, not even when I knew I'd earned it," she explained on her Web site. "I didn't want to join any club that would have me as a member." However, Dickerson would soon join a club that would turn her life around.

Transformed from Military Officer to Ivy Leaguer

In 1980, Dickerson joined the U.S. Air Force and it changed her life. "That was the place that told me I could, and should, aspire to anything," she told *Frontpage Magazine.* She applied the traits of hard work and discipline that she learned as a child, added her formidable intellect, and found herself sailing through a successful military career. After training as a Korean linguist, she was sent to Osan Air Base in South Korea. While serving fulltime, she took courses with the University of Maryland, earning an undergraduate degree in government and politics in 1984. Next, she attended officer training school where she was appointed Wing Commander in charge of 900 officer trainees.

After receiving a commission as a second lieutenant, Dickerson was posted in Texas where she continued her education, earning a master's degree in international relations from St. Mary's University. In 1989, she was promoted to captain and sent to Turkey as

chief of intelligence for the Ankara Air Station. Her next post was as an intelligence officer at the Pentagon where she remained until resigning in 1992. She later cited a culture of sexism as the reason. "Successful military women were routinely undermined," she remarked on her Web site. "The real issue, however, is the underlying belief that women just don't belong in certain situations, situations that always involve cream of the crop military jobs. I knew there was no unlimited future for me in the service and that's mainly why I left."

Dickerson applied to and was accepted into Harvard Law School's class of 1995. At Harvard, she struggled to find her place intellectually. She had begun to form distinct views on race, racism, and the black experience. Education and the military had taken her a long way from her impoverished childhood and she was interested in the connections and disconnections between her Ivy League life and her childhood ghetto life. She joined the Black Law Students' Association and left-thinking study groups, but found that they offered little tolerance for her independent thinking. She finally found her outlet in writing and began penning a column for the *Harvard Law Record.* It was a revelation. "I totally internalized the belief that a little girl from the ghetto could not be a writer," she told *Publishers Weekly.* Yet, Dickerson had finally found her calling.

Found Success as a Writer on Race

Soon after she graduated from Harvard, Dickerson's 16-year-old nephew was paralyzed in a drive-by shooting. The senseless crime, committed by a black man in her nephew's impoverished neighborhood, propelled her to analyze the political and cultural implications of the crime, as well as her personal anger and sadness. The result, "Who Shot Johnny," published in the *New Republic* in 1986, won a Best American Essay award and launched Dickerson's writing career. She went on to write for publications including the *Washington Times, New York Times Magazine,* and *Mother Jones.* She served as a senior editor at *U.S. News & World Report* and as a regular contributor to the on-line publications Beliefnet.com and Salon.com.

In 2000, Dickerson published *An American Story,* an astonishing memoir that documented her rise from the ghetto to Harvard. The book garnered critical acclaim and became a *New York Times* "Notable Book of the Year." In it, Dickerson laid bare the harsh realities of her childhood, her family, and her struggle to find her own voice. In doing she took a cold, hard look at race and the role it played in her life. The *New York Times Book Review* noted, "It is a startling thing to hear an American speak as frankly and un-self-servingly about race as Dickerson does." The issue of race in Dickerson's life deepened when she married a white architect, settled down to a comfortable middle-class in the mostly white suburbs, and bore two very pale-skinned children. She began to write more extensively on race issues, becoming a well-known essayist and a fellow at the New American Foundation, an organization dedicated to encouraging new public thinkers.

By 2004, Dickerson had isolated what she believed was the root of many of the problems African Americans faced and published her theory in *The End of Blackness*. The book extolled African Americans to stop focusing on a black/white dichotomy and get on with the business of living as an American period. "Race is a construct," she told the *Albany Union Times*. "Being a construct, it is neither biology nor destiny; you can set it down or walk away from it, or reshape it into anything you want it to be." The controversy that ensued thrust Dickerson into the limelight as an important modern thinker on race. Critics on all sides passionately engaged her in debate. As a women who stands in a very unique position with one foot in her hard-luck past and another in her hard-won future, she has accepted this dialogue gladly. As she said on her Web site, her life "makes me one of the chosen few who can act as a bridge between the working class and the mainstream." She does so with pen clutched bravely in hand.

Selected writings

Books

An American Story, Pantheon Books, 2000.
The End of Blackness, Pantheon Books, 2004.

Sources

Periodicals

Albany Times Union (Albany, NY), January 18, 2004, p. J1.
Publishers Weekly, July 17, 2000, p. 182.

On-line

Debra Dickerson, www.debradickerson.com (February 2, 2007).
"The End of Blackness," *Frontpage Magazine,* www. frontpagemag.com/Articles/ReadArticle.asp?ID= 12273 (February 2, 2007).
"The Fire Inside," *New York Times Book Review,* www.nytimes.com/books/00/10/08/reviews/ 001008.08scottt.html (February 2, 2007).

—Candace LaBalle

Michelle Ebanks

1962—

Corporate executive

Ebanks, Michelle, photograph. Rob Loud/Getty Images.

When Michelle Ebanks was a little girl visiting her grandmother's beauty salon in Dayton, Ohio, she loved to look at the pictures of stylish, confident black women in the *Essence* magazines in the waiting area. Years later, when she achieved the position of president of Essence Communications Partners, the memory of a young black child's hunger to see her hopes and dreams reflected in the glossy pages of a national magazine would give Ebanks a special sense of responsibility. Along with her professional goal of making sure that the 35-year old journal of African-American lifestyles continued to grow and prosper as a business, Ebanks felt a deep sense of connection with the magazine's most important goal—to reflect and improve the lives of all black people.

Ebanks came to Essence Communications after an impressive 20-year career in the business side of magazine publishing. Modest and reserved by nature, she nonetheless possessed a sharp business sense and a drive to succeed that led to recognition and promotion in a highly competitive field. As head of *Essence*, she has enjoyed the opportunity to combine her corporate vision with her values as an African American, a working woman, and a mother.

Grew up in Ohio and Florida

Ebanks was born Michelle Marie Washington on January 11, 1962, in Dayton, Ohio. She was one of three children of Thomas K. Washington Sr. and Charlotte Smith. During her early childhood, her father served in the U.S. Army, and was frequently transferred to bases throughout the country and even in Germany. Young Michelle lived in Ohio, California, and Texas before her parents divorced. After the divorce, she and her two brothers spent the school year with their mother in Dayton and in summer lived with their father in Miami where he had settled after leaving the army.

Charlotte Smith worked for the city of Dayton in a variety of positions, including the department of Housing and Urban Development. Ebanks was proud of her mother's self-assured professionalism, as well as the important work she did, helping to provide affordable housing for Dayton's poor citizens. In Miami, her father had opened a chain of dry cleaning businesses, and during the summers, she learned about work herself, helping out in her father's shops.

Thomas Washington was also a political activist who worked for civil rights, wrote a column for a Miami newspaper, and produced a local radio show. He defined himself as "pro-black," and taught his daughter to be proud of her heritage and to work for change. When Ebanks was only ten, her father took her with him to ring doorbells, campaigning for the election of Shirley Chisholm. Chisholm was a New York democrat who had been the first African-American woman elected to Congress in 1968, and who in 1972 became the first black woman to run for president.

Besides her parents, perhaps the greatest influences on Ebanks' childhood were her brothers. Growing up with two older brothers, she determined at a young age to do everything the boys did because she did not want to be left behind. She rode bikes with her brothers and played baseball and basketball, developing a love of competition and challenge that would propel her career in later years.

In both Dayton and Miami, Ebanks lived in communities that were almost completely African American. She did experience mixed-race situations in school. When she moved to Miami during her high-school years, she attended Gulliver Academy, a private school in nearby Coral Gables. Ebanks and her brother were

the first black students to attend Gulliver Academy, but she adapted well to the unfamiliar situation and continued to do well in school. Ebanks was quiet and reserved at school until one of her teachers, believing that she had a talent for leadership, suggested that she run for student government. She did and was elected, first president of her tenth grade class, then vice president of the student body. She also captained both the volleyball and tennis teams, learning that she liked taking a leadership role. During her sophomore and junior year, Ebanks took a heavy course load so that she could graduate a year early and leave high school when her brother graduated.

Studied Finance in College

After graduating from Gulliver in 1979, she entered the University of Florida. She had no particular career goal, but, having grown up working in a family business, she decided to study finance in order to help out in her future husband's business. She assumed that she and her long-term boyfriend would marry when they graduated. However, when he was not ready to get married so soon after college, she decided it was time to make a big change in her life. After graduating in 1983 with a degree in business finance, she neither married nor returned to Miami to work in her father's business. Instead, she went to California, where she could stay with relatives while seeking work. She got a job with an African-American-owned business called Univox California, Inc. Univox was a manufacturing company that made a variety of products including a water purification machine used by the U.S. Army.

Ebanks worked in the purchasing department at Univox for over a year, but she wanted to find a job where she could use the business skills she had learned during her college career. She answered an advertisement for a financial analyst with a Los Angeles magazine publisher called Knapp. Knapp published a wide variety of magazines, and Ebanks first worked on *Home*. Her natural drive to perform well combined with her ability to plan successful business strategies soon led to her promotion to business manager, then director of operations at another Knapp publication, *Bon Appétit*.

In 1993, a larger periodical publisher, Condé Nast Publications, bought Knapp. Condé Nast was based in New York City, and Ebanks moved to New York, where she became corporate business manager for 13 of the company's magazines. She was quickly gaining a national reputation for her astute business vision and able management. After three years with Condé Nast, she was hired away by another media giant, Time, Inc., where she became general manager of the respected *Money* magazine.

After two successful years on *Money*, Ebanks received another promotion. In 1998 she moved back to Florida to take the job of president and chief executive officer of another financial journal called *Mutual Funds Magazine.* Three years later, she returned to New York to take a job with *Essence,* the glossy magazine of African-American fashion and culture that she had first read as a child in her grandmother's beauty shop.

Went to Work at Essence

Essence Communications Inc. (ECI) was founded in 1968 by Clarence O. Smith and Edward Lewis with the goal of creating a woman's magazine that focused on the needs and interests of African-American women. They released the first issue of *Essence* in 1970, a full-size, glossy journal that featured articles on fashion, entertainment, and lifestyles, all from a black woman's perspective. *Essence* began with a circulation of 50,000 and grew rapidly. Readership had reached seven million and subscriptions over one million by 2000. That year, ECI signed a working agreement with Time Inc. and became Essence Communication Partners. Along with publishing the monthly journal, the company produces community events, many of which include charitable work. One such event is the annual three-day Essence Music Festival in New Orleans.

In 2001, Michelle Ebanks became group publisher for *Essence,* responsible for supervising production, advertising sales, and circulation. The magazine has thrived under Ebanks' management, and in 2003, it became the first African-American periodical to reach seventh place on *Advertising Age* magazine's "A-list" of outstanding publications. In 2005, Time Inc. became the owners of Essence Communication Partners, changed its name back to Essence Communications Inc., and placed Michelle Ebanks in charge of business operations.

As president of ECI, Ebanks has been able bring her vision and financial management skills to a business whose mission was close to her heart—entertaining, informing, and supporting black women and their families. She has found it especially satisfying to be part of projects that could offer help to members of the community. For example, after New Orleans was hit by Hurricane Katrina in August 2005, ECI contributed resources toward repairing the damaged city, including a partnership between the Essence Music Festival 2007 and the Children's Defense Fund, whereby a portion of the proceeds from the Festival will help expand the Fund's Freedom Schools Program in New Orleans. President Ebanks even picked up a hammer and joined a work party when Essence joined with Habitat for Humanity to rebuild houses in New Orleans.

Sources

Periodicals

Business Wire, April 26, 2001.
Essence, May 2000, p.28; May 2005, p. 32; November 2005, p. 14.
Jet, January 24, 2005, p. 17.
Playthings, July 2005, p. 9.

On-line

"The Barrier Breaker: Michelle Ebanks," *Min Magazine,* www.minonline.com/magazinesite/min_110106_p46_58.pdf - (January 25, 2007).
"Bios: Michelle Ebanks," *Essence,* www.essence.com/essence/bios/bio_ebanks (January 25, 2007).
"Chevrolet, Essence and Habitat For Humanity: Spreading Their Spiritual DNA," *Houston Style Magazine* www.stylemagazine.com/print_article.cfm?art_id=329 (January 25, 2007).
"*Essence* Turns 35," *AOL Black Voices,* http://blackvoices.aol.com/lifemain/lifemain_canvas/featurestory/_a/essence-turns-35/20050415161509990001 (January 25, 2007).
"Shakers: Expanding Essence," *AOL Black Voices,* http://blackvoices.aol.com/workmonmain/careers/shkebank0110200 (January 25, 2007).

Other

Information for this profile was obtained through an interview with Michelle Ebanks on February 8, 2007.

—Tina Gianoulis

Mike Epps

1970—

Comedian, actor

Among comedians there once were Bill Cosby, Richard Pryor, and a bunch of struggling unknowns. Everything changed in the 1990s when a new generation of young African-American comedians emerged, with the help of national exposure offered by HBO's *Def Comedy Jam* and its associated tours. Mike Epps became one of the brightest stars among that group. He built his reputation on the comedy circuit, however, he landed what he considered to be his "biggest break," as he told Jessica Williams-Gibson of the Indianapolis *Recorder,* in 2000, with a role in the hit film *Next Friday.* While more film roles came his way, Epps continued to do his comedy routine. Since 2001 he has been one of the most visible African Americans on the stand-up comedy circuit. His career has continued to rise toward genuine stardom, but that's not how Epps sees it: "I don't like the word star. Stars fall. I consider myself as a successful survivor," according to the Indianapolis *Recorder.*

Mike Epps was born on November 18, 1970, in Indianapolis, Indiana. Growing up, he split time between Indianapolis, where he lived in a house with his mother and eight siblings, and Gary, Indiana, where his spent summers in his grandparents' home. Epps has pointed to his large family, in which he had a lot of competition for his mother's attention, as the source of his natural inclination to entertain. He was always the class clown, sometimes taking it too far. He spent a few months in a juvenile detention center for a prank gone bad: sticking a classmates' hands together with Super Glue.

More trouble followed. Epps dropped out of high school, started dealing drugs, and spent some time in prison. Back on the streets, Epps one day followed an impulse that seemed obvious to everyone who knew him: He decided to try his hand at stand-up comedy. He entered a stand-up contest at an Indiana club called Seville's. Epps was an instant hit. Emboldened by his relatively easy early success in stand-up, he left the Midwest with $80 in his pocket and moved to Atlanta to launch a career in comedy. In Atlanta, he began to establish a reputation at the Comedy Act Theater, which held regular amateur nights on Tuesdays. Meanwhile, he paid his rent and grocery bills working in a manhole during the day. The style he developed during this period was modern in its sensibility, but in many ways his spontaneous approach was more a throwback to the comedy heroes he had admired as a youth, such as Richard Pryor, Bill Cosby and Redd Foxx.

So well was Epps received in Atlanta that the owner of the Comedy Act Theater suggested he try his luck in New York. At 21 years old, Epps hopped aboard a Greyhound bus and headed for the Big Apple. In New York, he immediately set out to find a place in the city's comedy clubs. The mainstream clubs proved to be exceedingly difficult to break into. However, a vibrant underground black comedy scene was emerging around this time, inspired by the phenomenon of HBO's *Def Comedy Jam.* Epps quickly found a home in this movement, and within half a year he had established himself as one of the best young African-American comics around. By 1995 he had appeared in two of HBO's *Def Comedy Jam* broadcasts and traveled with the Def Comedy Jam Tour. In 1997 he made his movie debut, appearing in *Strays,* Vin Diesel's first film as a director.

Epps landed a role in an episode of the hit HBO series *The Sopranos* in 1999. Later that year, he learned that Ice Cube was looking for somebody to cast as his co-star in *Next Friday,* a sequel to the movie *Friday.* In *Friday,* Ice Cube's debut as a film producer, Chris Tucker had filled the sidekick role, and it had made him a household name. Upon hearing that Tucker had bowed out of the sequel, Epps decided to make his best pitch for the part. He went to Los Angeles and invited Ice Cube to catch his stand-up act. Ice Cube was impressed and urged Epps to audition for the role of Day-Day, his suburban cousin being stalked by his obsessed ex-girlfriend and her thuggish younger sister. Epps soon landed the part. While much of the public already knew him from his stand-up exploits, *Next Friday* proved to be a breakout performance for Epps. The movie opened at the top of the box-office charts.

Other movie appearances, some of them rather small, followed on the heels of his role in *Next Friday.* He had a cameo in DJ Pooh's *3 Strikes,* and had a supporting role in the action comedy *Bait,* starring Jamie Foxx. The movie parts continued to pile up in rapid succession over the next few years. Epps had a voice role in the 2001 family comedy *Dr. Doolittle 2,* and later that year he played the wacky pimp Baby Powder in *How High,* a vehicle for hip-hop artists Redman and Method Man, whom some have described as the modern day, black Cheech and Chong. Epps then joined forces with Ice Cube once again in *All About the Benjamins,* in which he played the bumbling thief to Cube's bounty hunter. He teamed up with Ice Cube again for the third installment in the *Friday* series, *Friday After Next.*

Epps continued to land film roles over the next two years, but the movies he was in tended to be big flops, including the musical comedy *The Fighting Temptations* (2003) with Cuba Gooding, Jr. and Beyonce

Knowles, and *Resident Evil: Apocalypse* (2004), the sequel to the horror flick *Resident Evil.* In 2005 Epps portrayed Ed Norton to Cedric the Entertainer's Ralph Kramden in a new African-American film version of the classic 1950s situation comedy *The Honeymooners.* While the movie did not especially impress the majority of critics, it represented another step forward in Epps' Hollywood career. It was apparently a year of remakes for Epps; he also appeared in the film *Guess Who,* an update of the Sidney Poitier classic *Guess Who's Coming to Dinner,* in 2005.

Later that year, Richard Pryor himself tapped Epps to star in his planned biographical motion picture. "He never really told me why but I'm pretty sure he picked me because of my real life experiences," Epps told Janice Malone of the *Tennessee Tribune.* "I've been through a whole lot early in my life just as he has." To Epps, being cast as Pryor was the role of a lifetime. Unfortunately, the movie was delayed due to squabbles over the scripts. Epps remained hopeful about the project, telling the Indianapolis *Recorder* that "It's going to make a real change in my life and others. I'm hoping we get a good script, we get a good director and that I'm in the right frame of mind to represent Richard Pryor 'cause he is the greatest comedian." As of early 2007, there was still hope that the script issues would be resolved in time to start shooting later that year. Meanwhile, Epps remained busy with other projects, including another installment of the *Resident Evil* series and several other films still in the development phase. Yet stand-up comedy remained a vital part of Epps' career. As he explained to the *Tennessee Tribune:* "It will always be a part of my life no matter how big I become as an actor."

Selected works

Films

Strays, 1997.
Next Friday, 2000.
Dr. Doolittle 2, 2001.
How High, 2001.
All About the Benjamins, 2002.
Friday After Next, 2002.
The Fighting Temptations, 2003.
Resident Evil: Apocalypse, 2004.
The Honeymooners, 2005.
Guess Who, 2005.
Roll Bounce, 2005.
Something New, 2006.
Talk to Me, 2007.
Resident Evil: Extinction, 2007.

Television

Def Comedy Jam, 1997, 2006.
Inappropriate Behavior, 2006.

Sources

Periodicals

BackStage West, September 16, 2004, p. 7.
Essence, July 1, 2005, p. 100.
Houston Chronicle, April 3, 2003.
Interview, September 1, 2005, p. 144.
Real Detroit Weekly, December 27, 2006.
Recorder (Indianapolis, IN), October 6, 2006, p. 3.
St. Louis Post-Dispatch, December 24, 2003, p. 24.
Tennessee Tribune, October 20, 2005, p. D2.

On-line

"Def Comedy Jam: Interviews: In Steps Epps," *HBO,* www.hbo.com/defcomedyjam/interviews/index.html (February 12, 2007).
"Mike Epps Bio," *Sphinx Management Group,* www.sphinxmg.com/artist/mike_epps.asp (February 12, 2007).

"Mike Epps: The Honeymooners Interview," *Black-News,* www.blacknews.com/pr/mike-epps101.html (February 12, 2007).
"Mike Epps," *Richard de la Font Agency,* www.delafont.com/comedians/mike-epps.htm (February 12, 2007).
"Movie News: Hold The Laughter: Mike Epps Says Richard Pryor Biopic Being Rewritten," *VH1,* www.vh1.com/movies/news/articles/1548064/story.jhtml (February 12, 2007).
"Movie News: Mike Epps Compares Upcoming Richard Pryor Movie To 'Ray'," *VH1,* www.vh1.com/movies/news/articles/1503041/20050526/story.jhtml (February 12, 2007).

Other

Interview with Mike Epps by Tavis Smiley, *Tavis Smiley Show,* National Public Radio, December 12, 2002; September 26, 2003.

—Bob Jacobson

Adrian M. Fenty

1970—

Political leader

Elected mayor of Washington, D.C., in 2006, 36-year-old Adrian Fenty became the youngest individual ever to assume that post. With youth came energy, and Fenty was elected partly on the basis of his strong record of constituent services as a District of Columbia city council representative; residents of his district would sometimes say that Fenty would repair potholes or broken streetlights himself before city repair crews could get to them. Fenty himself, in a *Washington Post* profile, named endurance as his most distinctive characteristic, and political observers in Washington drew parallels between the mayor's political style and his athletic hobby—he is an enthusiastic distance runner who has completed several marathon races and has set his sights on the still more grueling Ironman triathlon event.

Motivated to Succeed

Adrian M. Fenty was a Washington native, born on December 6, 1970. He is biracial, with a black father and a white mother, and he told Marc Fisher of the *Washington Post* that this background gave him an advantage in a city whose politics were frequently split along racial lines. "I certainly don't think about it a lot," he said, referring to race, and he asserted that "there's no question [his background] gives me a tolerance and an appreciation for the views of everyone." His enthusiasm for distance running—and his concern for the problems of small businesses in Washington—was related to his family background; his father, Phil, operated a athletic-shoe store called Fleet Feet in the city's

Adams Morgan neighborhood, while his mother, Jan, taught school.

Fenty attended Mackin Catholic High School in Northwest Washington, where he ran track and finished his first two marathons. "He's very determined. He won't stop. He won't quit," friend Roger Reddock told Clarence Williams of the *Washington Times*. "He's got great stamina." At Oberlin College Fenty majored in English and economics, graduating in 1992. His ambition impressed classmate Earl C. Horton III, who told Williams that "[t]he one thing I was sure about was he has the motivation and the hustle. If you ever look at his eyes...he has that look on his face." The temptations facing young African-American men in Washington were no challenge. When a college friend suggested they could make money dealing drugs on the side, he recalled to Vanessa Williams of the *Washington Post,* "I remember thinking, 'What would my dad think if I got caught doing something like that?' What a letdown something like that would be for him." Fenty served as an intern for Ohio senator Howard Metzenbaum and later worked in the offices of Massachusetts congressional representative Joseph P. Kennedy II and of Eleanor Holmes Norton, the District of Columbia's nonvoting representative in the United States Congress.

Fenty went on to Howard University in Washington, earning his law degree and passing the District bar exam in 1996. He married a Howard classmate, and he and his wife Michelle, an international attorney, have twin sons, Matthew and Andrew. In the late 1990s, Fenty practiced probate law in Washington and

At a Glance . . .

Born on December 6, 1970, in Washington, DC; married Michelle (an international finance attorney); children: Matthew, Andrew. *Education:* Graduated from Mackin Catholic High School, Washington; graduated with double major in English and economics, Oberlin College, Oberlin, OH, 1992; Juris Doctorate degree, Howard University Law School, Washington, DC, 1996. *Religion:* Roman Catholic.

Career: Served several political internships; Washington, DC, lawyer, late 1990s; 16th Street Neighborhood Civic Association, president, late 1990s; Washington, DC, city council, Ward 4 representative, 2000; reelected 2004; Washington, DC, mayor, 2006–.

Addresses: *Office*—Office of the Mayor, John A. Wilson Bldg., 1350 Pennsylvania Ave., NW, Washington, DC 20004. *Web*—http://dc.gov/mayor/index.shtm.

was given business by the city, working on cases connected with individuals who were wards of the city. In one instance, he was charged with mishandling the affairs of an elderly Washingtonian, failing to file documents and monitor the man's finances properly. Fenty owned up to his errors and repaid the losses to the individual that had resulted. "I learned you have to cross every 't' and dot every 'i,' because one little thing can lead to a big problem," he told Williams. "I learned to show the type of attention to detail to make sure that never happens again."

Involved Himself in Community

Serving as lead attorney for the city council's Education, Libraries, and Recreation committee, Fenty became more and more involved in community affairs. He served as president of the 16th Street Neighborhood Civic Association and on a neighborhood commission in Ward 4, on the city's northern edge. "I saw that was what gave him passion," says Michelle Fenty told Williams. "He was the happiest when he was on the ANC [Advisory Neighborhood Commission]. He would come home very excited about having talked to all of these people and how he was going to help them with their problems." In 2000 he challenged Charlene Drew Jarvis, a 21-year officeholder, for her seat on the District's city council. With his shaved head, he was sometimes likened in appearance to professional basketball star Kobe Bryant. Energetically knocking on doors, he emerged victorious in the September 12, 2000, Democratic primary by a margin of 57 to 43

percent. An indication of his efforts was that voter turnout in Ward 4 was higher than anywhere else in the city. In overwhelmingly Democratic Washington, he cruised to victory in the November general election.

As a D.C. city councilman, Fenty earned a formidable reputation for paying attention to the welfare of his constituents. When touring his ward, he drove his city car rather than delegating the job to staffers, impatiently insisting that he knew local streets better than anyone else. Reelected in 2004, Fenty made few friends on the council. Members were annoyed at his habit of sending messages on his BlackBerry personal message device during meetings, and few supported him when, in 2005, he announced his candidacy for the post of mayor. But his Washington neighborhood overflowed with stories of city services delivered and on-the-ground police help in the crime-plagued area, and his 2006 primary campaign against council chair Linda Cropp gained momentum.

"You can't use my name, 'cause I'm expected to support Linda," one city employee told the *Washington Post's* Fisher, "but let me tell you this: My mother's block was getting real bad. The dealers were thick, corner to corner. I couldn't get the police to pay attention to it. Finally, we call Adrian. That same week, the cops flood the block and stay on it till the dealers abandon the place. See, I have to vote for Adrian." American University professor Brett Williams told Steve Goldstein of the *Philadelphia Inquirer* that Fenty had helped arrange for her water service to be restored, and that his staff, thinking that she might be in financial trouble, had sent Thanksgiving turkeys to her home. Cropp brought up Fenty's probate-law misdeed and portrayed him as inexperienced and as a micromanager. "I cherish being called too responsive," Fenty retorted, in conversation with Ian Urbina of the *New York Times,* taking credit for improvements in his ward's long-spotty city services.

Fenty favored an ultimately successful measure, opposed by Washington's food-service industry, that would ban smoking in indoor workplaces, including bars and restaurants. Though the city's political and business interests, including Mayor Anthony Williams, mostly lined up behind Cropp, Fenty touted his experience in his family's small business and presented himself as an advocate of the working poor. He picked up an endorsement from the city's populist former mayor, Marion Barry, and in the Democratic primary held on September 12, 2006, he trounced Cropp by a margin of about 57 to 31 percent.

An overwhelming victor in the November 7 general election, Fenty had already begun to implement his high-tech governing style with a "Webinar" or web-based seminar gathering input from advisors and city residents via e-mail, Web logs (or blogs), and Internet chat rooms. Fenty hit the ground running in January of 2007 with an ambitious list of 200 measures his administration planned to take during the first 100 days of his administration. His most widely reported action early in his term was an attempt to take over Washington's troubled public schools, removing many responsibilities from the city's board of education and placing them with a chancellor who would report to the mayor and city council. As of March, 2007, the plan seemed headed for council approval.

Sources

Books

Carroll's Municipal Directory, Carroll Publishing, 2006.

Periodicals

New York Times, September 14, 2006, p. A24.
Philadelphia Inquirer, September 10, 2006.
Washington Business Journal, September 22, 2000, p. 17.

Washington Post, January 6, 2005; August 24, 2006, p. B1; August 31, 2006, p. C1.
Washington Times, March 31, 2000, p. 4; September 14, 2000, p. 1; September 15, 2000, p. 4; June 6, 2005, p. B1; September 13, 2006, p. A1; November 7, 2006, p. B1; November 8, 2006, p. B3; January 5, 2007, p. A17; January 12, 2007, p. B1; February 11, 2007, p. C11; February 28, 2007, p. B1; March 19, 2007, p. C12.

On-line

"Adrian Fenty," Biography Resource Center, http://galenet.galegroup.com/servlet/BioRC (March 22, 2007).
"Biography: Adrian M. Fenty," Office of the Mayor, District of Columbia, http://dc.gov/mayor/bios/fenty.shtm (March 22, 2007).

—James M. Manheim

Felicia P. Fields

19??—

Actress, singer

Oprah Winfrey is a hard act to follow. But Felicia P. Fields has managed to pull off the feat with grace and power. Since 2005, Fields, a veteran of the Chicago professional musical theater scene, has charmed Broadway audiences with her portrayal of Sofia in the stage musical *The Color Purple,* the character played by Winfrey in the film version of Alice Walker's acclaimed novel. Already a regional star for several years, Fields has now taken Broadway by storm. Her work in *Color* has vaulted her to the highest peaks of the musical theater world, finally elevating her reputation to a level consistent with her immense singing and acting talent.

Felicia Pearl Fields was born and raised on the South Side of Chicago. Her father was a building inspector; her mother, whom Fields described in a November 2005 *Newsday* interview as "a pretty tough cookie herself," was proprietor of her own beauty salon. Like so many talented singers, Fields' performing career began with gospel. From an early age, she sang in the choir at her Baptist church in the Englewood neighborhood. Growing up, Fields was not thinking about a career in theater. She planned to become a schoolteacher. In fact, she never studied acting until after becoming a professional. She did, however, love the theater, recounting in a 1998 *Chicago Sun Times* interview her earliest theatrical experience as a child at the Drury Lane Evergreen Park. "I still remember sitting next to my father at shows and thinking 'I can do that'," she was quoted as saying in the *Sun Times.*

Church Choir Led to Professional Roles

Her voice stood out enough in the church choir that she caught the attention of two members of the congregation who were songwriters. They began regularly asking her to perform on their demo recordings. At one of these recording sessions in the late 1980s, another musician suggested that Fields audition for an upcoming production of *The Wiz* at the Marriott Theatre in the northern Chicago suburb of Lincolnshire. Fields ended up being cast as both Glinda the Good Witch and Auntie Em. Even with no formal acting training or experience, she proved to be a natural on the stage, and has been working steadily, mostly to glowing reviews, ever since.

Fields quickly became a fixture on the stages of Chicago's top professional theaters, including the Marriott Lincolnshire, The Goodman, Drury Lane, and Apple Tree. After making her debut in *The Wiz,* she followed up over the next several years with performances in such hit shows as *Hello Dolly, Ain't Misbehavin', Best Little Whorehouse in Texas,* and *Dreamgirls.* By the mid-1990s, she was widely recognized as one of the Windy City's leading performers in musical theater. The theater community was quick to recognize her extraordinary talent. She was nominated for numerous Joseph Jefferson Awards (or "Jeffs," as they are commonly known–Chicago's version of the Tony Awards), including one for her 1996 performance in the revue *Sophisticated Ladies,* two in 1998 for supporting

At a Glance . . .

Born Felicia Pearl Fields in Chicago, IL; children: two. *Religion:* Baptist.

Career: singer, actress, 1980s–.

Memberships: Actors' Equity Association; Artist Board, Apple Tree Theatre, Chicago.

Awards: Hattie McDaniel Award, for Best Featured Actress in a Play, *Ma Rainey's Black Bottom*, 1997; Joseph Jefferson Award, 7 nominations, 1993-98; Black Theatre Alliance Awards, nominated for Best Performance, *Stones*, 2003; Drama League Award, nominated for Distinguished Performance, *The Color Purple*, 2006; Tony Award, nominated for Best Performance by a Featured Actress in a Musical, *The Color Purple*, 2006; Theatre World Award, for Outstanding Broadway Debut Performance, *The Color Purple*, 2006.

Addresses: *Office*—c/o Apple Tree Theatre, 1850 Green Bay Road, Suite 100, Highland Park, IL 60035.

roles in *South Pacific* and *Elmer Gantry*, and another that year for her work in the review *Ain't Misbehavin'*. In 1997 Fields received the Hattie McDaniel Award— named for the first African American ever to win an Oscar—for Best Featured Actress in a Play for her performance in the title role in *Ma Rainey's Black Bottom*, a show she has appeared in several productions of over the years.

Became Mainstay of Chitown Theater Scene

Fields continued to work constantly, increasingly in featured roles, in the new century. In 2001 she reprised her role in *Ma Rainey* at Chicago's Goodman Theatre, and played Sister Moore in *The Amen Corner* both at the Goodman and at Boston University. She also made one of her less frequent forays into the classics that year, playing the Duchess of York in the Chicago Shakespeare Theatre's production of *Richard II*. The following year she played Nettie in *Carousel* at the Marriott Lincolnshire, and Assunta in *The Rose Tattoo* at The Goodman. Her 2003 performances included *Hot Mikado* and *Showboat* at the Marriott Lincolnshire.

While Fields was making a fine living in the Chicago theater scene, the stage was set, so to speak, for her big

break in 2002, while working on *Carousel* with director Gary Griffin. One day during a technical rehearsal, Fields decided that her costume made her look a little like Oprah Winfrey in the film version of *The Color Purple*. She spontaneously started hobbling down the aisle of the theater spouting some of Winfrey's lines from the movie. Amused, director Griffin said, "If I ever do *The Color Purple*, I already have Sofia (Winfrey's character)." Amazingly, just a month later Green called her to say he had been commissioned to direct a musical version of the Alice Walker novel.

Won Critical Acclaim

The Color Purple started out with a successful run at Atlanta's Alliance Theatre, before heading to Broadway for a hit run beginning in November of 2005 at the Broadway Theatre. Fields was instantly singled out as one of show's strongest elements. When much of the cast was invited to appear on Oprah's television show, Fields made it clear with her performance of her character's signature song, "Hell No!", that she had fully succeeded her host as the embodiment of the abused but strong-willed Sofia. Fields was nominated for a Tony Award for her performance on Broadway. She was also honored with a Clarence Derwent Award from the Actors' Equity Association (the main labor union for stage actors) and a Theatre World Award, 12 of which are awarded each year to actors and actresses making their Broadway debut.

In January of 2007 Fields announced that she was leaving the Broadway cast of *The Color Purple* in order to begin preparing for an upcoming national touring version of the show scheduled to begin a few months later. The tour would kickoff with a homecoming of sorts for Fields, opening at the Cadillac Palace Theatre in Chicago. Fields' remarkable ability to bring Sofia to life has left an indelible impression on audiences, especially the women among them. The tour allows her to reach a broader range of people.

"The real gratification is from the women who come up to you at the back stage door and say, 'You know, I've been abused, but I'm not going for it anymore'," she was quoted as saying in a July 2006 *Jet* article. With the acclaim she has received for her Broadway debut, Fields' career is set to soar as high in the future as her audiences' spirits do these days when the exultant strains' of "Hell No!" echo through the theater.

Selected works

Ain't Misbehavin', Apple Tree Theatre, 1993.
The Goodbye Girl, Marriott Lincolnshire, 1994.
Sophisticated Ladies, Drury Lane South, 1996.
Dreamgirls, Marriott Lincolnshire, 1996.
Ma Rainey's Black Bottom, The Goodman Theatre, 1997, 2001.
Carousel, Marriott Lincolnshire, 2002.

Hot Mikado, Marriott Lincolnshire, 2003.
Showboat, Marriott Lincolnshire, 2003.
The Color Purple, Alliance Theatre (Atlanta), 2004;
  Broadway Theatre, 2005-07.

Sources

Periodicals

Chicago Defender, February 28, 2007, p. 12.
Chicago Sun-Times, April 10, 1998, p. 9.
Jet, July 3, 2006. p. 61.

On-line

"Diva Talk: Chatting with *Color Purple's* Felicia P.
  Fields Plus Gravitte's 'Defying Gravity,'" *Playbill,*
  www.playbill.com/celebritybuzz/article/97437.html
  (April 2, 2007).
"Fields Brings Power to 'Purple,'" *Newsday.com,*
  www.newsday.com/entertainment/stage/ny-
  purple27,0,2767647.story?coll=ny-theater-
  headlines (April 2, 2007).
"Felicia Fields Exits *Color Purple* Jan. 28 to Prepare
  for Tour," *Playbill,* www.playbill.com/news/article/
  105212.html (April 2, 2007).
"Felicia P. Fields," *Broadway.com,* www.broadway.
  com/gen/Buzz_Story.aspx?ci=530470 (March 30,
  2007).
"Fields to Reprise Role of Sofia in *Color Purple* Tour,"
  www.playbill.com/news/article/103146.html (April
  2, 2007).

—Bob Jacobson

Sam Fine

1969—

Makeup artist

It is easy to assume that people like Halle Berry, Tyra Banks, Iman, and Beyonce Knowles achieve their peak beauty with little effort. In reality, they sometimes need help. Often that help comes from master makeup artist Sam Fine. Fine literally wrote the book on makeup and beauty techniques for African-American women. Through his work with big-name models and performers, as well as his efforts to educate ordinary women about how to look their best, Fine has helped change the way African Americans—and the cosmetic companies whose products they depend on—think about makeup. His ideas have played a huge role in teaching women how to accentuate the naturally beauty in a range of skin tones that was long neglected by the cosmetics industry.

Sam Fine was born on November 12, 1969, in Evanston, Illinois, just north of Chicago. He was adopted when he was six months old by the Denton family, who lived on Chicago's South Side. Fine knows little about his birth parents, beyond the fact that his father was black and his mother was Jewish. He grew up as Samuel Denton; only much later did he take on as his professional moniker the last name on his birth certificate. Fine was the youngest of the four Denton children, and the only boy among them. Growing up in a mostly female household, Sam was intrigued by the sight of his mother and sisters applying makeup and getting their hair done. "I used to pay my sisters $2 to let me style their hair," Fine was quoted as saying in a 1998 *New York Times* article. Fine remembered that they had to concoct much of their own makeup

because so few products appropriate for dark-skinned women were available commercially.

Focused on Fashion at Art Institute

Fine grew up in a typical middle-class environment that included Cub Scouts, piano lessons, and vacation bible school. Because his sisters were several years older, however, he spent a lot of time alone, especially once they went off to college. Always artistically inclined, he turned to drawing as his main form of solitary amusement. His artistic skill attracted attention early on, and he won local drawing competitions throughout elementary school and high school. In high school, Fine entered a portfolio review. His work impressed the judges enough that they awarded him a summer scholarship to the School of the Art Institute of Chicago, where he began to focus on a career as a fashion illustrator.

Upon graduating from Percy L. Julian High School on Chicago's South Side, Fine took the logical next step for anybody interested in a career in fashion: He moved to the New York area, taking up residence in Hackensack, New Jersey. His plan was to eventually enroll in one of the city's prestigious design schools, such as the Pratt Institute or Parsons: The New School for Design. Unfortunately, Fine was unable to swing the move financially, and he ended up returning home to Chicago within three months. During his short stay in the Big Apple, however, he managed to make a few industry connections. One of them was with a small company called Naomi Sims Cosmetics. He began

At a Glance . . .

Born Samuel Fine on November 12, 1969, in Evanston, IL; adopted in 1970 and renamed Samuel Denton. *Education:* Graduated from Percy L. Julian High School, Chicago; summer scholarship to The School of the Art Institute of Chicago.

Career: Freelance fashion illustrator, 1987-89; Naomi Sims Cosmetics makeup counter, A&S Department Store, New York, 1989; professional makeup artist, 1991–.

Addresses: *Web*—Fine Beauty, Inc., finebeauty@samfine.com; samfine.com.

doing some work for them on a freelance basis, and in 1989 the company invited him to work at their first New York City cosmetics counter, located in the A & S Department Store on 34th Street. Fine leaped at the opportunity, and at age 19 he moved to New York once again, this time settling in Brooklyn.

Second Move to New York Successful

In New York, Fine began to assemble a portfolio of his work by testing his skills out with aspiring models and photographers. His best friend at the time was an established makeup artist, who was able to provide guidance and career advice. In 1991 Fine began working as an assistant with top makeup artists Fran Cooper and Kevyn Aucoin. He helped out on fashion shows and photo shoots, which brought him into contact with top models, photographers, designers, and others who made the fashion industry tick. At one fashion show, Fine met supermodel Naomi Campbell, and shortly thereafter she called him at his cosmetic counter day job and asked him to work with her on *People Magazine*'s "50 Most Beautiful People" issue.

Soon after that, Fine's career began to flourish. He started working regularly with quite a few prominent African-American women, including Patti LaBelle, Vanessa Williams, Tyra Banks, and Iman. In 1993 he landed his first makeup job for an *Essence* magazine cover, with actress Jackee Harry. Over the next several years, his work could be seen on the covers of such other magazines as *Cosmopolitan, Harper's Bazaar, Vibe,* and *Marie Claire.* He increasingly evolved into the "go to" makeup artist for black women, and as a result he became the first African-American spokesperson for the Revlon and CoverGirl cosmetic brands. As his reputation soared and his client list ballooned, Fine became an important voice not just for particular products aimed at African Americans, but for a whole new approach to beauty. Fine's embraces and celebrates dark complexions and African-American fea-

tures, rather than attempting to mask or de-emphasize them.

Book and Tour Reach Mainstream Audience

In 1998, Fine summed up what he had learned about making African-American women beautiful in his book, *Fine Beauty: Beauty Basics and Beyond for African-American Women,* published by Riverhead Books. The book features makeup tips tailored for the range of African-American skin tones, and photos of the effects of those techniques on famous performers and models as well as ordinary people. *Fine Beauty* brought to the general public many of the concepts Fine had been applying successful for years to the faces of celebrities. Already one of the most sought-after makeup artists in the fashion and entertainment industries, by the turn of the century his name and ideas were well-known to African-American women in every part of the county, in every line of work.

Fine has further expanded his efforts to reach a broad audience. His "Fine Beauty Tour," sponsored by *Essence,* beauty retailer Sephora, AMBI Skincare, and nail care specialists OPI Products, brought a series of makeup seminars to women in at least 10 cities beginning in 2005. Also in the works are an instructional video, and his own line of cosmetics, both of which will likely further solidify Fine's place among the elite makeup artists of his time.

Selected writings

Fine Beauty: Beauty Basics and Beyond for African-American Women, Riverhead Books, 1998.

Sources

Periodicals

Black Elegance, February/March 1998, p. 15.
Houston Chronicle, April 23, 1998; October 2, 2005, p. 3.
New York Times, April 12, 1998, p. 9.

On-line

"Celebrity Makeup Artist and Chicago Native Sam fine Returns Home for Educational Tour," *Bahiyah Magazine,* http://bwmmag.com/magazine/index2.php?option=com_content&task=view&id=459&pop=1&page=0&Itemid=201 (February 15, 2007).
Sam Fine, www.samfine.com (February 15, 2007).

Other

Additional information for this profile was obtained through an interview with Sam Fine on February 15, 2007.

—Bob Jacobson

Norman C. Francis

1931—

Educator

Norman C. Francis has been one of the nation's most respected educators for half a century. As an administrator, and, later, as president, of Xavier University of Louisiana (XULA), he has worked for justice and equality, not only at XULA but throughout the United States. Francis has fought for civil rights and acted as a civic leader, working tirelessly to create fairer political and financial institutions in the city of New Orleans and the state of Louisiana. Moreover, Francis has played an important role in the recovery of Louisiana in the aftermath of Hurricane Katrina as chair of the board of the Louisiana Disaster Recovery Authority, an agency established by the governor to direct the state's efforts to rebuild areas damaged by the hurricane in the summer of 2005. In each of his leadership roles, Francis has gained respect and admiration.

Norman C. Francis was born on March 20, 1931, in the south central Louisiana city of Lafayette, one of five children of Joseph A. and Mabel F. Francis. His early years were marked by the economic slump of the Great Depression, which made jobs scarce. Joseph Francis supported his family shining shoes and painting houses, while everyone in the family did what they could to help. Norman himself began working at the age of six, milking and pasturing the family cow. In later years, his father worked as a barber, and his shop was a community gathering place for African-American men. When he was grown, Francis remembered that it was while playing checkers with the men at his father's barbershop that he learned how to plan ahead, recognize opportunities, and consider all his options.

Received Work Scholarship to College

The population of southern Louisiana is largely Roman Catholic, and Joseph and Mabel Francis, devout members of the church, sent their children to Catholic schools. When Norman Francis graduated from Lafayette's St. Paul High School in 1948, he planned to enter the U.S. Army because his family had no money to pay for higher education. However, one of the nuns who had taught him at St. Paul contacted a member of the Sisters of the Blessed Sacrament, the order that directed Xavier University of Louisiana in New Orleans. The nun arranged a work scholarship for Francis, and he entered Xavier that year, working in the college library to pay his tuition.

XULA is the only historically black Catholic university in the entire Western Hemisphere, as well as the only one founded by a Saint. During the early 1900s, Katharine Drexel, a member of the religious order Sisters of the Blessed Sacrament, received a large inheritance from her father. She used the money to open many schools across the country, with the goal of providing a good education for African American and Native American children. One of these was a coeducational high school for black students in New Orleans. By 1925, that high school had grown to become Xavier University of Louisiana. Katherine Drexel's work was honored by the church when she was made a Saint by Pope John Paul II in 2000.

Francis graduated from XULA in 1952. He planned to become a lawyer and entered Loyola University, a

Jesuit college that had been founded in New Orleans in 1912. In 1955, he became the first African American student to earn a law degree there. Upon completing his degree, he entered the U.S. Army, joining the Third Armored Division and earning the rank of corporal specialist four.

After completing a two-year tour of duty, Francis left the army and began to consider his civilian career. The civil rights movement was beginning, and Francis was deeply inspired by the cause of justice and racial equality. He wanted to do something to improve the condition of black people in the United States, and he began to feel that working in education might be the best way to do that. He took a job in 1957 as dean of men at his old alma mater, XULA.

Appointed First Lay President of XULA

Between 1957 and 1968, Francis had several different jobs in the XULA administration. He was director of student personnel services, assistant to the president for student affairs, assistant to the president in charge of development, and executive vice president. During this time, the Sisters of the Blessed Sacrament had continued to take responsibility for running the university, but in the late 1960s, the nuns decided it was time for a XULA graduate to become president.

They asked Francis to take the job, and in 1968 he became the first president of XULA who was a layperson, not a member of the clergy. As Francis said in a 2004 interview in *The Black Collegian,* "My appointment was a major decision by an order of white nuns who thought that it was time for them to step back and let the people they had educated run the institution they had built. That was a big decision, a big decision. Catholic colleges did not have lay presidents, to say nothing of a Black lay president."

Francis has remained president of XULA for almost four decades, becoming the longest sitting university president in the United States. The university has thrived under his administration, more than tripling enrollment and greatly expanding both its course offerings and its campus. By the early 2000s, XULA was awarding more doctor of pharmacy degrees to African Americans and sending more black graduates to medical schools than any other U.S. college. Francis has been awarded 35 honorary degrees in recognition of his academic achievement.

Became Community Leader

In his own life, Francis lives out "the ultimate purpose" of the university that he leads. The XULA Web site states that purpose as "the promotion of a more just and humane society." Francis himself has demonstrated this mission. In addition to working for increased access to academic excellence for African-American students, Francis has continued his work for justice and civil rights in the city of New Orleans, the state of Louisiana, and the United States as a whole. He has served on dozens of boards, task forces, and commissions on a city, state, and national level and has acted as an advisor to five U.S. presidents.

During the 1960s, as a XULA administrator, Francis supported the civil rights movement by allowing freedom riders to stay in student dorms after their bus was attacked. He continued to work for racial equality by helping to organize black primaries to place more African American candidates in Louisiana elections. In 1972, in order to improve the access of working-class African Americans to financial institutions, he helped found the Liberty Bank of New Orleans, which grew into one of the largest black-owned banks in the country with Francis as chair of its board of directors. He also served on the National Commission on Excellence in Education, helping to write its 1983 report, titled, "A Nation at Risk," which outlined racism and classism within the school system and called for education reform.

When Hurricane Katrina hit the Gulf Coast on August 29, 2005, the community once again called on Francis to help. Governor Kathleen Blanco asked him to chair the Louisiana Recovery Authority (LRA), which had been set up to coordinate the state's massive rebuilding efforts. She also asked him to head the Louisiana Disaster Recovery Foundation, which would coordinate funding and donations for the project. Francis was already immersed in repairing and rebuilding the XULA campus, which had been flooded during the storm and suffered extensive damage. However, he readily agreed to take on the additional responsibilities to the community, while still meeting his goal of reopening XULA by January 2006. As reconstruction in New Orleans continued in 2007, Francis remained a high profile leader at XULA and in the community at large. Francis' service to his community earned him respect from a broad range of his fellow citizens.

Sources

Periodicals

Black Collegian, February 2004, pp. 79-84.
Black Issues in Higher Education, February 10, 1994, pp. 38-9.
Jet, June 19, 2006, p. 8; January 8, 2007, p.8.
New Orleans CityBusiness, July 7, 2003.
Times-Picayune (New Orleans, LA), December 16, 2006.

On-line

"Dr. Norman C. Francis Receives the Presidential Medal of Freedom," *Xavier University of Louisiana,* www.xula.edu/president/award.html (January 25, 2007).
"Eleven Awarded Honorary Degrees," *Harvard University Gazette,* www.news.harvard.edu/gazette/2003/06.05/01-honorary.html (January 25, 2007).
"Norman C. Francis," *Biography Resource Center,*

http://galenet.galegroup.com/servlet/BioRC (January 25, 2007).

"Students Return To Campuses That Are Forever Changed," *Luno Concerns,* http://loyno.info/ chronstudents.html (January 25, 2007).

Other

Information for this profile was provided by the office of the president, Xavier University of Louisiana.

—Tina Gianoulis

Marilyn Hughes Gaston

1939—

Physician, author

The first African-American woman to assume leadership of a bureau of the U.S. Department of Health and Human Services, Dr. Marilyn Hughes Gaston has dedicated her career to the goal of making quality health care accessible to all individuals regardless of income, race, or other factors. As head of the Bureau of Primary Health Care (BPHC) of the Health Resources and Services Administration, she brought health care to thousands of sites across the country that serve needy populations. Officially retired from government service since 2001, Gaston continued to promote the goal, identified in a 1998 government initiative, of "100 percent access [to health care] and zero health disparities." In 2003, Gaston co-founded the Gaston and Porter Health Improvement Center, a non-profit organization with a mission to provide outreach programming to promote health. She also spoke frequently on health issues, and indicated her interest in starting a program to recruit youth to work toward removing barriers that can limit access to medical care.

A native of Cincinnati, Ohio, Gaston was born Marilyn Hughes on January 31, 1939. She grew up with her younger brother and older half-brother in a three-room apartment in a public housing project. Her mother, Dorothy Hughes, was a medical secretary and her father, Myron Hughes, worked as a waiter. Money was scarce, but the family, as Gaston described it in an interview published in *Notable Black American Women,* was rich in love and happiness. From an early age, Gaston thought of becoming a doctor, but she received little encouragement. Medical schooling was extremely expensive, and Gaston's teachers and school

counselors told her she would never be admitted. They warned her that she faced too many obstacles: she was a woman; she was an African American; and she was poor. Despite these warnings Gaston persisted with her seemingly impossible dream.

Gaston's family encouraged her ambitions, which were further strengthened when, home alone one day, Gaston saw her mother faint in the living room. Mrs. Hughes had cervical cancer but, as Gaston noted on the National Institutes for Health Web site, "We were poor, we were uninsured, she was not getting health care." The experience, Gaston emphasized, made her determined to "do something to change that situation." When Gaston was 12 years old the family moved out of public housing, and she attended a college preparatory school. Though teachers tried to talk her out of pursuing a medical education, she listened instead to the advice of her mother, who told her not to give up and emphasized that racism was not an excuse for failure. Gaston was also inspired by her godmother, who led a movement to desegregate the public swimming pool in their neighborhood. With these two strong women as role models, Gaston was able to persevere in her struggle to qualify as a physician.

Gaston graduated from Miami University in 1960 and entered the University of Cincinnati Medical School, where she earned her medical degree in 1964. She did her internship at Philadelphia General Hospital and her residency in pediatrics at the Children's Hospital Medical Center. Upon completion of her training, Gaston chose not to enter private practice but to focus instead on pubic health, where she felt she could be most

At a Glance . . .

Born Marilyn Hughes on January 31, 1939, in Cincinnati, OH; married Alonzo Gaston; children: two. *Education:* Miami University, BA, 1960; University of Cincinnati Medical School, MD, 1964.

Career: Associate professor of community pediatrics, 1968-1970; community health center, Lincoln Heights, OH, founder and director, 1969-1972; sickle cell research center, Cincinnati, OH, founder and director, 1972-1976; National Institutes for Health, Bethesda, MD, medical expert and deputy branch chief of Sickle Cell Center, 1976-1990; U.S. Public Health Service Commissioned Corps, medical expert, 1979-2001; U.S. Health Resources and Services Administration, Bureau of Primary Health Care, director, 1990-2001; Gaston and Porter Health Improvement Center, Potomac, MD, co-founder and co-director, 2003–.

Memberships: American Academy of Pediatrics, fellow; National Academy of Sciences, Institute of Medicine.

Awards: State of Ohio Governor's Award, 1987; National Medical Association Scroll of Merit, 1999; Dr. Nathan Davis Award, American Medical Association, 2000; Capital Breast Care Center Award for Outstanding Achievement in Women's Health and Wellness, 2006; National Medical Association Lifetime Achievement Award; Civic Ventures, Purpose Prize (with Gayle Porter), 2006; three honorary doctorates.

Addresses: *Agent*—Publicity Department, Random House, 1745 Broadway, 18th floor, New York, NY 10019; *Office*—Gaston & Porter Health Improvement Center, 8612 Timber Hill Lane, Potomac, MD 20854; *Web*—www.gastonandporter.org.

effective in meeting the medical needs of the poor. She applied for and received government funding to open a health center in Lincoln Heights, an all-black city near Cincinnati, Ohio.

As director of the Lincoln Heights facility, Gaston became interested in finding better ways to treat sickle cell anemia, an inherited blood disease that is seen almost exclusively among African Americans. At the time, the majority of children diagnosed with sickle cell disease were not expected to survive into adulthood.

With grant money from the National Institutes for Health, Gaston set up a sickle cell center in Cincinnati, where she served as director until 1976. When she moved in 1976 to Washington, D.C., where her husband had accepted a position at Howard University, Gaston took a job at the Sickle Cell Center in the National Heart Lung and Blood Institute, part of the National Institutes for Health. Her research team found that infants with sickle cell disease who received penicillin at birth were much less likely to die from sickle cell disease than babies who did not receive this medication. This discovery led to the implementation of national screening tests to ensure that newborns with the disease could be identified and treated promptly. Gaston joined the U.S. Public Health Service Commissioned Corps in 1979, and by 1990 was promoted to the rank of Assistant Surgeon General and Rear Admiral in the U.S. Public Health Service, becoming the second African-American woman to do so.

In 1990 Gaston moved to the Bureau of Primary Health Care (BPHC) of the Health Resources and Services Administration (HRSA). There her job was to improve access and quality of health care, especially among those living in poor and isolated communities. With a $5 million budget, Gaston oversaw programs that brought medical workers, facilities, and supplies to some of the country's neediest neighborhoods and improved health outcomes for more than 12 million people. During her administration, BPHC delivered health care to more than 4,000 critical sites across the country, including community centers, migrant health centers, homeless shelters, public housing, and schools. Other programs in her bureau targeted the special medical needs of the elderly, pregnant women, and new immigrants.

Realizing the importance of preventive medicine in improving health outcomes for women and minorities, Gaston worked with clinical psychologist Gayle K. Porter to write *Prime Time: The African American Woman's Guide to Midlife Health and Wellness*. The book, Gaston explained in the interview for *Notable Black American Women*, "is about living a lifestyle of prevention," an especially important consideration for black women who, in Gaston's view, often neglect their own health because they are busy caring for others. "We as Black women are dying at rates greater than any other group of women," Gaston said in the interview, but many if not most of these causes of death are preventable. The book urges readers to improve their health and well-being by proper diet, exercise, and attention to emotional needs. A reviewer for *Essence* called the book a "groundbreaking" work. To further the goal of the book, Gaston partnered with Porter to co-found the Gaston and Porter Health Improvement Center, a non-profit organization dedicated to providing outreach programming to help people make lifestyle changes to improve their health. One of the most successful programs is the Prime Time Sister Circles, support groups created to help women achieve their health goals, which in 2006 earned Gaston and Porter the first Purpose Prize awarded by Civic Ventures.

Gaston's work to improve public health has earned her numerous individual honors. In addition to numerous city and state awards and honorary degrees, she was awarded the National Medical Association's highest honor, the Scroll of Merit, in 1999. The following year she received the American Medical Association's Dr. Nathan Davis Award. The University of Cincinnati created the Marilyn Hughes Gaston Scholarship in 1999, which grants full-tuition medical scholarships to two low-income minority students each year. In 2006 the Capital Breast Care Center (CBCC) in Washington, DC created the Marilyn Hughes Gaston Award for Outstanding Achievement in Women's Health and Wellness. In a press announcement published on the Georgetown University Web site, the CBCC noted that "Dr. Gaston has dedicated her life to improving the health of our nation, focusing on poor and minority families."

Selected works

Books

(With Gayle K. Porter) *Prime Time: The African American Woman's Complete Guide to Midlife Health and Wellness*), Ballantine, 2001.

Sources

Books

Notable Black American Women, Book 3, Gale Group, 2002.

Periodicals

Essence, August 1, 2001, p. 64.
Publishers Weekly, May 7, 2001, p. 244.

On-line

"Changing the Face of Medicine: Dr. Marilyn Hughes Gaston," *National Institutes for Health*, www.nlm.nih.gov (January 5, 2007).
"Inaugural Marilyn Hughes Gaston, MD, Award for Outstanding Achievement in Women's Health Given," *Georgetown University*, http://explore-georgetown.edu (January 5, 2007).

—E. M. Shostak

Truman K. Gibson Jr.

1912-2005

Attorney, boxing promoter

Truman K. Gibson Jr. was the first black American to be awarded the Presidential Medal of Merit, for his service advocating for the rights of black soldiers during World War II. He organized the American Negro Exposition of 1940 and was involved in a major legal battle to end racial segregation in Chicago housing. In the 1950s Gibson became the first black boxing promoter and president of the International Boxing Club (IBC).

Studied Law

Truman Kella Gibson Jr. was born on January 22, 1912, in Atlanta, Georgia. His early years were spent in the black intellectual enclave of Atlanta University, where he attended school with his brother and sister. Their mother, Alberta Dickerson Gibson, was a teacher. Truman K. Gibson Sr., one of the country's most successful black businessmen, had put himself through Atlanta and Harvard Universities and rose to prominence with the Atlanta Mutual Insurance Company.

In the early 1920s increasing racial tensions in Atlanta prompted Gibson Sr. to move the family to Columbus, Ohio, where he founded Supreme Life and Casualty, which became one of the nation's premier black businesses. On the streets of Columbus, Gibson Jr. sold *The Crisis*, published by family friend W. E. B. DuBois. Gibson Jr. attended a nearly all-white high school where he was an athlete, but as a light-skinned black he experienced animosity from both races.

In 1929 Gibson Sr. formed the Supreme Liberty Life Insurance Company and moved his family to Chicago's South Side. Hoping to play Big Ten football, Gibson Jr. won a scholarship to Northwestern University in Evanston, Illinois. However after being warned about segregation in Evanston, he looked in the phone book for another college and enrolled at the University of Chicago. During the summers he sold burial insurance in black communities throughout the Midwest.

During his sophomore year Gibson was hired as a research assistant to Harold F. Gosnell, contributing to Gosnell's book *Negro Politicians* and becoming acquainted with the city's black power elite. Gibson graduated from the University of Chicago Law School only to find that the Chicago Bar Association did not admit blacks. He joined the board of Supreme Liberty Life and went to work in a private law firm. In one of his first cases Gibson successfully fought off an attempt to unseat Evanston's first black alderman.

Supported His Race

During the Great Depression gambling was an economic mainstay in the black community and accounted for much of Gibson's law business. However he took on racial discrimination cases. He won $25 in damages for Isabelle Carson, a Northwestern alumna and graduate student in social work at the University of Chicago, who had been denied service at a restaurant. They married on February 12, 1939.

Gibson served as a *pro bono* attorney in one of the most important civil-rights cases of the day, *Lee v.*

Hansberry, challenging real-estate covenants that barred blacks. Supreme Liberty Life bankrolled the original Hansberry mortgage and the subsequent legal battle. Hansberry's 1940 U.S. Supreme Court victory was based on a technicality resulting from Gibson's tireless research. The case was the basis for Lorraine Hansberry's play *A Raisin in the Sun*.

Gibson became executive director of the American Negro Exposition of 1940, commemorating the 75th anniversary of emancipation. The *Chicago Defender* called it "the greatest show of educational advancement ever exhibited by any race of people." It included the first national exhibition of black artists, 120 historical exhibits, a sports hall of fame, and musical productions under the direction of Duke Ellington. However the expo's success was eclipsed by the spread of war in Europe.

Joined War Department

In 1940 Gibson campaigned for President Franklin Roosevelt's reelection. Late in that year he was named assistant to Bill Hastie, whom Roosevelt had appointed Special Aide on Negro Affairs to the Secretary of War. It had been a token pre-election offering to black soldiers. Military leaders were determined to maintain racial segregation and black soldiers were drastically underutilized, performing the most menial jobs. They were confined to training camps in the South where they were abused, assaulted, and murdered. It was Gibson's job to investigate the multitude of complaints from black servicemen and their families. He traveled the country defending black soldiers and attempting to forestall race riots.

In January of 1943 Hastie quit in frustration and Gibson took over his job. Gibson recalled writing a memo to Assistant Secretary of War John J. McCloy: "The issue…is not one of changing fundamental attitudes. It is little more than getting the attitude across to our civilian Army that all soldiers engaged in a common task should be treated as soldiers regardless of race." Gibson's helplessness made him a target of the black press and black leaders. He wrote: "I was becoming a lightning rod absorbing all the venom that the army's racist policies would understandably generate among African Americans."

Gibson did have a few successes. His efforts led to the radio program *America's Negro Soldiers*, for which he lined up performers and gathered information from black training camps. He was involved in producing and distributing Frank Capra's 1944 film *The Negro Soldier*, which depicted the heroics of black soldiers and airmen, as well as the realities of black army life. Gibson not only saved baseball player Jackie Robinson from a court martial for knocking-out an officer, he got him accepted into Officers Candidacy School.

Attacked from Both Sides

In 1945 the "Buffalo Soldiers" of the 92nd Infantry Division were finally deployed to Italy, only to be accused of cowardice. The army threatened to withdraw the black division and Gibson was sent to investigate. He interviewed 800 officers and hundreds of enlisted men. He found that the black troops were scapegoats for replacement soldiers without combat training and inexperienced white commanders. As Gibson wrote in his memoir, "the army had a stake in trying to prove that black soldiers couldn't fight." However at a press conference in Rome Gibson reported that, although the black troops were as brave as whites, most of them were illiterate or semi-illiterate and poorly trained. A furious black public demanded Gibson's resignation. It was only many years later that the brave 92nd was vindicated.

Next Gibson visited the European theater where he reported on the successes of the first integrated combat units. As the war ended, Gibson was instrumental in the integration of redistribution centers for returning servicemen and in enabling black psychologists and psychiatrists to treat patients in integrated military hospitals.

Gibson left the War Department in December of 1945. He wrote: "I had had enough. Enough of the obstacles the army threw up at every turn to frustrate the aspirations of black soldiers. Enough of the persistent racism of the officer corps. Enough of the preconceived determination that African American soldiers would fail in combat. Enough of the incredible balancing act I was performing—behind the scenes waging war against all that, while on the surface endeavoring to put the best face on War Department dictates and policies. All the while I was being damned in the black press as a traitor to my race." Nevertheless Gibson's efforts broke ground for the desegregation of the military in 1948.

Back in Chicago Gibson reestablished his law practice with his brother Harry and accountant Theodore Jones. With the establishment of a universal draft, President Harry Truman appointed Gibson to the Advisory Commission on Universal Training, which recommended the desegregation of the military. He testified before congressional committees on several occasions and in 1948 participated in the National Defense Conference on Negro Affairs.

Introduced Televised Boxing

Gibson first met future world heavyweight champion Joe Louis in 1935 when they shared an interest in horseback riding. As an enlisted man Louis refused to box for segregated army audiences. Gibson negotiated for integrated audiences and arranged for Louis to lead a troupe of black boxers on a tour of military bases in Europe and North Africa. He also arranged the second Joe Louis-Billy Conn title fight to benefit the Army Relief Fund. In 1947 Gibson and Jones took charge of Louis's finances, legal issues, and Internal Revenue Service (IRS) troubles. Gibson established Joe Louis Enterprises, Inc.

Gibson set out to revive the sport of boxing, moving its capital from New York to Chicago. He initiated an elimination series to determine Louis's successor. The IBC was formed in 1949 with Gibson as secretary and later president. Gibson recognized the potential of the television sets that were appearing in homes across America. Soon he had built a multimillion-dollar business with televised boxing almost every night of the week. Gibson wrote: "Boxing, which had seemed in the doldrums at the end of the war, had roared back, and its popularity soared to new heights. Boxing and TV complemented each other and grew together. Here was a place where race didn't seem to matter, or at least not so much as in society in general." The IBC consolidated its ownership of professional boxing, which later became the basis for government antitrust charges.

With Sugar Ray Robinson under contract, Gibson attacked IRS regulations that required professional athletes to be credited immediately with their entire winnings. His success meant that athletes could spread their winnings out over time to avoid huge tax bills.

Connected to Organized Crime

The Ring magazine wrote in 1957: "Gibson may look and sound, at times, like a church deacon. But he is no babe in the woods. He is crafty, he knows the angles." Although his partners were involved in organized crime, Gibson maintained that the IBC was clean and that no fight had ever been fixed while he was running the club. However in 1959 the U.S. Supreme Court ruled that the IBC was an illegal monopoly.

Gibson's purported connections to crime mobs made him a focus of both Estes Kefauver's Senate subcommittee and the Justice Department under Attorney General Robert Kennedy. In the Pittsburgh Courier of January 2, 1960, chairman of the Illinois State Athletic Commission, Frank Gilmer, attacked "those vindictive and jealous individuals who are trying to crucify" Gibson. "To include Gibson in that situation is a travesty on justice and a reflection on the democratic system under which we live. He is one of the finest men I have ever met, and one of the most honest executives in the entire business world." In 1961 Gibson was convicted in federal court on two counts of conspiracy, fined $5,000, and sentenced to five years' probation. In his memoir Gibson described it as "Guilt by association combined with the enmity of Bobby Kennedy." Although his career as a boxing promoter was over, Gibson maintained that the IBC's promotion of black athletes and interracial matches influenced the victories of the Civil Rights Movement of the 1950s and 1960s.

Gibson returned to his law practice. In 1977 he was convicted in a stock-swindling case. His law license was suspended for two years and he was ordered to pay $1,000 monthly to the federal government, which he defaulted on. In 1987 he was given five years probation for bank fraud.

As the last surviving member of the "black cabinet" of Presidents Roosevelt and Truman, Gibson wrote his memoirs detailing his struggle to integrate the U.S. military. Gibson died at Mercy Hospital in Chicago on December 23, 2005.

Selected writings

(With Lestre Brownlee and Michael Reuben) *The Lord Is My Shepherd*, Children's Press, 1970.
(With Steve Huntley) *Knocking Down Barriers: My Fight for Black America,* Northwestern University Press, 2005.

Sources

Periodicals

American Quarterly, December 2004, pp. 945-973.

Chicago Defender, May 9, 1940.
Chicago Tribune, December 27, 2005.
New York Amsterdam News, January 5-11, 2006, p. 30.
New York Times, January 2, 2006, p. B.7.
Pittsburgh Courier, November 7, 1959, p. 12; January 2, 1960, p. 26; April 30, 1960, p. 22; June 10, 1961, p. 31.
Ring, August 1957, pp. 8-9.
Times (London), February 2, 2006, p. 61.

—Margaret Alic

Grandmaster Flash

1958—

Rap musician, music director, disc jockey

One of the founding fathers of hip-hop, Grandmaster Flash was one of rap's earliest technical pioneers. The deejay (DJ) innovative turntable techniques he experimented with in the 1970s have become synonymous with rap and hip-hop today. Flash and his group, the Furious Five, became one of the best-known rap acts of the early 1980s, with popular singles such as "The Message," "The Adventures of Grandmaster Flash on the Wheels of Steel," and "White Lines (Don't Do It)." Their music signaled the transition of rap from simply party music to a platform for serious political and social commentary. Flash split from the Furious Five and went on to record on his own, but faded from mainstream popularity in the 1980s. Flash came back into view in the 1990s as an elder statesman of the genre, revived and celebrated by contemporary hip-hop groups and media. He was inducted into the Hip Hop Hall of Fame in 2002; yet his status as a groundbreaker was further cemented in 2007 when he and the Furious Five became the first rap musicians inducted into the Rock and Roll Hall of Fame.

Innovated DJ techniques

Grandmaster Flash was born Joseph Saddler on January 1, 1958, in Barbados, West Indies, but was raised in the Bronx, New York. Recognizing her boy's fascination with electronics, Saddler's mother sent him to Samuel Gompers Vocational High School. His musical tastes were shaped by what he snuck from his father's and sister's record collections—he plucked Glenn Miller, Louis Armstrong, Miles Davis, Ella Fitzgerald, Dinah Washington, and Stan Kenton from his father; his sister's collection exposed him to Michael Jackson, Tito Puente, Eddie Palmieri, James Brown, Joe Corba, and Sly and the Family Stone, among others. He attended early DJ parties thrown by DJ Flowers, MaBoya, and Peter "DJ" Jones as a teen. Jones took an interest in the young Saddler, and the upstart DJ began to engineer his own turntable style.

Flash was not the first person to experiment with two turntables, but his discoveries are among the most known in contemporary hip-hop. Among the innovative turntable techniques Flash is credited with developing are "cutting" and "scratching" (pushing the record back and forth on the turntable), "phasing" (manipulating turntable speeds), and repeating the drum beat or climatic part of a record, called the "break." He developed a way to segue between records without missing a beat, using a mixer. He also was known for his technical tricks, mixing records behind his back or under tables, and manipulating mixing faders with his feet. In the late 1980s, he was the first DJ to design and market his own DJ device, the Flashformer.

After nearly a year spent practicing in his 167th Street apartment, Saddler started spinning records at free block parties and parks in the Bronx, often illegally pilfering power for his sound system from intercepted power mains until being shut down by police. He soon earned the nickname "Flash" for his rapid hand movements and general dexterity on the decks. Not completely satisfied that his wily turntable tricks were enough in themselves to completely entertain an audi-

At a Glance . . .

Born Joseph Saddler on January 1, 1958, in Barbados, West Indies; raised in the Bronx, New York.

Career: Began spinning records at block parties in the South Bronx in the early 1970s; formed Grandmaster Flash and the Furious Five with MCs Cowboy, Kid Creole, Melle Mel, Rahiem, and Scorpio, 1977-83; solo artist, 1984–; *Chris Rock Show,* musical director and DJ, late 1990s; Sirius radio program, host, 2007; Adrenaline City Entertainment, founder, 2007–.

Awards: Hip Hop Hall of Fame, inductee, with Furious Five, 2002; Rock and Roll Hall of Fame, inductee, with Furious Five, 2007.

Addresses: *Office*—Grandmaster Flash Enterprises, 600 Johnson Avenue, Suite E-7, Bohemia, NY 11716. *Web*—www.grandmasterflash.com.

ence, Flash invited friend and vocalist Keith Wiggins, later known as Cowboy, to share the stage with him. Wiggins would become one of rap's first "MCs," rapping lyrics over Flash's beats.

Until he was approached by promoter Raymond Chandler, Flash performed in the style of the times—for free. Chandler was among the first to see the commercial viability, and Flash agreed to let Chandler promote him and charge entrance fees, though Flash could not believe anyone would pay to see him spin records.

Formed Grandmaster Flash and the Furious Five

In the mid-1970s, friends Grandmaster Melle Mel (Melvin Glover) and Kid Creole (Nathaniel Glover) joined with Flash and Wiggins to form Grandmaster Flash and the Three MCs. Two more rappers, Kurtis Blow (Kurt Walker) and Duke Bootee (Ed Fletcher) joined and were later replaced by Rahiem (Guy Todd Williams) and Scorpio (Eddie Norris, aka Mr. Ness) and the sextet became known as Grandmaster Flash and the Furious Five, which became one of rap's first groups. The crew was known for its choreography, studded leather stage wear, and solid rapping skills. According to the GrandmasterFlash Web site, Furious Five MC Cowboy pioneered phrases like "Throw your hands in the air, and wave 'em like ya just don't care!," "Clap your hands to the beat!," and "Everybody say, ho!" which are echoed tirelessly in contemporary hip-

hop. The early days of live rap fostered head-to-head rapping competitions between rival MCs, often competing for their competitor's equipment in lieu of prize money.

Flash and the group recorded a number of singles for the Enjoy label, the first of which, "Super Rappin'," was released in 1976. Though an underground hit, the song went mostly unnoticed, as did the subsequent singles "We Rap Mellow," and "Flash to the Beat." Joe Robinson Jr. bought out Flash's Enjoy contract for his Sugarhill record label, and one of the most legendary artist-label teams was born. Robinson's wife, Sylvia, began writing songs for the group, and they released "Freedom," which was pushed to gold-selling status by the first major tour in rap history. The single "Birthday Party" followed, but the revolutionary "Grandmaster Flash on the Wheels of Steel" was released soon after and became a smash hit. The first song to incorporate samples, "Grandmaster Flash on the Wheels of Steel" dramatically showcased Flash's singular talent and changed the way music was recorded.

Cowritten by Sylvia Robinson, 1982's "The Message" was decidedly darker and more focused on urban issues than the group's previous party anthems and, though Flash and the Five recorded it reluctantly, the record became a platinum-selling hit within a month of its release. During recording of the anti-cocaine single "White Lines (Don't Do It)," Flash and Mel had a falling out. Also, despite the group's success, Flash had not seen much in the way of profits, so he left Sugarhill Records and took Kid Creole and Rahiem with him to sign a deal with Elektra Records. The rest of the group stayed as Melle Mel and the Furious Five, and achieved nearly instant success with the single "White Lines." The popular anthem was ironic, as Flash himself had become a freebasing cocaine addict. Flash and Mel later appeared together on a 1995 cover of the song by Duran Duran.

Flash drifted out of mainstream culture for much of the 1980s. His solo record, 1985's *They Said it Couldn't be Done*, met with low critical response. Songs like "Alternate Groove" and "Larry's Dance Theme," critic Ralph Novak wrote in *People*, were fun, enjoyable, and incorporated the lyrical phrasing and turntable and synthesizer manipulations that Flash was famous for. But those two strong songs were lost in the sea of "homogenized pop" that dominated the record, Novak continued. Novak declared Flash could not "be forgiven for forsaking the rhythmic rapping that made him" a hip-hop star. 1986's *The Source* noted that the album was a bitter and boastful declaration that alleged all other rappers had only copied Flash and his style. The record's strong point, noted *People* critic David Hiltbrand, was Flash's "feverish…turntable scratching technique" on what he considered the "best tracks," "Fastest Man Alive," and "Style," but those skills were hidden throughout most of the record.

Honored for Pioneering Work

Grandmaster Flash and the Furious Five reunited on-stage for a charity concert hosted by Paul Simon in 1987, but a proper reunion did not occur until 1994, for a rap-oldies show that also featured Kurtis Blow, Whodini, and Run-DMC. Flash returned to mainstream consciousness in the 1990s, celebrated by hip-hop culture and media as an elder statesman of hip-hop. He co-produced Public Enemy DJ Terminator X's solo record, Super Bad, and hosted a call-in radio show that showcased hopeful MCs. A slough of greatest hits records were released in the late 1990s, and Flash worked as musical director and DJ of HBO's *Chris Rock Show.*

At the end of 2001 Flash was busy at work on a new solo project built around the sounds he experimented with at the South Bronx block parties of the late 1970s. *Essential Mix* was released in 2002. It was followed in 2004 with *The Official Adventures of Grandmaster Flash,* with cuts from original block party tapes and exclusive interview footage with Flash himself. Flash also prepared a 28-page booklet to be included with the release, featuring rare photographs from the period and a detailed history of the era. In addition to these recording projects, Flash remained an attraction on the Las Vegas strip, performing in various casinos including the Bellagio and the Mirage. He also mixed music for a weekly Sirius radio program in 2007. He also started his own recording label, Adrenaline City Entertainment, to promote the music of other artists.

As Flash continued to mix fresh sounds, his reputation as a pioneer of hip-hop grew. In 2002, Flash and the Furious Five were inducted into the Hip Hop Hall of Fame. By 2007 their import on the development of modern music was honored with their induction into the Rock and Roll Hall of Fame. Proud that the hall of fame had recognized hip-hop, Flash remarked to Jon Pareles of the *New York Times* that "it opens the gates to our culture." And his part in unlocking the door was forever memorialized.

Selected discography

Greatest Messages, Sugarhill, 1983.
They Said It Couldn't Be Done, Elektra, 1985.
The Source, Elektra, 1986.
Ba Dop Boom Bang, Elektra, 1987.
On the Strength, Elektra, 1988.
Grandmaster Flash Vs. the Sugarhill Gang, Recall, 1997.
Greatest Mixes, Deep Beats, 1998.
Adventures on the Wheels of Steel, Sugarhill, 1999.

Official Adventures Of Grandmaster Flash, Strut, 2002.
With Melle Mel/Furious Five, *The Message*, Sugarhill, 1982.
Work Party, Sugarhill, 1984.
Stepping Off, 1985.
On the Strength, 1988.
Greatest Hits, Sugarhill, 1989.
Message from Beat Street: The Best of Grandmaster Flash, Melle Mel & the Furious Five, Rhino, 1994.
More Hits from Grandmaster Flash & the Furious Five, Vol. 2, Deep Beats, 1996.
Adventures of Grandmaster Flash, Melle Mel & The Furious Five: More of the Best, Rhino, 1996.
Right Now, Str8 Game, 1997.
Old Scholl Rap 3, Thump, 1998.
Sal Soul Jam, 2000.
Essential Mix, 2002.
The Official Adventures of Grandmaster Flash, 2004.

Sources

Books

Larkin, Colin, editor, *Encyclopedia of Popular Music*, Muze UK Ltd., 1998.
Rolling Stone Encyclopedia of Rock & Roll, Third ed., Fireside/Rolling Stone Press, 2001.

Periodicals

Entertainment Weekly, June 24, 1994, p. 14.
Flagpole, August 14, 2002, p. 27.
New York Beacon, March 27, 2002, p. 27.
New York Times, March 13, 2007, p. B3.
People, March 25, 1985, p. 22; June 23, 1986, p. 18.
Sacramento Observer, November 16-22, 2006, p. E5.
Wall Street Journal, March 16, 2007, p.

On-line

"Grandmaster Flash," *All Music Guide*, www.allmusic.com (March 21, 2002).
New Musical Express, www.nme.com (January 7, 2002).
Rolling Stone, www.rollingstone.com (January 7, 2002).
Grandmaster Flash, www.grandmasterflash.com (April 6, 2007).

—Brenna Sanchez and Sara Pendergast

Ice Cube

1969—

Rap musician, songwriter, music producer, actor

"With an eye that magnifies brutal characters and violent situations, Ice exposes a world that seems on the brink of exploding in the ear of the listener," wrote Havelock Nelson and Michael Gonzales in their book, *Bring the Noise: A Guide to Rap Music and Hip-Hop Culture.* A native of South Central Los Angeles who recorded with the notorious group N.W.A. before going solo, Ice Cube has often been a lightning rod for controversy; his N.W.A. song "F— tha Police" and solo raps like "Black Korea" have elicited angry denunciations, threats, and protests. Yet Ice Cube has argued repeatedly that his lyrics simply hold a mirror up to the reality of inner-city life. In the meantime, his records have gone multiplatinum, he developed an avid following among young white rock fans, and he gained even more fame by highlighting his kind, comedic personality in two spectacularly profitable film franchises: *Friday* and *Barbershop.* The contrast between his gangsta rap career and his film comedies seem perfectly reasonable to Ice Cube. As he told UPI NewsTrack: "You can't pigeonhole me into anything."

Rap Grabbed His Attention

Ice Cube was born O'Shea Jackson in 1969—four years after the Watts Riots shook the foundations of Los Angeles and placed the race relations crisis in focus for the nation. His mother, Doris, who, like O'Shea's father, Hosea, hailed from the southern United States, named her son after her favorite football player, O. J. Simpson. A better-than-average student, he attended Hawthorne Christian School where he dabbled in sports. Like many of his friends, O'Shea committed a few petty crimes but was not involved in heavy gang violence. While funk and soul dominated inner-city radio during his youth, nothing caught O'Shea's ear quite the new sounds of rap that arrived toward the end of the 1970s. "When I first heard [the Sugarhill Gang's] 'Rapper's Delight,' I couldn't stop rewinding it," he told *Art Form.* "It did nothing but grab me. By the age of 14, I was writing my own raps, and seeing [influential "gansta" rapper] Ice-T in concert for the first time."

O'Shea—who now called himself Ice Cube—was also hanging around with his friend Jinx, who shared his passion for rap. After hearing Ice Cube's first rap—written during typing class—Jinx agreed to make a tape with him. Ice Cube admitted to *Rolling Stone* that this early effort was "pathetic. The beat was going, and I was over in the left corner. The lyrics, they were cool, but they wasn't no exciting type of mind-boggling shit. I was only 15, you know." In 1986, Jinx's cousin, Dr. Dre, hooked Ice Cube up with Eric "Eazy E" Wright, who had financed an independent record label—Ruthless Records—with proceeds from his drug dealing. Eazy asked Ice Cube to write material for a New York-based group called HBO, which had signed with Ruthless.

Ice Cube collaborated with Dr. Dre on a track called "Boyz-n-the-Hood," an uncompromising tune about life on the streets of Compton. HBO didn't want the song, so Eazy recorded the song himself in 1986. Then he, Ice Cube and Dr. Dre became Niggas With Attitude, or N.W.A. The group's records—many written and rapped by Ice Cube—garnered them a following, and they seemed embarked on a lucrative career. But Ice Cube's mother insisted that he get an education, so at age 18, he headed off for the Phoenix Institute of Technology. After a yearlong drafting course, Ice Cube returned to Los Angeles and started up with the group in earnest.

Founded Gangsta Rap with N.W.A.

Ice Cube wrote material for Eazy's solo effort, *Eazy-Duz-It, Ruthless* released in 1988. N.W.A.'s first LP, *Straight Outta Compton*, appeared on the Priority label in 1989. Featuring the controversial single "F—tha Police," which prompted a threatening letter to the record company from the FBI, the album went platinum in three months without the benefit of any radio airplay. Listening to the album, Nelson and Gonzales wrote in *Bring the Noise*, "is like sitting in the Theatre of Urban Mojo, staring at rapidly changing images of ghetto angst." While the authors charge that the band received harsh criticism because it told the truth about young black men's lives, they admit that the songs are an assault on the listener. Yet, they add, "in some way one cannot help but become attracted to the brutal images—it's like staring at an auto accident."

Despite N.W.A.'s massive success, Ice Cube got into a dispute with the group's manager, Jerry Heller. After a 50-city tour and record grosses of over $3 million, Ice Cube found he'd earned a mere $32,000. Following further negotiations he was compensated, but decided to leave the group. "N.W.A.'s still a strong group without Ice Cube," the rapper remarked to *Musician*. "But Ice Cube is not as strong with N.W.A. as he is by himself." He formed his own label, Street Knowledge, hiring new talent such as female rapper Yo-Yo. His first

solo album, *AmeriKKKa's Most Wanted*—released on Priority in 1990—was quickly certified platinum. Produced in collaboration with Public Enemy's Chuck D. and the Bomb Squad, the album convinced many that Ice Cube was the real force behind N.W.A.'s hardest-hitting work, and that as a solo artist he would be a major force. *Spin* called it "a masterpiece." Yo-Yo debuted on the track "It's a Man's World," matching Ice Cube's well-known sexism with savvy responses; some listeners viewed her inclusion as a tempering of Ice Cube's alleged misogyny. Indeed, Ice Cube also produced Yo-Yo's 1990 album *Make Way For the Motherlode* and would serve as executive producer on her 1992 sophomore effort, *Black Pearl*. Still, Nelson and Gonzales declared that "the sexism found on [*AmeriKKKa's Most Wanted*] is counterproductive to the goals of the struggle" for black liberation.

In 1991, Priority released Ice Cube's *Kill At Will*, another highly successful record that earned strong reviews. *Art Form* praised the single "Dead Homiez" as "a harrowing and sorrowful tale of a funeral for a friend." That same year, Ice Cube made his acting debut in John Singleton's hit movie *Boyz N' the Hood*, playing the haunted, violent Doughboy to generally favorable reviews.

With the release of *Death Certificate*, Ice Cube once again plunged into controversy. Apparently anti-Semitic references to Heller in "No Vaseline" and hostile words for Korean grocers in "Black Korea" triggered a wave of protests from organizations like the Simon Wiesenthal Center and the Southern Christian Leadership Conference; even *Billboard* condemned the record in an editorial. Ice Cube's apparent racism and misogyny sparked considerable comment, though he and some of his defenders noticed that critics were silent on the subject of black-on-black violence.

At the same time, however, Ice Cube impressed many critics with his prowess as a rapper and observer of life on the streets: *Entertainment Weekly* called 1991's *Death Certificate* "20 tracks of the most visceral music ever allowed in public," awarding it an "A-" grade. *Spin* admired the record's "big, slap-happy beats" but took Ice Cube to task for what critic Dimitri Ehrlich deemed racist, sexist, and homophobic material. Side one—the "Death Side"—begins with the sound of a funeral; "the life side" commences with a birth. "The 'death' side is the condition we're in now," Ice Cube explained to Ehrlich in *Interview*, adding that "There are more positive records on the 'life' side, because while the 'death' side shows you where we at, 'life' shows you where we going."

Broadened Appeal

Following Ice-T's successful run on the first Lollapalooza traveling rock festival in 1991, Ice Cube appeared on the bill for Lollapalooza 2 in 1992, sharing the stage with funk-rockers the Red Hot Chili Peppers, Seattle-based grungemeisters Soundgarden, and Pearl Jam, among many others. Almost every rock act on the bill heaped praise on Ice Cube, and the Chili Peppers went so far as to appear in a video for his 1992 album *The Predator*. Another, much more important event came between *Death Certificate* and *The Predator*, however: the Los Angeles riots in the spring of 1992. After a group of white police officers who were videotaped beating black motorist Rodney King were acquitted by an all-white jury, the city exploded in acts of random violence. Fans looked to Ice Cube for a definitive statement on the riots.

The Predator earned an "A-" from *Entertainment Weekly's* Greg Sandow, who observed that "what's most striking here are songs—Ice Cube's strongest, most cohesive work yet—about the perils of everyday South Central life." Robert Hilburn of the *Los Angeles Times*—who called Ice Cube's first and second LPs "two of the most compelling albums *ever* in rap "—found that despite its consistencies, the album's best moments make it "essential listening." Still, Hilburn criticized the rapper for "failing to deal more directly with the events of [the riots]." The album debuted at Number One on the *Billboard* pop and rhythm and blues charts simultaneously, the first album to do so since Stevie Wonder's *Songs in the Key of Life* in 1976.

On top of enhanced fame from his new hit record, Ice Cube would soon become even better known thanks to another film role. This time he starred with Ice-T in the film *Trespass*, a crime thriller whose working title had been Looters but was changed in response to the 1992 riots. Meanwhile, *Reflex* magazine reported that Ice Cube had donated $25,000 to the Los Angeles-based Minority AIDS Project, and *Option* noted his donation of proceeds from a new single to post-riot relief efforts.

Struck Out on His Own

Just as *The Predator* was raiding the charts, *Rolling Stone* announced that N.W.A. had apparently disbanded. Ice Cube, however, appeared on top of his game. His 1993 release *Lethal Injection* was one of the year's most eagerly anticipated albums. While some critics praised it, Kevin Powell of *Vibe* declared it "not the masterpiece it could have been." *Time*, meanwhile, claimed that "Ice Cube's raps about police brutality and white immorality enter the ear and expand in the brain like a Black Talon bullet; his lyrics are sometimes inexcusable, but his logic is often inescapable. Ignore his high-caliber insights at your peril."

Bell Hooks, a feminist theorist, explored Ice Cube's perceived misogyny and thoughts on attaining black self-love in an interview with the rapper published in *Spin*. "Black women have always been the backbone of the community," he declared, "and it's up to the black man to support the backbone." He also insisted that "I do records for black kids, and white kids are basically eavesdropping. White kids need to hear what we got to say about them, and their forefathers, and uncles, and everybody that's done us wrong." Additionally, he admitted wanting to move into "straight political records" but didn't want to change the content of his records too abruptly.

By 1994, Ice Cube's life had undergone some changes. Reported *Vibe*, "He's happily married, a follower of the beliefs of the Nation of Islam, and the father of a little namesake (O'Shea Jackson, Jr.), with a baby girl on the way. Fans and detractors alike will tell you that Ice Cube seems a lot less angry these days." He starred in Singleton's feature *Higher Learning*, directed some music videos, and announced plans to eventually move into feature film direction. Although the scourge of white America appeared to have gone mainstream, *Lethal Injection* had done little to rehabilitate Ice Cube in the eyes of his critics; in interviews, Ice Cube's more conciliatory remarks were still tempered with flareups of the old fury. He also trumpeted the Nation of Islam's demand for a separate black country. Yet the "new" Ice Cube reflected a more pragmatic sensibility; as he insisted to *Vibe*, "I know that killing a nigga' down the street ain't going to solve none of my problems at all. And I don't put that into my records, unless I'm explaining a situation. I ain't stupid no more. And some people can't deal with that."

Created Successful Films

The more mature and sensible Ice Cube also began to solidify the new direction in his professional life. The next few years would paint the rapper as more of a producer of movies than music. Ice Cube made his film writing debut in 1995 with the release of the hugely successful movie *Friday*. The film featured F. Gary Gray in the director's chair and comedian Chris Tucker in the costar seat. The movie launched the big screen career for both Gray—who had done videos for Ice Cube and Queen Latifah—and Tucker, who had experienced success with HBO's *Def Comedy Jam*. With a budget of $2 million, *Friday* has since grossed more than $80 million dollars.

Ice Cube acted as executive producer and star in his next movie, *Dangerous Ground*, and costarred in horror flick *Anaconda* with Jennifer Lopez. And as he planned, his ever-changing position in Hollywood filmmaking was approaching a milestone. His next role would be as director, writer and actor in *The Players Club*. This directorial debut for Ice Cube had a bigger budget than *Friday*—$5 million—and proved with opening week returns of more than $8 million, to be a financial success as well. *The Players Club* boasted the highest per-screen gross of the movies opening during the same weekend. Ice Cube, now a rapper, writer, producer, actor and director, was also now a member of the small Hollywood Club of moneymaking film directors.

With the confidence that success was possible in the

film world, Ice Cube went back to his roots recording *War & Peace*, a two volume disc set that dropped Volume 1, in 1998. *War & Peace, Vol. 1 (The War Disc)* debuted with mild reviews. The rap artist, however, was still applauded for his impressive rhyme flow. He also tackled more movie roles, staring in *Three Kings* with George Clooney and Mark Wahlberg in 1999. *War & Peace, Vol. 2 (The Peace Disc)* was released in 2000 and has sold close to 750,000 units. To promote the release, Ice Cube joined the successful Up In Smoke Tour during the summer. Along with Ice Cube, the tour featured Dr. Dre, Eminem, and Snoop Doggy Dogg.

Ice Cube also revisited his early success with a follow up to *Friday—Next Friday*. His production company, CubeVision, produced the movie for New Line Cinema as part of production pact that had extended through 2002. The production pact folded after New Line turned down several projects recommended by Ice Cube. He then began working on two films slated for release in 2001: *Ghost of Mars* and *All About the Benjamins*. Ice Cube has placed great stock in advice his mentor, John Singleton, has offered. "He said if you can write a record, you can write a movie," Ice Cube explained in *Jet*. Following that advice, Ice Cube has found great success as a filmmaker, as well as a musician.

As a filmmaker Ice Cube continued the *Friday* franchise with another sequel, *Friday After Next*. The three films were blockbusters. He followed that success up with another comedy *Barbershop*. *Barbershop* included several controversial statements by a character played by Cedric the Entertainer. Cedric played a grumpy barber who spouted off about his grievances against Martin Luther King, Rosa Parks, and Jesse Jackson. The comments sparked conversations throughout communities and even prompted Rosa Parks to decline an invitation to an NAACP Image award presentation ceremony in which both *Barbershop* and her life story were nominated for an award in 2002. The sequel, *Barbershop 2: Back in Business,* contained decidedly tamer material. These films too were box office hits.

Ice Cube continued his comedy output and box office success with *Are We There Yet?* in 2005 and its sequel *Are We Done Yet?* two years later. The films are comic romps about Nick Persons, played by Ice Cube, a once-carefree bachelor who tries to adjust to married life with stepchildren. In 2007 Ice Cube was developing a reality-based television show for the A&E network entitled *Good in the Hood* about reformed criminals who help others turn their lives around.

Comfortable with Dual Image

Ice Cube's attention to his softer sensibilities did not cloud his vision for his harder edges. He grew increasingly frustrated with the direction rap music was going:

toward innocuous party music and away from social commentary. To inform young rappers and rap music listeners of his desires for change, Ice Cube wrote and produced a new album *Laugh Now, Cry Later*. He included songs about child support, the perils of drug dealing, and assessments of President George Bush and California Governor Arnold Schwarzenegger governance. Cutting through the lighter fare played on rap radio stations, singles from *Laugh Now, Cry Later* quickly rose to the top of the charts. "Why We Thugs" stayed among the top ten for over a month and the album was named by *Jet* among the top 20 albums not long after its release. His acting also included serious fare; he appeared in *xXx: State of the Union* as a NSA agent involved in stopping a military overthrow of the U.S. government.

His phenomenal success with both his intense music and his comedy films reveal Ice Cube's interest in expressing himself and connecting to his audience. "I have never worried about being hard or soft. I have always just been myself," Cube told Lydia Martin of the *Miami Herald*. "I'm concerned about being a man. Being a badass doesn't turn me on. That's an image; that's a gimmick. I mean, I still have hardcore records left in me…and hardcore movies. But I thought this was the perfect time in my career to make some movies for the whole family and reach another generation. I figure my core audience has kids who need something to connect to." Still married, Ice Cube's own family had grown to four children. With a solid family foundation and thriving business ventures, Ice Cube's desire to turn his creative impulses into marketable projects predicted much future success for him.

Selected works

Albums with N.W.A.

Boyz-n-the-Hood, Priority, 1986.
Straight Outta Compton, Priority, 1989.

Albums, solo

AmeriKKKa's Most Wanted, Priority, 1990.
Kill at Will, Priority, 1991.
Death Certificate, Priority, 1991.
The Predator, Priority, 1992.
Lethal Injection, Priority, 1993.
War & Peace, Vol. 1, (The War Disc), Priority, 1998.
War & Peace, Vol. 2, (The Peace Disc), Priority, 2000.
Laugh Now, Cry Later, Lench Mob, 2006.

Films

Boyz N' the Hood, 1991.
Trespass, 1993.
CB4, 1993.
Higher Learning, 1994.
Friday, (also writer) 1995.

Dangerous Ground, (also executive producer) 1997.
Anaconda, 1997.
Players Club, (also writer and director) 1998.
I Got the Hook Up, 1998.
Three Kings, 1999.
Next Friday, (also writer) 2000.
Shadow Man, 2000.
Ghost of Mars, 2001.
All About the Benjamins, 2002.
Barbershop, 2002.
Friday After Next, 2002.
Barbershop 2: Back in Business, 2004.
Are We There Yet?, 2005.
xXx: State of the Union, 2005.
Are We Done Yet?, 2007.

Sources

Books

Nelson, Havelock, and Michael Gonzales, *Bring the Noise: A Guide to Rap Music and Hip-Hop Culture*, Harmony Books, 1991, pp. 87-89.

Periodicals

Art Form, 1992, pp. 42-49.
Daily Variety, November 23, 1992, p. 6; March 13, 2007, p. 3.
Entertainment Weekly, November 15, 1991, p. 90-91; November 20, 1992, p. 88; May 12, 1995, p. 43; April 17, 1998, p. 48; October 8, 1999, p. 22; April 13, 2007, p. 55.
Hollywood Reporter, January, 2001.
Interview, December 1991, p. 89.
Jet, February 28, 2000, pp. 58.
Los Angeles Times, November 15, 1992, p. 64.
Men's Health, September 2006, p. 104.
Miami Herald, April 5, 2007.
Musician, March 1991, pp. 58-61.
Newsweek, December 2, 1991, p. 69; April 27, 1998, pp. 72; June 19, 2006, p. 58.
Option, July 1992, p. 146.
Pulse!, August 1992, p. 65.
Reflex, November 10, 1992, p. 11.
Rolling Stone, October 4, 1990, pp. 78-86, 166.
Spin, January 1992; March 1992, pp. 33-37; April 1993.
Time, January 3, 1994, p. 85.
Variety, January 17, 2000, pp. 50.
Vibe, February 1994; March 1994, pp. 41-46.

On-line

Ice Cube, www.icecube.com (April 9, 2007).

Other

UPI NewsTrack, April 5, 2007.

—Simon Glickman , Leslie Rochelle, and Sara Pendergast

Mwai Kibaki

1931—

Politician, economist

Kibaki, Mwai, photograph. AP Images.

Economist and politician, Mwai Kibaki was swept to power in 2002, becoming the third president of independent Kenya, ending 24 years of Daniel Arap Moi's rule, and breaking the hegemonic grip over national politics that the Kenya African National Union (KANU) had maintained since Kenya won its independence from Britain in 1963. As in other countries in Sub-Saharan Africa that have, for the first time since independence, recently witnessed a handover of power through the ballot box, the elections were hailed as a historical landmark, a "second liberation." Also in common with these countries, however, the return to multiparty democracy has not borne the fruits of its promise. Under Kibaki, euphoria gave way to disillusionment as governmental corruption appeared as intractable as ever, jobs were scarce, and 20 million of the country's 30 million continued to live below the poverty line of one dollar per day in East Africa's largest economy. Dubbed by *New African's* Tom Mbakwe "one of the eternal faces of Kenyan politics," Kibaki has played a role in government uninterrupted since independence, rising up the ranks to prominence—before falling out with his predecessor in the 1980s, founding his own

party, and resolutely launching three bids for the presidency.

The youngest of eight children, Kibaki was born on November 15, 1931, to tobacco and cattle farmers Kibaki Githinji and Teresia Wanjiku. The family, members of Kenya's largest single tribal group, the Kikuyu, lived in Gatuyaini Village near Mount Kenya—homeland of the Kikuyu and Kenya's highest mountain and the second highest in Africa. Kibaki attended three primary schools and received his secondary education at one of Kenya's best schools, Man'gu High School, where his academic performance earned him a scholarship at Uganda's Makerere University to read economics, history, and political science. At Makerere—a prestigious institution where a significant number of those who were to play key roles in post-independence Africa were educated—Kibaki thrived. He graduated in 1955 with first class honors, and was chairman of the Kenya Students Association, and vice chairman of the Makerere Students Guild. On graduation, Kibaki accepted a job as assistant sales manager with Shell's Uganda division, but very quickly left when he was awarded a scholarship to study at the London School of Economics. Equipped with a distinction in economics and public finance, Kibaki returned to Makerere in 1958 to take up a post as assistant economics lecturer.

Four Decades in the Kenyan Government

During a visit to Kenya, while he was still teaching, Kibaki helped to draft what was to become independent Kenya's first constitution—a process which according to Kibaki and others involved took just a few hours at a Nairobi bar. Kibaki left Makerere and returned to Kenya in 1960, serving as executive officer for two years in KANU, the largest Kenyan political party at the time. Kibaki left this role the same year that he married Lucy Muthoni, a pastor's daughter, with whom he was to have four children. In 1963, when Kenya won its independence, KANU, led by Jomo

Kenyatta, took the helm of government and Kibaki was elected Member of Parliament. He served in Kenyatta's government in a number of positions before being made minister of finance and economic planning in 1970. On Kenyatta's death in 1978, Moi became president and appointed Kibaki as his vice-president. Under Moi, vibrant debate became stifled, culminating in a constitutional amendment in 1982 which made KANU the only legal political party. Moi and Kibaki fell out over the 1988 elections which consolidated Kenya as a one party state, and the president demoted Kibaki, granting him the ministry of health portfolio. Kibaki resigned from KANU in December 1991, days after the one-party state stipulation in the constitution was repealed, to found the Democratic Party (DP) on Christmas Day and launch a bid for the presidency.

Despite a nominal return to multi-party democracy, Moi retained his tenacious grip on power, winning the vote in 1992 and 1997 through rigged elections marred by violence and bloodshed. Kibaki ran both times, placing third in 1992 and second in 1997. Kibaki presided over the forging together of fifteen disparate groups to form the National Rainbow Coalition (NARC) that would run against KANU in the 2002 elections. In the months before the elections several prominent KANU members defected to NARC due, in large part, to Moi's obstinate insistence that Uhuru Kenyatta, son of Kenya's first post-independence president, be the presidential candidate.

Kibaki's campaign centered on four central pledges: a crackdown on corruption, rapid economic growth and the creation of 500 000 jobs, constitutional reform, and free primary education for all. With these promises, Kibaki tapped into the thirst for change, and in elections largely free from violence, was swept to victory on a wave of euphoria, winning 62.2% of the vote. Three days later, on December 30, 2002, Kibaki was inaugurated—still in a wheelchair due to a car accident he had suffered on the campaign trail. The atmosphere was jubilant, chaotic, and hopeful; people were singing a NARC campaigning slogan, "Everything is possible without Moi." Indeed, when Moi arrived, his convoy was pelted with mud and his faltering speech was booed and jeered throughout. Kibaki, on the other hand, delivered from his wheelchair, what, according to *New African* journalist Wanjohi Kabukuru, was one of the best speeches given in the East African region. Promising to "lead this nation out of the present wilderness and malaise onto the promised land" through "responsive, transparent and innovative leadership" and announcing that "the era of 'anything goes' [was] gone forever", the speech was stirring and did little to temper the enormity of the expectations of the Kenyan electorate.

From the Wilderness to the Promised Land?

The first move of the new government was to initiate the free primary education policy just one week after

Kibaki took office. Moi had bequeathed a foundering economy isolated from the international community. Citing endemic corruption, the IMF had, apart from a few months in 2000, frozen its funding to Kenya since 1997, and other bilateral and multilateral donors had consequently done the same. Kibaki's pledge to turn the economy around meant restoring investor confidence and encouraging the resumption of international aid—and so was intimately linked to his pledge to crack down on corruption.

Towards the end of 2003, international donors resumed aid and lending, citing Kibaki's tough stance on corruption and judicial reform. In the first two months of Kibaki's rule, the equivalent of $198 million stolen from public coffers was recovered. Investigations led to the suspension of a number of judges and magistrates accused of bribery and related offences. Kibaki's government opened an inquiry into the notorious Goldenberg Affair—a high-profile scandal in the early 1990s involving non-existent companies, fabricated claims, and central bank payments of billions of dollars for fake export credits for gold and diamond. It was this investigation in particular that was meant to convey the message that the top echelons of Kenyan government would no longer be able to plunder the state with impunity.

Despite early signs of improvement, however, high-level sleaze, corruption, and mistrust continued to characterize the economic and political landscape during Kibaki's presidency. In a move that was perceived by many as proof of his commitment to stamp out corruption, Kibaki had appointed John Githongo as chief anti-corruption investigator. Less than two years later, however, in 2004, Githongo announced his resignation during a trip to the United Kingdom, days after the British High Commissioner had caused a diplomatic storm accusing Kenyan government officials of "eating like gluttons" and "vomiting on the shoes of foreign donors," as quoted by Neil Ford writing for *African Business*. Githongo claimed that he had been prevented from investigating the activities of high-ranking officials in Kibaki's government, and in a dossier he had prepared, exposed the Anglo-Leasing scandal, which revolved around a $20 million passport computer system, and led to the resignation of a number of Kibaki's ministers and to the suspension of some money flows from the United States and Germany.

As part of an effort to reduce Kenya's reliance on multilateral and Western donors, Kibaki's government intensified economic co-operation with China and the Asian Tigers. Perhaps more crucially, it, with Tanzania and Uganda, has sought to move forward with the establishment and institutionalization of the East African Federation, which would entail economic integration and the creation of a single market.

Troubled Leadership

Constitutional reform, one of Kibaki's central electoral pledges, was seen by many as essential to the consolidation of democracy. The process of drawing up a new constitution exacerbated and brought to the fore deep frictions and fissures within Kibaki's National Rainbow Coalition. Disagreements were particularly acrimonious when it came to the issue of how much power would be concentrated in the president. The final draft was put to a national referendum. According to critics and opponents of this draft—amongst whom were a quarter of Kibaki's cabinet—it did not place sufficient limits on the president's extensive powers. In a country where a third of the adult population are illiterate, fruits were used to represent the opposing camps. Kibaki's yes campaign used a banana, and the no campaign, an orange. After weeks of incendiary and sometimes violent campaigning, on November 21, 2005, the orange camp carried the day with 57 percent of the vote. Kibaki's immediate response to his humiliating defeat was to sack his entire cabinet, running the country for a fortnight with his vice-president, attorney general and permanent secretaries constituting his only team. After drawing up a new sympathetic cabinet, Kibaki was plunged further into crisis when several of the people he had named turned down their appointments.

Tribal affiliations and loyalties, thought to have become less politically significant since the end of the Moi-era, clearly played out in voting patterns; most dramatically, in the Kikuyu Mount Kenya region, the yes campaign took 92% of the vote. For a number of commentators, however, the results of the constitutional referendum are better understood as an indictment of Kibaki's rule. In the words of Magesha Ngwiri, opinion editor of Kenya's *Daily Nation* newspaper, the vote was "a countrywide protest against the fact that he seems to have retreated into some laager of his own creation." It will be in the 2007 elections—which Kibaki announced that he would contest in January 2007—that Kibaki's popularity with the Kenyan electorate will be more accurately gauged.

Whilst Moi's rule was characterized by his adept political maneuverings which played ethnic differences off against one another, Kibaki's hands-off approach has not incited ethnic tensions. Accusations, however, that Kibaki, himself a Kikuyu, has fallen under the influence of a clique of Kikuyu politicians dubbed the "Mount Kenya mafia," have stirred up fears of domination by the Kikuyu, who constituting just over a fifth of the Kenyan population, are the country's largest ethnic group. The principally Kikuyu based Mau Mau rebellion—in which Kibaki's brother fought and died—was a key part of Kenya's path to independence. Rather than celebrate it, however, independent Kenya has shied away from official commemoration for fear that it would have divisive and disruptive consequences in a multiethnic state. Kibaki has sought to reverse this trend, so that this bloody chapter in Kenya's struggle for independence can be officially remembered.

Elected on a mandate to eliminate corruption, transform the economy, and implement constitutional reform, Kibaki has, despite presiding over increased economic growth rates and an expansion of the democratic space, spectacularly failed to bring about dramatic change. The continued prevalence of corruption in high places is matched by the disappointment and disenchantment amongst the Kenyan electorate, who in 2002 had such high hopes and aspirations of Kibaki. Ugandan journalist and editor, Charles Onyango-Obbo, writing for *openDemocracy,* argued, however that, "When the history of Kenya is finally written in the years to come, Kibaki will probably be judged more favorably than current events suggest." Measured against realistic expectations—rather than the promises of a new dawn that would herald a complete break with the past—perhaps Kibaki will indeed be seen to have played a positive role for Kenya.

Sources

Books

Munene, Macharia, *The Politics of Transition in Kenya, 1995-1998,* Quest & Insight Publishers, 2001.

Mutunga, Willy, *Constitution-Making from the Middle: Civil Society and Transition Politics in Kenya, 1992-1997,* Sareat, 1999.

Duel of the Decade: In perspective, Hon. Mwai Kibaki's 1997 General Election Campaign, Up-market Solutions Ltd., 1998.

Periodicals

African Business, February 2003; May 2003; January 2004; March 2004; June 2005; January 2006; October 2006.

Daily Nation, November 23, 2005.

Diamond Intelligence Briefs, December 13, 2004.

Global Agenda, July 22, 2004.

New African, February 2003; December 2003; March 2005; February 2006; March 2006; July 2006.

The Guardian, December 31, 2002.

Time International, January 13, 2003.

World Press Review, March 2003.

On-line

"Kenya after Mwai Kibaki," *openDemocracy* www.opendemocracy.net/democracy-africa_democracy/kenya_3285.jsp (January 22, 2007).

"President Kibaki's Speech to the Naiton on his Inauguration as Kenya's 3rd President, 30/12/2002," *State House Kenya,* http://statehousekenya.go.ke/speeches/kibaki/2002301201.htm (January 22, 2007).

—Naira Antoun

Martin Lawrence

1965—

Comedian, actor

Comedian Martin Lawrence has been one of the busiest entertainers in show business. As star of the FOX-TV series *Martin* and host of HBO's *Def Comedy Jam*, Lawrence has found a wide and varied audience for his humor based on the black urban experience. Ratings for Lawrence's situation comedy in particular indicate that the young performer has found a "young, multiracial audience," to quote *New York Times* writer Mark Stuart Gill. The reporter added that most of the appeal of *Martin* "emanates from Mr. Lawrence himself…. He resembles a teddy bear on caffeine." Lawrence's star continued to rise at the turn of the millennium with a mix of adult-oriented stand-up concerts, comedy films, and even a G-rated animated movie. Yet in 2007, his comedy in *Martin* remained a strong foundation for his audience appeal, and a DVD of the show's first season was released. His unique, irreverent style continued to endear him to audiences.

Celebrated Positive Urban Life in Martin

In the *Source*, Eric D. Hatcher wrote: "Despite [the 1992-93 television] season's explosion of new sitcoms featuring black casts, *Martin* is perhaps the only one that successfully portrays a slice of urban reality. The show tends to exemplify the comedian's own beliefs in love, cultural pride and the black family unit. And the on-screen love thang between Martin and upscale girlfriend Gina (Tisha Campbell) is a true-to-heart depiction of a '90s brotherman, his woman and their relationship." Lawrence himself told the *New York Times* that *Martin* is closely based upon his own experiences, his own joys and pain. "Martin is a black man in his own world," the entertainer said. "He does hard, physical comedy. But he can be silly and gentle and romantic. His persona is about trying to find a place in society and a loving relationship that works." He added: "I'm portraying me, my personal experience. Young black men struggling to be the head of their households. Not always doing it right."

Upscale magazine contributor Sonya Jenkins wrote of Lawrence: "At a very young age, he was on a mission to make it as a comedian or nothing at all." Martin Lawrence was born in 1966 in Frankfurt, Germany, while his father was stationed there with the Air Force. While Lawrence was still a baby, the family moved to Landover, Maryland, a suburb midway between Baltimore and Washington, D.C. There Lawrence's father left the family, so the youngster grew up in a one-parent household with five siblings. Times were hard for the Lawrences. Martin's mother supported the family by working as a cashier in a series of department stores. The hours were long and the paychecks slender. Lawrence told *People* that when his mother would come home from work tired, "I would lie on the end of her bed, trying to make her laugh. I knew when I made my mother laugh, I had something."

Lawrence credits his mother and siblings with keeping him out of trouble as a youth. He did not live in a particularly deprived or dangerous neighborhood, but drugs and petty crime were common all the same. "I avoided [crime] because I had a family that stayed on top of it," he told *TV Guide*. "Me and my friends were

At a Glance . . .

Born on April 16, 1965, in Frankfurt, Germany; raised in Landover, MD; son of John (a former Air Force serviceman and policeman) and Chlora (in retail sales) Lawrence; married Patricia Southall 1995 (divorced 1996); children: one daughter. *Education*: Eleanor Roosevelt High School, Landover, 1984.

Career: Comedian and actor, 1984–; writer for and star of *Martin*, FOX-TV, 1992-1997.

Selected awards: NAACP Image Awards, 1995 and 1996, for *Martin*; BET Comedy Icon Award, 2005.

Addresses: *Agent*—Jim Berkus, United Talent Agency, 9560 Wilshire Blvd., Suite 500, Beverly Hills, CA 90212. *Manager*—The Firm, 9465 Wilshire Blvd., Suite 212, Beverly Hills, CA 90212.

smart enough to know we didn't want to go to jail—we didn't want to be behind somebody's bars. We had people who talked to us and helped us stay out of trouble by channeling our energy into sports and boxing, things that weren't destructive." Lawrence in particular found a niche as a boxer. As a teen he was a 90-pound Golden Gloves contender in the Mid-Atlantic region.

School held little appeal for Lawrence. He preferred clowning over studying and was constantly being scolded for his attitude. "I was always a hyper kid and could never stay still," he told *The Source*. "I'd much rather be up in front of the class makin' them laugh, so it became practice for me." Indeed, one of Lawrence's teachers finally made a deal with him: if he would behave through class, he could test his comedic abilities for the last five minutes of the period. He was a hit, and he became determined to make a living from comedy. "For me, this was all or nothing," he said in *Upscale*. "I left no room for anything else. That goal was just for my own push—my own self-esteem. The fear of not being a success in my life made me push even harder."

Launched Career with Stand-Up Comedy

With the encouragement of his family and friends, Lawrence began to seek work as a stand-up comic as soon as he had graduated from high school in 1984. He began his career in comedy clubs in Washington, D.C., while holding down a day job as a janitor in a Kmart department store. He was not an overnight

success. "I went onstage with my wild street humor and needless to say, the audience just didn't get it," he recalled in *Upscale*. "It was like a nightmare." Such rejection can shatter confidence, especially in a young performer. Lawrence kept his faith in himself, however, and he kept experimenting with new material, drawing special ideas and inspiration from comedian Richard Pryor. "Richard taught me that honest emotions about sex could be really funny onstage," Lawrence told the *New York Times*.

Eventually Lawrence moved to New York City. There he performed for free in Washington Square Park, a noted proving ground for would-be entertainers. In 1986 he got his break, so to speak, when he appeared on the television show *Star Search*. A variety show that allows unknown performers to compete for prizes and exposure, *Star Search* marked Lawrence's debut on national television. He did not win the night he was on the show. In fact he had to fly back to Washington, D.C., and return to his janitorial work for a time. Then, some months later, a Hollywood producer telephoned him and asked him to come to California for a screen test at Columbia Pictures.

Lawrence's first regular television work was for the comedy series *What's Happening Now!* He also made progress as a stand-up comedian, appearing in Los Angeles comedy clubs and in cable television comedy shows. His stand-up work drew the attention of director Spike Lee, who gave Lawrence a small but significant role in the 1989 movie *Do the Right Thing*. After *Do the Right Thing*, Lawrence landed the part of Bilal in *House Party* and *House Party II*, both successful black comedies.

Adapted to Different Audiences

From the outset Lawrence showed an ability to mold his comedy to the level of sophistication of his audience. Movies and network television featured a hyper but somewhat respectable Lawrence. Cable television was an entirely different matter. There, in the less restrictive, pay-TV environment, Lawrence indulged himself in raunchy monologues about sex and masculinity in the modern world—precisely the same earthy, personal brand of humor that had won fans for Richard Pryor. That type of comedy helped establish him as host of HBO's *Def Comedy Jam* as well as the star of several made-for-cable specials. And in September of 1993, Lawrence produced his first comedy album, *Talkin' Shit*, recorded live at The Comedy Store in Los Angeles and The Funnybone in Philadelphia.

Lawrence found the national spotlight in 1992. First he appeared with Eddie Murphy in the comedy movie *Boomerang*. The experience of working with Murphy was particularly helpful to Lawrence, who had long admired the established star. *Boomerang* also reunited Lawrence with Tisha Campbell, an actress he had worked with before on the *House Party* films.

Lawrence and Campbell became the nucleus of a cast for a new situation comedy to be produced by FOX Television.

Lawrence worked with the producers at FOX to create *Martin*, a 30-minute weekly comedy about a young Detroit disc jockey, his executive girlfriend, and his buddies. The show is more than a mere light treatment of the battle between the sexes: in it, Martin must struggle with his dual impulses to be macho *and* needy, to assert himself with his girlfriend and to depend upon her for emotional support. Topper Carew, the executive producer of *Martin*, told *TV Guide*: "I think the reason so many people love [Martin] is they can see that he's not perfect. He's expressive, animated, tender, sincere, and very honest. He represents the voice of the young African-American male in his mid-20s. One who doesn't have the benefits of an Ivy League education, who comes from the housing projects and had to struggle through all the social and economic obstacles that so many young black men face."

Developed Martin into a Hit

Martin first aired in 1992 in the time slot just after FOX's most successful comedy, *The Simpsons*. Figures from the A.C. Nielsen television ratings company in 1993 showed that the program ranked in the top five nationally among viewers from ages twelve to seventeen, and even in the top ten among viewers from ages two to eleven. The teen and young-adult audience is a particularly sought-after one by broadcasters and advertisers. Yet for all its mainstream appeal, *Martin* did not sacrificed its allegiance to black dialogue and attitude. Lawrence told the *Source*: "Coming up in the business I had people telling me what I could say, what I couldn't say, what I could do, what I couldn't do. Now I'm doing things the way I want to do them…. I am doing exactly what I want to do."

Some observers found fault with *Martin* and its modern, urban-romantic themes. In a speech in 1992, entertainment mogul Bill Cosby expressed the opinion that shows like *Martin*, among others, reinforced negative black stereotypes, including the idea that black men are oversexed and insensitive. Other critics faulted Lawrence for the two female characters he plays on the show—his mother and Sheneneh, an "around the way girl." Lawrence took exception to the criticism. He told *TV Guide* that he tried to make sure his show reflected his own perception of life—both comically and seriously. "These are characters that I've always wanted to play and have fun with," he told *Upscale*. "They're people I knew while growing up. 'Sheneneh'—the round-the-way girl and my mother—who's better to play my mother? I grew up with her." He added that he tried not to take the criticism personally. "It's like anything else in life. If you don't believe in yourself, then who will believe in you? The next man's way of getting there might not necessarily work for me, so I have to create my own ways of getting there."

Lawrence created one way of "getting there" to which audiences responded with sympathy and humor. During the February ratings "sweeps" in 1993, FOX broadcast three episodes of *Martin* that featured a running argument between Martin and his sweetheart. Viewers were given a telephone number and invited to vote on who should apologize to whom for the argument, and the winning vote was written into the final script. Response to the phone-in poll was overwhelming, and the majority of the callers felt that Martin should be the one to apologize. The stunt helped boost *Martin*'s audience share past its competitors on the other three major television networks.

In January of 1993, the National Association for the Advancement of Colored People (NAACP) gave *Martin*—and Martin Lawrence—its prestigious Image Award for outstanding television series. The award reflects the respect Lawrence is receiving for attempting to field a television comedy about some very serious subjects: being African American, young, and involved in a serious monogamous relationship, as the 1990s progress. *Newsweek* correspondent Harry F. Waters wrote: "The message of *Martin*—and what probably accounts for its huge teen following—is engagingly unique. The show's leading man poignantly struggles to be just that: *the man*. What sitcom has ever shown us that?"

Continued to Refine his Comedy

Lawrence told the *Source* that his comedy seeks to poke fun at the very things that produce pain and anxiety in life. "No one is immune to a joke," he said. "When you look at laughter, you look at hurt. With a smile comes a frown. So if something happens that is terrible, I can take it and find a way to make you laugh at it and say, 'Hey, yeah it is f—ed up, but let's try to laugh while we're up here.'"

Two years into his hit television show, film became a more dominant facet of Lawrence's acting career. In 1995, Lawrence co-starred with Will Smith in *Bad Boys*. Lawrence played detective Marcus Burnett, a financially pressed father and partner of Mike Lowry (Smith), a well-to-do bachelor. *Bad Boys* brought in $15.5 million in sales in its first weekend at the box office. The dynamics between the two detectives made the movie a hit. Producer Do Simpson told *Jet*: "Martin and Will are uniquely, inherently, and definitively funny. When you put them together they're screamingly funny."

In 1995, Lawrence married Patricia Southall who he reportedly met two years prior during the "Def Comedy Jam" concert. The former beauty pageant winner and Lawrence were married at the Waterside Marriott Hotel in Northfolk, Virginia. A year later, in early 1996, Patricia gave birth to their daughter, Jasmine.

Suffered from Fatigue and Stress

Lawrence's professional career continued to progress. While still continuing with his own show, he filmed *Nothing to Lose*, which was released in 1997. The stress and success of a comedic acting career, however, began to take its toll on Lawrence. He was known for frequent outbursts on the set of *Martin* and had difficulty while filming *Nothing to Lose*, forgetting his lines and breaking into hysterical laughter without reason. Being sent home one day from the set, Lawrence was found wandering the streets and even rambling in a carwash with a concealed and loaded gun. He spent the night in the hospital, reportedly to be treated for dehydration and exhaustion, returning to the set the next day to finish the remainder of the film without a problem.

On July 29, 1996, Lawrence attempted to walk through a metal detector at a Phoenix airport with a concealed 9mm gun. He eventually received two years probation and his family sent him to a drug rehabilitation center. He soon checked himself out and returned home. A few months later, Lawrence's instability and alleged abuse prompted his wife of less than two years to file for a divorce.

Tisha Campbell, the costar on *Martin*, left the show citing an unreasonable and unsafe working environment which she attributed to Lawrence's frequent outbursts and alleged sexual harassment. Competing lawsuits were settled out of court and she agreed to finish the season provided that Lawrence was not present when she was being filmed, a difficult feat for the show's writers as Campbell and Lawrence played an intimately married couple. Campbell's decision, nonetheless, brought the five-year hit series to a premature end and had in excess of $65 million in syndication sales.

Later in 1997, Lawrence was charged with battery after allegedly punching a man in a nightclub. According to *Jet*, the two men had gotten into a scuffle on the dance floor. Lawrence pleaded no contest and was sentenced to two years probation, 240 hours of community service, and to hold a fund-raising show in which he raised over $10,000 for two nonprofit organizations in July of 1998.

Found Renewed Success in Hit Films

After this period of turmoil, attributed by some to the pressure of success, Lawrence returned to the screen, acting with Eddie Murphy again in *Life*, released in 1999. In this prison comedy the two 1930s bootleggers make an emergency run down to Mississippi where they stumble onto a crime scene and are falsely accused of murder. Both are sentenced to "life" terms in prison. The film takes Lawrence and Murphy through sixty years of time, showing their emotional and physical changes as well as the growth of their friendship.

After *Life* Lawrence geared up for two more movies. But before he began filming, he suffered through another obstacle in 1999. While jogging in triple-digit temperatures in warm clothing he slipped into a coma with a temperature of 107 degrees. He managed to make a miraculous recovery. A hospital spokesperson told *Jet*: "He's made an amazing recovery. We nicknamed him our Miracle Man. It's not often that someone with a 107 [degrees] temperature makes such a recovery." After he recovered, he filmed two movies that were major successes: *Blue Streak* and *Big Momma's House*. *Big Momma's House*, a $120 million-plus success, led to *Black Knight*, a film for which he will reportedly made $16.5 million. *Black Knight* is about a restaurant employee who finds himself in medieval times.

Despite lending his talents to such family fare as *Rebound* and the animated film *Open Season,* Lawrence continued to gravitate back toward adult humor projects. Lawrence told Mike Szymanski of *Word Magazine* that "I'll always like adult humor more, that's my favorite," but added that he likes "mixing it up...I just love not being pegged into one specific thing." He filled his plate with projects that ran the gamut, from giving voice to Boog the bear to the delight of children in *Open Season,* to playing a middle-aged man on a motorcycle road trip with his buddies in *Wild Hog,* to contemplating another sequel to the hit *Big Momma* films, to seeking out a film role to play a villain.

His flexibility stopped with his acting roles, however. Lawrence kept his stand-up comedy separate. For his stand-up comedy concert *Runteldat* released as a film in 2002, Lawrence offered unflinching looks into his personal life—including his erratic behavior—stinging social commentary, and a stream of cuss words. Comparisons to Richard Pryor were plentiful. The box office receipts topped $20 million, a huge success for a comedy routine, which made Lawrence think long and hard about creating a follow up. But as he admitted to Szymanski, "I'm always thinking about standup, but you can't follow 'Runteldat' with just anything. If I have something to say and it's funny and the subject matter is interesting, then I'm right there." Testament to his prominence in comedy came in 2005 when Lawrence was honored with the BET Comedy Icon Award for his body of work and contribution to the field of comedy. While yet to release another stand-up performance, Lawrence kept busy. He hosted a new series for Starz Entertainment to feature little known comedians, *Martin Lawrence Presents 1st Amendment Stand-Up*, starting in 2007, and had begun work on two new films.

Selected works

Films

Do the Right Thing, 1989.
House Party, 1990.
House Party II, 1991.
Talkin' Dirty After Dark, 1991.
Boomerang, 1992.
Bad Boys, 1995.
Nothing to Lose, 1997.
Blue Streak, 1999.
Big Momma's House, 2000.
What's the Worst That Could Happen?, 2001.
Rebound, 2005.
Open Season, 2007.
Wild Hogs, 2007.

Television

Martin, FOX-TV, 1992-1996.
Martin Lawrence Presents 1st Amendment Stand-Up, Starz Entertainment, 2007.

Other

Talkin' Shit (comedy album), Atlantic, 1993.
You So Crazy (stand-up concert film), 1994.
Runteldat (stand-up concert film), 2002.

Sources

Periodicals

Newsweek, February 15, 1993, p. 47.
Jet, October 4, 1999, p. 38; April 19, 1999, p. 28; July 27, 1998, p. 37-39.
Hollywood Reporter, July 24, 2000.
New York Times, August 1, 1993, p. H-31; August 2, 2002, p. B12.
Newsweek, August 14, 2000, p. 60.
People, April 12, 1993, p. 53-54.
People Weekly, May 12, 1997, p. 194-197.
Source, April 1993, p. 46-48.
Spin, September 1993.
Tennessee Tribune, October 5, 2006, p. D6.
TV Guide, March 6, 1993, p. 28-30.
Upscale, February 1993, p. 78-79.
Variety, August 5, 2002, p. 21.
Washington Post, July 1, 2005, p. C5.

On-line

"Martin Lawrence, Not Turning into a Family Man," *Word Magazine,* www.wordmag.com/Film/FILM-FEAT_2006.12_Martin.htm (April 10, 2007).

—Anne Janette Johnson, Laura L. Brandau, and Sara Pendergast

A. Leon Lowry Sr.

1913-2005

Civil rights leader, minister, educator

The Reverend Dr. A. Leon Lowry Sr. earned a place in American history by serving as one of the teachers of civil rights leader Rev. Dr. Martin Luther King Jr. when King was a theology student at Morehouse College in Atlanta. For the citizens of Tampa, Florida, however, Lowry was more than a page in the history books. He was a leader in the fight for civil rights in Tampa in the 1950s and 1960s, going on to become the first African American elected to countywide office in Florida's Hillsborough County. In later life he became a Tampa institution who had touched the lives of numerous people in the community. "What I found in doing...research was that people genuinely loved him—from city and county officials to the people in his church," documentary filmmaker Spencer Briggs, who made a film about Lowry, told Walt Belcher of the *Tampa Tribune.*

The first part of Lowry's life was marked by moves between Georgia and the northeastern United States. Born Alfonso Leon Lowry in Savannah, Georgia, on June 12, 1913, he grew up in New York City, in a multiethnic neighborhood in Brooklyn that was home to recent immigrants from various parts of Europe. In 1935 he returned to Georgia to enroll at Morehouse College in Atlanta, graduating in 1939. His initial aim was to study medicine, but he felt a calling to the priesthood and furthered his education in theology. In 1942 he received a graduate degree from Andover-Newton Theological School near Boston and continued taking classes at Harvard and Boston universities.

Becoming pastor at Massachusetts Avenue Baptist Church in Cambridge, Massachusetts, Lowry seemed

on track for a distinguished career in the ministry there. He decided to return to the segregated South, however, in order to take a position as professor of theology and dean of men at Morehouse, his alma mater. In 1945 one of his students was a young Martin Luther King Jr., who had enrolled at Morehouse at age 15. When asked about King, Lowry sometimes quipped (as Hillsborough County Judge Perry Little recalled to Chris Echegaray of the *Tampa Tribune*) that "He showed some promise." Although Lowry soon left Atlanta, the bond between teacher and student continued and deepened as the struggle for civil rights intensified in the 1950s.

In 1946 Lowry returned to preaching as pastor of Tabernacle Baptist Church in Augusta, Georgia. There he married Claudia Whitmore, and the couple raised two sons, A. Leon Lowry II and Benjamin William Lowry. The family moved to Tampa, Florida, in 1956 so that Lowry could become pastor of Beulah Baptist Institutional Church. He remained in that post until 1995. Soon after his arrival in Florida, Lowry was elected president of the state branch of the National Association for the Advancement of Colored People (NAACP).

The University of South Florida opened its doors in 1956, and Lowry campaigned to help African Americans to be accepted for enrollment there. Organizing new NAACP chapters in small Florida towns, he was sensitive to the position of potential activists in small towns. He gave a chapter in Plant City, Florida, the innocuous name of the Ridge Improvement Society in order to protect its members from reprisals by employ-

At a Glance . . .

Born on June 12, 1913, in Savannah, GA; raised in Brooklyn, NY; died on August 20, 2005, in Tampa, FL; married Claudia Whitmore, 1946 (deceased 1994); married Shirley, 2000; children: A. Leon Lowry II and Benjamin William Lowry. *Education:* Morehouse College, Atlanta, GA, BA, 1939; Andover-Newton Theological School, Massachusetts, DD, 1942; studied theology at Harvard University, Boston University. *Religion:* Baptist.

Career: Morehouse College, Atlanta, GA, professor and dean of men, mid-1940s; Tabernacle Baptist Church, Augusta, GA, pastor, 1946-56; Beulah Baptist Institutional Church, Tampa, FL, pastor, 1956-95, pastor emeritus, 1998-2005; Hillsborough County, FL, leader of civil rights initiatives, 1960s; Hillsborough County School Board, member, 1976-92.

Memberships: National Association for the Advancement of Colored People (Florida chapter president).

Awards: Florida State Bar Association, Medal of Honor, 1987.

ers. "It was during the time where, if your name appeared on the rolls, you were automatically fired so you had to find a way to deal with that and get the job done," Hillsborough County NAACP president Sam Horton recalled to Sherri Day of the *St. Petersburg Times*. "Sometimes when you are renowned across America, you don't have time to deal with the little folks. He never forgot the little people."

As the lunch counter sit-in grew in importance as a means of nonviolent resistance to segregation, Lowry formed teams of students from Tampa's Booker T. Washington Junior High School and Blake and Middleton high schools to occupy counters at local stores. Segregationists peppered Lowry's home with gunshots, nearly hitting Lowry and his wife. The NAACP office was besieged with bomb threats, and a man with a baseball bat half-concealed under a coat tailed Lowry for weeks. But Lowry refused to back down, organizing a group of sympathizers who would quickly post bail for protesters who had been arrested. Finally Tampa restaurant owners agreed to begin serving African Americans on an equal basis.

Lowry was involved in further civil rights campaigns in Florida, including the ultimately successful effort to desegregate buses, railroads, and transportation terminal buildings in the state. He met with President John F. Kennedy in 1961 to discuss desegregation initiatives. "A lot of times the hard work of the movement was done beyond the scope of the TV cameras and after the national figures had left town," historian Ray Arsenault told Day. "Leon Lowry was one of the figures who did the heavy lifting. Within the history of the movement of this part of Florida, he is a towering figure of great historic importance." He co-founded a black-owned bank in Tampa and served for 16 years on the board of directors of the local public television station, WEDU.

In 1976, Lowry was urged by Hillsborough County School Board member Pat Frank to run as her replacement when she left the board to run for higher office. "He responded, very quietly and firmly, with the answer 'No,'" she told S.I. Rosenbaum of the *St. Petersburg Times*. Never one to seek out the spotlight, the soft-spoken Lowry was persuaded to change his mind and eventually won the election by a greater margin that Frank had achieved in her last campaign, becoming the first African American elected to countywide office in Hillsborough County. He won reelection several times and retired from the school board in 1992. The following year, Tampa's A. Leon Lowry Elementary School in Tampa was dedicated in his honor.

Recognized for his social justice campaigns with the Florida Bar Foundation's Medal of Honor in 1987, Lowry remained active until the end of his life. After retiring from Beulah Baptist, he wrote a religion column for the *Florida Sentinel-Bulletin* and established a three-times-a-week ministry for inmates at Tampa's Orient Road Jail, using a scooter to ride through the halls. Lowry's first wife died in 1994, after which the 87-year-old minister wooed a 39-year-old teacher at a church school by cooking her liver-and-onion dinners; she became Shirley Lowry upon the couple's marriage in 2000. The Rev. A. Leon Lowry died in Tampa of congestive heart failure on August 20, 2005. At his funeral, Dr. Michael Harris told mourners, as quoted by Rosenbaum: "We're not mourning a loss. We're celebrating a victory: his victory in life over forces that would hurt his people, his victory in terms of letting us know that love is more powerful than hate."

Sources

Periodicals

St. Petersburg Times, August 21, 2005, p. B1; August 27, 2005, p. A1; August 28, 2005.
Tampa Tribune, January 16, 2005, p. 1; August 21, 2005, p. 1; August 28, 2005, p. 1; October 13, 2005, p. 1.

—James M. Manheim

Ludacris

1978—

Rap musician

Most radio stations can only play clean versions of Ludacris's hit singles, and most of his lyrics "cannot be reprinted in a family magazine," wrote *Entertainment Weekly* critic Tom Sinclair. However, the Atlanta-based rapper is a multi-platinum-selling, Grammy-award-winning star. His 2000 major-label debut, *Back for the First Time*, sold more than three million copies, fueled by the hit singles "What's Your Fantasy" and "Southern Hospitality." His 2001 release, *Word of Mouf*, was similarly successful. He is "more than just a party- and sex-obsessed MC (though he is that, too)," claimed music critic Touré in *Rolling Stone*. "He's a guy with a bagful of flows and tones, whose voice is an instrument that he's taking full advantage of." The humor and danceability of his songs can sometimes get him off the hook for his often harsh and sexually demeaning lyrics. Having catapulted to fame with such music, Ludacris then explored more serious themes in his music and acting, to critical acclaim.

Born a "Little Entertainer"

Ludacris was born Christopher Bridges and spent his first 12 years in Champaign, Illinois. As a child, he was a natural talent. "Since I was a kid, I was always a little entertainer," he told *Fridge* magazine. His parents, who were still in college when their only child was born, used to take him to parties to provide entertainment. He grew up around hip-hop music, and recalled writing and recording demo tapes when he was just a child; his first song included the lyrics "I'm cool, I'm bad, I might be ten, but I can't survive without my girlfriend," he told

Teen People. He was only nine when he wrote it, he continued, "but I needed something to rhyme with 'girlfriend.'" He moved with his family to Atlanta when he was 12 years old.

Ludacris told Fahiym Ratcliffe in an interview with the *Source* that despite his years in the Midwest, "Atlanta is where I spent most of my life and [where] my years of real growth and development took place." He wrestled and played baseball at Banneker High School, and his high school cohorts eventually became his Disturbing tha Peace entourage. After graduating in 1995, he attended Georgia State University as a music business major for a while, but dropped out to pursue his rapping aspirations. He also developed Ludacris, his outlandish alternate persona. "I have a split personality," he joked in *Showcase*. "The nickname is something I made up—part of me is calm, cool, and collective, while the other side is just beyond crazy." The rapper counts MCs Scarface, Q-Tip, and Rakim among his influences, as well as comedians Richard Pryor, Eddie Murphy, and Cheech & Chong.

Ludacris competed in local hip-hop talent shows, and sent a demo tape to Atlanta's Hot 97-FM, which earned him an internship at the radio station. He started recording promotional spots that aired on the station, graduating to his own primetime show under the moniker "Chris Lova Lova," where his voice was heard throughout Atlanta. A major break came when hip-hop producer Timbaland hired him to work on the single "Fat Rabbit" from his 1998 album *Tim's Bio*, after he heard Ludacris's demo. Soon after, popular hip-hop artist Jermaine Dupri hired him to voice the

At a Glance . . .

Born Christopher Bridges, c. 1978 in Champaign, IL. *Education*: Attended Georgia State University.

Career: Rapper. Interned at Atlanta Hot 97-FM radio station; Disturbing tha Peace, record label, founder, 2000–; Def Jam South, recording artist, 2000–; Ludacris Foundation, founder, 2001–.

Awards: Grammy Award, for Best Rap/Sung Collaboration, 2004; Grammy Award, for Best Rap Album, 2006; Grammy Award, for Best Rap Song, 2006; Spirit of Youth Award, 2007.

Addresses: *Web*—www.defjam.com/site/artist_home. php?artist_id=308.

John Madden 2000 video game. Motivated by the hype he was getting, but with no sign of a record deal, Ludacris decided to release his first record on his own. His debut, *Inconegro*, on his own Disturbing tha Peace label, hit Atlanta record stores in 2000. It ended up selling 30,000 copies and generating considerable word of mouth for the artist. The success resulted in his signing on as the first artist to Def Jam Records' then-new Def Jam South imprint.

Part of the Dirty South Sound

Ludacris is part of a surge of hip-hop that has risen out of the South, overtaking the national charts, and he is one of a list of contemporary R & B and hip-hop luminaries, including Jermaine Dupri, Dallas Austin, Arrested Development, TLC, OutKast, Goodie Mob, Organized Noise, and Too Short. "The East Coast had a time when it was reigning supreme," Ludacris explained in *Vibe*. "The West Coast had a time when it was reigning supreme. And now the South's reigning supreme."

Def Jam South repackaged *Inconegro* and released it as *Back for the First Time* in 2000. The release was a breath of humorous fresh air on the serious hip-hop scene. "When my album came out," Ludacris told *New York*, "it seemed like no one wanted to be fun or crazy anymore." According to writer Kris Ex in *XXL*, "What's Your Fantasy," the album's first single, "established [Ludacris] as an NC-17 rapper: full frontal nudity, but more artistic than sleazy." On the second single, "Southern Hospitality," Ludacris declared his love for his adopted hometown and the song became a smash hit. *Back for the First Time* sold more than three

million copies and "solidified him as the South's prince of rhyme," according to the *Source*. Though he was known for his outlandish lyrics, Ludacris maintained that he was a more complex artist. "I don't worry about being typecast as one type of rapper," he said in the *Source*, "because if they really listen…then they'll find that there's more to acting crazy and being stupid. Sometimes it's being…serious and talking about real-life situations on stuff that I go through."

Ludacris turned out his follow-up release, *Word of Mouf*, during the next year. Swizz Beatz, Timbaland, Mystikal, and Organized Noise were among the hot hip-hop talents Ludacris called upon to help out on the album. Ludacris explained in *Rolling Stone* that "Cold Outside" and "Growing Pains" recall his struggle to the top, and "Saturday" describes "what people do on their best days." On the Timbaland-produced "Rollout," Ludacris not-so-subtly urges people to mind their own business instead of his. The hit single "Area Codes" is about having girlfriends all over the country, features rapper Nate Dogg, and is "one of the high points" of the album, according to *Boston Globe* critic Keri Callahan, who declared the album "not for innocent ears." "They say the number-one promotion is word of mouth," Ludacris said in *Fridge*. "So I'm trying to tell everybody that if there was no radio and there was no television, this album is going multi-platinum by word of mouth alone. That's how good I feel it is." It was a hit album, as was his next two, *Chicken-n-Beer*, which released in 2003 and *Red Light District*, released in 2004.

Expanded His Horizons

While working on new albums, Ludacris also dabbled in acting. He appeared in *2 Fast 2 Furious, Hustle and Flow*, and *Crash*. He also narrated for *The Heart of the Game*, a film about the triumphs and tribulations of a high school girls' basketball team. Ludacris told Geoff Boucher of the *Los Angeles Times* that rapping prepared him well for acting. As a rapper, "you got to be able to do your thing with a bunch of people staring dead at you waiting for something to happen," Ludacris explained. "That all gets you ready to be an actor…. That's why rappers have been doing all right in movies. But I still think they have something to prove." Ludacris proved himself as an actor in *Crash*. The film's producer Cathy Schulman called him "the great, great discovery of this movie," according to the *Los Angeles Times*. His performance as a car thief in *Crash* won Ludacris a Screen Actors Guild award in 2006.

Ludacris' commercial appeal as a musician had generated millions in album sales and garnered him several multi-platinum albums. Yet with his *Release Therapy* album of 2006, Ludacris also won critical praise. The songs included serious messages, as in a song imploring prisoners to stay strong during their sentences, and a song about an abused child who runs away, as well as a song commenting on the commercialization of rap. Ludacris took the serious messages further. With his charitable foundation, he partnered with the National Runaway Switchboard to help address the issue of youths running away from home in America. He and the Ludacris Foundation were honored for their efforts with a Spirit of Youth Award in 2007. The serious slant to his music struck a chord with listeners. The songs "Money Maker" and "Runaway Love" from the album both reached the top of the *Billboard* charts. Ludacris won two Grammy Awards in 2006 for Best Rap Album and for "Money Maker" as Best Rap Song. His awards in 2006 marked an apex of Ludacris' status in both the music and film industry. Yet it seemed a high point that he might be able to surpass.

Selected discography

Albums

Inconegro, Disturbing tha Peace, 2000.
Back for the First Time, Def Jam South, 2000.
Word of Mouf, Def Jam South, 2001.
Chicken-n-Beer, Def Jam, 2003.
Red Light District, Def Jam, 2004.
Ludacris Presents Disturbing Tha Peace, DTP/Def Jam, 2005.
Release Therapy, Def Jam, 2006.

Sources

Periodicals

Boston Globe, January 3, 2002, p. CAL12.
Entertainment Weekly, December 7, 2001, p. 102.
Fridge, fall-winter 2001-02, p. 67.
Los Angeles Times, May 8, 2005, p. E18; September 24, 2006, p. E42.
New York, September 10, 2001.
Rolling Stone, December 6-13, 2001.
Showcase, December-January 2002.
Source, February 2002, p. 80.
Teen People, summer 2002, p. 68.
Vibe, November 2001, p. 102; June 2002, p. 92.
XXL, December 2001, p. 91.

On-line

All Music Guide, www.allmusic.com (August 20, 2002).
The Ludacris Foundation, www.theludacrisfoundation.org (April 6, 2007).
"Ludacris Official Website @ defjam," *Def Jam,* www.defjam.com/site/artist_home.php?artist_id=308 (April 6, 2007).

Other

Additional information was provided by Def Jam South publicity materials, 2002.

—Brenna Sanchez and Sara Pendergast

Rick Mahorn

1958—

Professional basketball player, coach, broadcaster

A power forward on the Detroit Pistons "Bad Boys" squads that terrorized National Basketball League opponents in the late 1980s, Rick Mahorn had a long career in the game he was told as a high school student that he was not good enough to play professionally. Although he had a justified reputation for rough behavior on the basketball court, Mahorn was described by friends as warm and supportive away from the game. An intelligent and articulate basketball thinker, Mahorn enjoyed a successful career as a coach and broadcaster after he retired from playing in 1999, at the age of 40.

Lacked Athletic Ability as Youth

Derrick Allen Mahorn was born in Hartford, Connecticut, on September 21, 1958. Mahorn's father, Owen, a milk plant dispatch manager, abandoned the family when Mahorn was eight months old. With his mother, Alice, supporting the family by doing domestic work in the city's mansions, Mahorn was raised partly by his older brother, Owen Jr., who showed basketball talent early and later joined the varsity squad at Fairfield University. There were few signs, however, that Rick Mahorn had an athletic career ahead of him. As a child he was chubby and often came out on the losing end of scraps with his older brother.

The situation changed, however, when Mahorn grew from six feet one to six feet seven over the space of a few months as a 16-year-old and kept growing up to his adult height of six feet eight and a half inches. He played football (as a tight end and defensive end) at Hartford's Weaver High School and then made the

basketball team in his senior year. College scholarship offers were more numerous for football than for basketball, but Mahorn stuck with the sport in which he liked to compete with his older brother in one-on-one matches, finally starting to win them during his sophomore year of college. "That was the sweetest feeling in the world," he recalled to *Sports Illustrated* after he achieved professional stardom. "Now I'm living Owen's dream. He doesn't know he could never be as proud of me as I am of him."

Mahorn decided to focus on basketball even though he did not receive a scholarship from the school he wanted—the University of Connecticut, with its powerhouse basketball squads. Coaches there told Mahorn he did not have the skills to compete at a Division I school, so he enrolled at Hampton Institute (now Hampton University), a historically African-American school in Virginia, with its Division II basketball team. "When I ended up going to Hampton, I was discouraged," Mahorn told John Brennan of New Jersey's Bergen County *Record*. "But it ended up being a blessing. It was a way to let me know that my skills weren't up to par." His mother urged him to focus on his educational goals, and he graduated from Hampton with a B.S. degree in business administration in 1980.

Drafted by Bullets

While he focused on his studies, he also improved his basketball skills. But Mahorn told Brennan, "I never thought about playing in the NBA." The National Basketball Association took notice of him, however, when he led all Division II players in rebounds during the 1979-80 season. The Washington Bullets selected Mahorn in the second round of the 1980 draft, making him the first Hampton Institute player ever drafted by an NBA team. Mahorn made his NBA debut in 1981 with the Bullets, getting into 52 games that year. Until 1992, when he took a year off to play basketball in Europe, he exceeded that total as a starter who played in nearly all his team's outings.

The legend of Mahorn as enforcer or on-court thug began to grow during his years with the Bullets as the team signed another big forward, six feet eleven, 275-pound Jeff Ruland. A sportscaster dubbed the pair McFilthy and McNasty, with Mahorn in the latter role. "If anybody is my beef brother, bruise brother, whatever, it's Ruland," Mahorn told *Sports Illustrated.* "We had the same kind of dog—black Dobermans. Our kids were the same age. His license plate was GTM 677. And by coincidence, mine was GTM 877. We were the same kind." The offspring Mahorn referred to was his daughter Moyah, whom he called (according to *Sports Illustrated*) "my heart, my light, my life." He later

married, and he and his wife Donyale raised three more children.

Mahorn's game quickly improved after his rookie year with the Bullets, and he posted a career-best average of 12.2 points per game in the 1982 season. Through 1984 he was a consistent performer who averaged around ten points per game and was a formidable defensive presence in the center of the foul lane. In 1985 his offensive production dropped slightly as he averaged just 6.3 points per game, and he was traded in June of that year to the Detroit Pistons. "I was shocked," he told *Sports Illustrated.* "I learned the game from [Bullets center] Wes Unseld, alongside Jeff Ruland. I felt at home in Washington." Unseld told the magazine that Mahorn "had endeared himself to me. Ninety-nine percent of the guys don't want the job Rick has. A lot of people have problems with the way he plays. I have no problem with it. If you come in there weak, Rick will make you pay."

Accumulated Fines

As it turned out, Mahorn's aggressive style of play found a good home in Detroit. It didn't take Mahorn long to announce his highly physical presence on the court. In 1987 he sent star Boston Celtics shooter Larry Bird scooting across the floor of the Pistons arena with a sharp hip bump. The 1989 season was a banner year of on-court Mahorn violence: he was fined $5,000 for elbowing Cleveland Cavaliers guard Mark Price in the head, and that was just one of three fines levied against him that year, at a total cost of $11,000. He had regular run-ins on the court, one of them involving the entire Chicago Bulls squad.

Mahorn acquired the nickname Ricky Mayhem, and Atlanta Hawks player Dominique Wilkins recalled to the *Atlanta Journal-Constitution* that "[i]f you took the ball down the middle against Ricky, you knew you were gonna get whacked." Many players defended Mahorn's style. One was New York Knickerbockers center Patrick Ewing, a Mahorn opponent since the days when both were college players. "He's a great defender," Ewing told *Sports Illustrated.* "He knows all the tricks. He can push you out, then pull the chair and make you fall flat on your butt. Until this day, when I play Rick Mahorn, I know it's going to be a war." Mahorn himself simply told the same magazine that "I can play. I wouldn't have been in this league for nine years if I couldn't play. Thug this, enforcer that. I take 48 minutes very seriously, that's all."

In Detroit, Mahorn found another on-court partner in toughness: Pistons center Bill Laimbeer. The combination was a potent one; fans flocked to the Pistons' new Palace of Auburn Hills arena to see the "Bad Boys" in action, and in 1989 the team put any doubts to rest by cruising to an NBA championship. That year Mahorn was sent to the Minnesota Timberwolves in the league's expansion draft but quickly moved to the Philadelphia 76ers, where he was teamed with power forward Charles Barkley. Mahorn's salary ballooned from $600,000 in 1989 to an estimated $965,000 in 1990 and $1,330,000 in 1991. In 1990 he made the NBA's All-Defensive second team, and he played in four postseason all-star games over the course of his career.

Maintained Athleticism Longer than Most

Well past the point where the games of most NBA big men have begun to slow down, Mahorn's remained viable and consistent. He played in Italy for the Virtus Roma and Il Messagero clubs in 1992 and was then signed to the New Jersey Nets, remaining with that club from 1993 until 1996. He returned to the Pistons from 1996 to 1998 and closed out his career with the Philadelphia 76ers in 1999, receiving a million-dollar salary at age 40. Over 13 seasons he appeared in 1,117 games, averaging 6.9 points and 4.6 defensive rebounds per game. His achievements on the court were honored with an induction, in 2003, into the Central Intercollegiate Athletic Association's John B. McLendon Jr. Hall of Fame.

Mahorn quickly set his sights on a basketball coaching career. Paying his dues as coach of the Rockford Lightning in the minor-league Continental Basketball Association for a year (and leading the team to a conference title), he was hired in the fall of 2000 as an assistant coach by the Atlanta Hawks. "I was in Washington when Rick was there," Miami Heat assistant coach Jeff Bzdelik observed to the *Atlanta Journal-Constitution*. "You could see at that age he was going to be a coach. Even when he was a rookie out of Hampton, you could tell by his demeanor on the practice court. Rick had ideas, and he understood the game, and older guys paid attention."

Considered for the post of Pistons head coach in 2001 but passed over in favor of Rick Carlisle, Mahorn finally succeeded in returning to the city whose rough-and-tumble personality fit his own. He served as color analyst for Pistons games broadcast on radio station WDFN, and in 2005 he became assistant coach of the Detroit Shock team in the Women's National Basketball Association (WNBA). The job reunited Mahorn with Bill Laimbeer, who served as head coach, and the pair proved as potent on the sidelines as they had been on the court: the Shock were WNBA champions in 2006.

Sources

Periodicals

Atlanta Journal-Constitution, October 29, 2000, p. E5.
Grand Rapids Press, April 25, 2001, p. C1.
Record (Bergen County, NJ), March 17, 1996, p. S7.
Sports Illustrated, April 10, 1989, p. 66.

On-line

"Coach Bio: Rick Mahorn," *Detroit Shock,* www.wnba.com/shock (March 3, 2007).
"Rick Mahorn," *Basketball Reference,* www.basketball-reference.com/players/m/mahorri01.html (March 3, 2007).
"Rick Mahorn," *National Basketball Association,* www.nba.com (March 3, 2007).

—James M. Manheim

Tyron McFarlan

1971(?)—

Circus performer

As the 34th Ringmaster of the famed Ringling Bros. Barnum & Bailey Circus, Tyron "Ty" McFarlan Jr. faces more physical demands during a show even than the acrobats and clowns with whom he performs. "I hope I make it fun; it really is a very taxing job," he explained to Allison Perkins of the *Stars and Stripes*. "Most performers are on for ten minutes and done for much of the rest of the show. I'm the only performer on the floor for the entire show." McFarlan came to the organization without any previous experience in circus performing. "I had no preconceived notions of what to expect," he told Marty Clear of the *St. Petersburg Times*. "But I tell you, it's been a wonderful trip."

A native of Columbia, South Carolina, Tyron Stucks McFarlan Jr. was born around 1971. His father was a United States Army warrant officer who became a South Carolina state trooper, and his mother a third-grade teacher. An atmosphere of military discipline served McFarlan well in his future career, as he became master of ceremonies to a large and diverse group of performers and animals. At a young age he showed an interest in following his father into the military; he enlisted in the Army National Guard at 16 and enrolled in the Reserve Officers' Training Corps (ROTC) during his college years at the University of South Carolina. He graduated from that institution in 1996 with a degree in criminal justice and considered applying to law school.

McFarlan rose to the rank of captain in the Army National Guard, but all through his military development and his studies at the University of South Carolina he felt the importance of creative impulses growing in his life. At Columbia's Keenan High School he played the trumpet in honors bands and also took to the stage as a vocalist. He formed an R&B group that gained some regional fame and seemed within reach of a recording contract at one point. "Whatever is truly inside you is going to come out—sooner or later," McFarlan observed, as quoted on the *Ringling Bros. Barnum & Bailey* Web site. After finishing school, McFarlan landed roles in musicals such as *Ragtime* and *Jesus Christ Superstar* at Columbia's Workshop Theater.

Landing some modeling and advertising jobs, McFarlan was featured as one of the "Tough Guys" in commercials for Ford's F-150 pickup truck. Still, he was slow to begin thinking of performing as a career. He made a living as a state driver's license examiner in South Carolina, with his 13-year National Guard career providing an important income supplement. McFarlan married, settled in Columbia, and had a daughter, Nymah. His drive toward self-expression went unfulfilled, and he began to seek out any chance he could to sing, whether at military-base worship services or even improvising slight variations on drill cadence calls.

Finally, in 2004, McFarlan gave in to his creative impulses. He applied for and received a leave of absence from his state job, auditioned for a role in a production of the musical *Show Boat* at the Circa '21 Dinner Playhouse in Rock Island, Illinois, and was accepted. During the show's run, the theater company's manager mentioned an advertisement he had seen in *Backstage* magazine, seeking a new Ringmaster for the Ringling Bros. Barnum & Bailey Circus, and said he

At a Glance . . .

Born 1971(?) in Columbia, SC; married; children: one daughter. *Education:* University of South Carolina, BS, criminal justice, 1996. *Military Service:* U.S. Army National Guard.

Career: South Carolina Department of Motor Vehicles, driver's license examiner, 1990s and early 2000s; R&B band, Columbia, SC, member; Workshop Theater, Columbia, singer and actor, early 1990s; Circa '21 Dinner Playhouse, Rock Island, IL, performer; Ringling Bros. Barnum & Bailey Circus, 34th Ringmaster, 2005–.

Awards: South Carolina State Senate resolution, 2006.

Addresses: *Office*—c/o Feld Entertainment, Inc., 8607 Westwood Center Dr., Vienna, VA 22182.

thought McFarlan had the right set of talents for the job. The Illinois show's run was ending, and McFarlan was preparing to return home to Columbia. He knew little of what the job might entail as he had attended a circus only once, as an adult. Moreover, auditions for the position were held in Florida and were set to close the following day. And McFarlan's Department of Motor Vehicles supervisor refused to extend his leave.

Notwithstanding these obstacles, McFarlan jumped into his car and drove to Florida, practicing songs for his audition at the wheel. Auditions had actually closed by the time he arrived, but a phone call from the dinner-theater manager in Illinois got him in the door. He sang a Stevie Wonder song to lukewarm response from his interviewers, but they perked up at his rendition of David Lee Roth's "Just a Gigolo." Soon after McFarlan finished his audition, the job was his; he was chosen over 34 other aspirants. On January 6, 2005, he became Ringling Bros. Barnum & Bailey's 34th Ringmaster, or master of ceremonies. He became part of a long tradition with little turnover, noting that there had been fewer Ringmasters than presidents of the United States. McFarlan was the second African American to hold the position; the first was Johnathon Lee Iverson, in 1999. Part of his motivation for joining the circus may have been disenchantment with U.S. military policy; he was quoted in *Time* as saying that "I could either run away and join the circus or be stuck in the middle of a war not wanting to be there."

McFarlan's new life was a hectic one. "The circus is a year-round job, and we do as many as three shows in one day," he told the University of South Carolina's *Carolinian* magazine. "We recently played Madison

Square Garden and did 13 shows in four days. It can be exhausting. But you can be so excited about something that you forget you're tired." Sometimes McFarlan flew his wife and young daughter to cities where he was performing so that he could see them. Allergic to pet dander, he had to adjust his vocal technique as he learned to perform in a tent full of animals.

Despite these challenges, McFarlan found the his new position brought together the performing-arts and military sides of his background. "First of all, I love to perform, whether it's singing or acting," he told Clear. "I just love that reaction from the audience. But what I'm finding also is that a lot of the disciplines I learned in the military I can use as a ringmaster." During rehearsals, for example, he made a point of addressing other performers by name, after the fashion of military commands. McFarlan also enjoyed becoming a role model and cultural ambassador. "I'm learning different languages," he enthused to the *Washington Informer.* "It's also great seeing so many African Americans who are happy to see an African American ringmaster. While the circus is for people of all ages and nationalities, demographically, I am seeing more African Americans and Hispanics come to the shows. I think the word has gotten out."

A two-year tour living in a studio apartment on the circus's mile-long train—one of the longest trains in the world—McFarlan noted—did not dim McFarlan's enthusiasm. "What I love most is the jaw-dropping faces I see," he told Perkins. "I look at the audience and see people grabbing their faces. It's fantastic to look at the audience and see their reaction." In 2007 he entered his third year as Ringmaster of the extravaganza known as the Greatest Show on Earth.

Sources

Periodicals

Arkansas Democrat-Gazette, January 2, 2007.
Free Times (Columbia, SC), August 10, 2006.
Jet, January 31, 2005, p. 32.
New York Beacon, February 24-March 2 2005, p. 27.
Record (Bergen County, NJ), January 9, 2005, p. A2.
St. Petersburg Times (FL), January 6, 2005, p. W32.
Stars and Stripes, March 19, 2006.
Time, January 31, 2005.
Washington Informer, March 30, 2006.

On-line

"Our 34th Ringmaster: Tyron McFarlan!," *Ringling Bros. Barnum & Bailey,* www.ringling.com/explore/135/stars/tmcfarlan.aspx (March 4, 2007).
"Tyron McFarlan: Rousing Ringmaster," *Carolinian,* www.sc.edu/carolinian/kudos/kudos+05nov_01.html (March 4, 2007).

—James M. Manheim

Simon Nkoli

1957-1998

Gay rights activist, anti-apartheid activist

Simon Nkoli's personal courage and fierce pride in his identity as a black South African and a gay man made him a leader in both the anti-apartheid movement and the South African gay liberation movement. More, his refusal to keep his gay identity hidden and his tireless work within the anti-apartheid movement helped change long-held anti-gay attitudes among those who worked for social justice in South Africa. Nkoli not only helped found the first black-led gay rights groups in his homeland, but he also paved the way for South Africa to become the first country in the world to include the protection of gay and lesbian rights in its national constitution.

Tseko Simon Nkoli was born on November 26, 1957, in Phiri township in, Soweto, South Africa. Soweto, a contraction of the words "South Western Townships," is the name given to a group of small black communities outside the South African city of Johannesburg. His parents and their four children lived in poverty and fear under the extreme segregation of the South African apartheid system. One of Nkoli's earliest memories was of hiding his parents from the police because the white government's restrictive pass law policy made it illegal for the family to live together.

His parents separated when Simon was a young child, and he was sent to live with his grandparents, who worked as tenant farmers in the Free Orange State, a province south of Johannesburg. The children worked long hours on the farm and faced whippings from the white landlord if their work was not finished on time. Even as a child Nkoli quickly understood that education was his best hope of a better life. Until he was 13, he

walked 14 kilometers, or almost nine miles, to attend school in addition to his farm work.

When he turned 13, both the white landowner and his grandparents agreed that Nkoli should quit school in order to work full time on the farm. Unwilling to give up his dream of improving his life, he ran away to Johannesburg where he found his mother, Elizabeth, and his stepfather, Elias, and continued his education. His stepfather worked in a hotel as a chef, and his mother worked as a domestic servant and later as a clerk in a shop.

Nkoli began to realize that he was gay when he was a teenager. When he was 19 he became involved in his first romantic relationship with a man, a white bus driver he had met through a pen pal magazine. On his 20th birthday, he told his family about his sexual orientation. His family remained steadfast in their love of Nkoli, yet knew little about homosexuality, and were angry and fearful about his revelation. Nkoli's male friend's parents were also upset by the relationship. They had accepted their son's gayness, but refused to allow his relationship with a black man. The two young men were so devastated by their families' reactions that they made a plan to commit suicide together. When Nkoli's mother discovered the plan, she gave up her opposition to the relationship and convinced the two not to kill themselves.

In hopes of changing his sexuality, Nkoli's mother and stepfather had taken him to priests, traditional folk healers, and a psychiatrist. By coincidence, the psychiatrist was a gay man who offered Nkoli support in

At a Glance . . .

Born Tseko Simon Nkoli on November 26, 1957, in Phiri, Soweto, South Africa; died on November 30, 1998, in Johannesburg, South Africa.

Career: Congress of South African Students, member, 1979; Gay and Lesbian Organization of Witwatersrand, co-founder, 1989; Township AIDS Project, co-founder, 1990; National Coalition for Gay and Lesbian Equality, co-founder, 1994.

Selected memberships: Congress of South African Students; African National Congress; United Democratic Front; Gay and Lesbian Organization of Witwatersrand; National Coalition for Gay and Lesbian Equality.

Selected awards: Stonewall Award (United Kingdom), 1996; International Gay and Lesbian Human Rights Commission, Felipa Award (posthumous), 1999.

his choice. He even suggested a way that Nkoli and his partner could live together, with Nkoli posing as a servant. When they both entered college in Johannesburg, they did live together in this way.

Struggled Against Culture and Law in South Africa

From hiding his parents from the police in their own house to pretending to be a servant in order to live with his partner, and in hundreds of other large and small ways, the unjust system of racial segregation called apartheid had affected Nkoli all of his life. To understand Nkoli's accomplishments, it is necessary to understand a little of the history of the nation where he grew up.

Southern Africa had been colonized by both Dutch and British settlers, beginning in 1652 when the Dutch East India Trading Company established an outpost there. First attracted by trade, then by vast pasturelands which could support herds of sheep and cattle, Dutch settlers began to leave the coastal areas to settle inland. By the late 1700s, the British had also established a large colonial presence in the south of Africa. Both groups had enslaved local black inhabitants as well as importing slaves from other African countries and the West Indies. The role of slavery increased as diamonds, gold, and other valuable minerals were discovered and exploited during the 1800s.

The Union of South Africa was formed in 1910 as a result of a series of wars between the British and Dutch

colonists. That same year, a system of government-sanctioned racial segregation was introduced. Though slavery had been abolished, a series of "separation" laws ensured that black South Africans, who were in the vast majority, would remain on the bottom of society. One of these was the Native Land Act of 1913, which set aside only 7.3 percent of the country's land as reserves where black people could live, prohibiting blacks from buying land outside the reserves. Another, the Mines and Works Act of 1911, legislated segregation in the workplace by limiting black workers to the lowest level jobs.

The black people of southern Africa had resisted their conquest since the first colonists had begun taking over their land and enslaving them, but they had been overcome—first by military power and disease, then by government-enforced legislation. The African National Congress, which formed in 1910 in response to the segregation laws, was one of the major organizations of resistance.

During the late 1940s, the right-wing National Party gained power. They introduced the word "apartheid" to describe South Africa's system of racial separation and increased the inequities, launching a dual education system that ensured that most blacks would remain uneducated and powerless.

First Stirrings of Activism

It was this unfair system of education that led to Simon Nkoli's first experiences with resistance to apartheid. In 1974, a new law was passed requiring all black schools to use and teach the white South African language Afrikaans. Most black South Africans associated Afrikaans with the hated apartheid regime and did not want to use it. Unrest over this issue along with general anger at the treatment of blacks exploded in 1976 in the Soweto uprising.

As a student at the time, Nkoli joined his fellow students in protesting the Afrikaans requirement. Students went on strike, refusing to go to class. On June 16, 1976, 23 people died when police greeted a peaceful rally with tear gas and guns. Though the Soweto Massacre was tragic, it demonstrated the callousness of the white regime and injected a new energy into the anti-apartheid movement.

In 1979, Nkoli joined a student resistance group called the Congress of South African Students (COSAS), soon becoming the secretary for the Transvaal region. However, his participation in the movement to end apartheid would always go hand-in-hand with his fight for gay rights. He "came out" to his comrades in COSAS, who, after discussing the issue, decided that he should remain in the office of secretary.

Became a Leader

Nkoli realized that he needed the support of other gay and lesbian people in order to go on with his work. In

1980, he joined the Gay Association of South Africa (GASA), a largely white gay group. However being one of very few black members of GASA was difficult and painful. Apartheid restrictions often prevented him from attending events, and the indifference of the white gay community angered Nkoli. He decided that he needed to find black gays and, placing an advertisement in a black newspaper, he set about forming a black South African gay and lesbian organization. Together with those who answered his ad, he started The Saturday Group, South Africa's first black gay organization.

Nkoli continued to work for the rights of black people, joining the African National Congress (ANC) and the United Democratic Front (UDC). However, the South African government responded harshly to those who resisted its laws. In 1984, Nkoli was arrested with 21 other activists and charged with treason and murder. The case, which became known as the Delmas treason trial, lasted for four years, and Nkoli remained in prison until he was released on bail on June 30, 1987. As always, he was honest and open about his sexual orientation, stating that he could not have committed the crime he was charged with, because he had been at a meeting of a gay and lesbian group.

Nkoli's work to end apartheid and his courage during his years in prison earned the respect of those who worked with him. Even those who had been prejudiced against gay people began to understand their issues in a new way. Ken Davis of *Green Left Online* quotes Terror Lekota, another defendant in the Delmas trial who later became national chair of the ANC, "All of us acknowledge that Simon's coming out was an important learning experience…. How could we say that men and women like Simon, who had put their shoulders to the wheel to end apartheid, should now be discriminated against?"

Nkoli was finally acquitted of all charges in the Delmas trial in 1988. He then returned to his activism and formed a new and important organization: The Gay and Lesbian Organization of the Witwatersrand (GLOW). GLOW was the first gay and lesbian organization that was based in the black townships surrounding Johannesburg. Though membership in GLOW was open to all, it was largely black.

Affected Political Change

GLOW took an important role in South African politics. As resistance to the injustice of apartheid increased around the world, GLOW worked hard both to end the segregated state and to insist that equal rights must apply to all. With Simon Nkoli as its first chair, GLOW spoke out in the media and organized demonstrations, including South Africa's first gay pride in 1990. The group also spoke out against homophobia within the anti-apartheid movement. David Beresford, a writer for the *Guardian Unlimited,* quotes Nkoli at the first gay pride march in Johannesburg, "With this march, gays and lesbians are entering the struggle for a democratic South Africa where everybody has equal rights and everyone is protected by the law: black and white; men and women, gay and straight."

By the end of the 1980s, it had become apparent to most white South Africans that apartheid was a failed system. President F.W. de Klerk began removing some of the most oppressive legislation and released Nelson Mandela, the president of the ANC, from prison, where he had been held for twenty-seven years. By 1994, Mandela himself had been elected the first black president of South Africa. One of the first goals of the new government was to draft a new constitution. It is largely thanks to the work of Simon Nkoli and the gay and lesbian organizations that he brought together that the new South African constitution, ratified in 1996, became the first in the world to forbid discrimination against gays and lesbians. The government would soon recognize gay partners, allow gay adoption, and extend health and tax benefits to gay families, becoming one of the most progressive nations on earth in terms of gay and lesbian rights.

In 1994, Nkoli initiated more growth in the gay and lesbian movement in South Africa when he helped found the National Coalition for Gay and Lesbian Equality (NCGLE). Connecting progressive organizations throughout the country, NCGLE was a racially mixed group with black leadership.

Battled AIDS Epidemic

While the battle against apartheid was being won, an even more desperate battle was beginning. During the late 1980s, the dramatic increase of the AIDS epidemic on the African continent was becoming an important issue for gay and lesbian Africans. What government support there was for people with AIDS was largely unavailable to gay people, who were too often either blamed or ignored. To counter such attitudes, Nkoli helped found the Township AIDS project in 1990, which worked with GLOW to educate gays about the disease and to fight for improved treatment.

Sadly, Nkoli himself contracted the disease and fell victim to society's inadequate response to the epidemic. He died on November 30, 1998 in Johannesburg, largely because he could not afford medication to treat his AIDS-related illness. His funeral was a testament to his lifelong work to connect the many different struggles for social justice in South Africa. His coffin was draped with a rainbow flag, a symbol of tolerance and diversity, as activists from a wide variety of groups came to say goodbye to a friend and leader. His speech at the first gay pride in 1990, quoted by Beresford on *Guardian Unlimited* captured much of the spirit if Simon Nkoli's life, "I am black and I am gay. I cannot separate the two parts of me into secondary or primary struggles…. So when I fight for my freedom I must fight against both oppressions. All those who believe in a democratic South Africa must fight against all oppression, all intolerance, all injustice."

Sources

Books

Gevisser, Mark, and Edwin Cameron, *Defiant Desire: Gay and Lesbian Lives in South Africa,* Routledge, 1995.

Krouse, Matthew, and Kim Berman, eds., *The Invisible Ghetto: Lesbian and Gay Writing from South Africa,* Gay Men's Press, 1995.

Periodicals

Advocate, January 16, 1990, pp. 44-5; November 17, 1992, pp. 44-47; May 28, 1996, pp. 35-7.

Gay Community News, September 13-19, 1987, p. 9; 1998, pp. 18-21.

Progressive, March 1990, p. 14.

Films

Simon & I, Women Make Movies, 2001.

On-line

"Hamba kahle (farewell) Simon Nkoli," *Green Left Online,* www.greenleft.org.au/1999/345/19684 (February 24, 2007).

"Queer State funeral in Sebokeng," *Q Online,* www.q.co.za/regulars/cohen/981215-nkolifuneral.htm (February 24, 2007).

"Simon Nkoli," *glbtq: an encyclopedia of gay, lesbian, bisexual, transgender and gay culture.* www.glbtq.com/social-sciences/nkoli_ts.html (February 24, 2007).

"Simon Nkoli," *Biography Resource Center,* http://galenet.galegroup.com/servlet/BioRC (February 24, 2007).

"South Africa: Pride and Prejudice," *Guardian Unlimited,* www.guardian.co.uk/elsewhere/journalist/story/0,,1981395,00.html (February 24, 2007).

—Tina Gianoulis

Yannick Noah

1960—

Tennis player, singer

The winner of the French Open in 1983 as well as the Italian Open in 1985, Yannick Noah became the first French international tennis celebrity. Often ranked among the Top Ten players of the game early in his career, Noah was discovered by tennis star Arthur Ashe. Over his three-decade-long career he became renowned for his powerful serve, acrobatic net game, electrifying play, winning smile, and flashy dreadlock hairstyle. Leaving tennis in 1992, Noah reinvented himself as a pop star, touring the globe and selling millions of reggae-inspired pop albums.

Began with Homemade Racket

Born on May 18, 1960, in Sedan, France, Yannick Simon Camille Noah is the oldest of three children. His father, Zacharie Noah, was a professional soccer player; his mother, Marie-Claire, was a teacher. When Noah was two years old, his father moved the family to his native Cameroon after an injury ended his soccer career. When the elder Noah took up tennis to keep in shape, he taught Yannick the game. The capital city of Yaounde, where the Noahs lived, had few courts, but Yannick practiced as much as he could by using a wooden racket that he crafted himself. On the day he turned ten years old, Yannick celebrated by arranging a tennis tournament among his friends. He had each contestant pay a dollar to purchase the trophy he won himself.

A year later, Yannick was chosen to attend a clinic at a local tennis club where Arthur Ashe and other professionals were visiting on a tour of Africa. When he was given the chance to play with Ashe—a U.S. Open and Wimbledon champion—Yannick aced the pro once and matched him point for point across the net. Ashe soon contacted Philippe Chatrier, head of the French Tennis Federation, to invite Yannick to attend a special tennis academy in Nice, France. Noah spent the next five years at the academy while attending a local secondary school. Opting to leave secondary school one year short of graduation to focus on tennis, he moved to Paris and came under the instruction of the coach of the French national team, Patrice Hagelauer. The young Yannick went on to win the French junior title in 1977.

By 1980 Noah was ranked the Number One player in France after a series of Grand Prix titles and impressive showings in Grand Slam tournaments. Negative press regarding his confession of smoking hashish periodically—as well as his charge that other athletes used stronger drugs to improve their play—undermined his confidence.

Won French Open

He struggled the next year, but his form returned when he won the French Open in 1983. Suddenly a French celebrity, Noah moved to New York to avoid the harrowing publicity in France. He recuperated from injuries and the loss of his grandfather, a village chief who was murdered during a political coup in Cameroon, playing infrequently in 1984. Strengthened by his rest, Noah won the Italian Open in 1985. Although he reached the finals of many tournaments in the intervening years and was ranked fifth in the world in 1987, Noah failed to win the more prestigious titles, including another French Open.

Marital woes and injury plagued Noah during the late 1980s. Wed to Swedish model Cecilia Rodhe in 1984, Noah divorced her three years later after the births of his son, Joachim, and daughter, Tara. He suffered many defeats, including his loss to John McEnroe in the second round of the 1989 Davis Cup. Noah divulged about McEnroe in the *New York Times*, "He played very, very well. What can I say? It was very difficult. My knees were fine. I don't even have that excuse."

Despite his athletic prowess, Noah did not advance beyond the quarterfinals in Grand Slam tournaments throughout most of the 1980s. The *New York Times* stated in 1989, "Yannick Noah has always entertained tennis fans with his flamboyant style of play. His physical ability on sky-high overheads, diving volleys and thunderous serves has always made him stand out on the court. But he has been a bit of an enigma in his years on the circuit." In the U.S. Open that same year, Noah, ranked 23rd in the world, was defeated by Boris Becker in yet another quarterfinal.

"Yannick Noah is back in all his glory and threatening to crash a party that seemed reserved for the usual big names in tennis," crowed a *New York Times* correspondent in a review of his early play in the 1990 Australian Open. His comeback was short-lived, however, with his loss at the tournament. His malady of seesawing in and out of retirement at the end of the 1980s afflicted Noah into the 1990s. By August of 1990, Robin Finn of the *New York Times* dubbed the player "a dependable loser" at the U.S. Open. "I'm living one week after the other right now," Noah told Finn. "It's a difficult situation where I'm not playing very well and getting very frustrated." His coach, Dennis Rolston, predicted that if Noah did not improve his training regimen and confront his ambivalence toward the game, he would reach a crisis decision. Noah continued playing, though, capturing the title of captain of the French Davis Cup team the next year.

Led French to Davis Cup

In his debut as captain of France's Davis Cup team, Noah startled the tennis world when he announced on November 28, 1991, that he would play only if another team member was injured. A defending champion who played in the Davis Cup final in Grenoble in 1982 and the Davis Cup quarterfinal in San Diego in 1989, Noah selected Guy Forget and Henri Leconte to lead the team. He explained in the *New York Times*, "The emotions are still there, but I don't feel like I'm the one who must hold the racquet. I believe the players we have are good enough to win." Under Noah's tutelage, Guy Forget spurred the team to take the Davis Cup on December 1, 1991, when he defeated Pete Sampras three sets to one. With great emotion, Noah joined the team on the courts of Lyon, France, when they celebrated their victory.

After viewing television reports of disturbances between security officers and antiapartheid demonstrators at the world doubles championships in Johannesburg, South Africa, Noah made news again in 1991 when he decided to boycott tennis matches in that country. Although South Africa had just been allowed re-entry into international sports at the beginning of the decade, Noah was quoted by *Jet* as saying, "Frankly, I can't see myself going there as a player or as captain of France's Davis Cup team. I would have the feeling of being used."

Ranked among the Top Six highest-paid male tennis stars, Noah indicated that his devotion to tennis was waning in the 1990s and began investigating the possibility of a career in music. He had begun playing guitar in the 1980s, and found that he loved it. He had formed a 10-man band called Zam Zam and began recording pop and rock music. His first recording went gold in France in 1990—"because I'm popular as a tennis player, not because of the quality of the music," Noah remarked to Rick Marin of the *New York Times*. An employee of a Parisian record store confirmed Noah's assessment, saying, according to *Sports Illustrated*, "I suppose it's not too bad...for someone who doesn't sing."

France's loss to Switzerland in the 1992 Davis Cup competition marked the end of Noah's tennis career. To the consternation of the French Tennis Federation, Noah resigned as captain of the 1992 French Davis Cup team. Guy Forget echoed the hope of French officials that Yannick Noah will be persuaded to reconsider his resignation. Although he was publicly criticized by Noah after the French loss to the Swiss team, Forget commented in *Sports Illustrated* about France's magnetic athlete, "Yannick is irreplaceable." Noah did not reconsider his decision to leave tennis, however, he continued to serve as commentator for tennis tournaments and play occasionally in senior tennis matches.

Reinvented Himself

Noah turned immediately to his passion for music. He and his band began an extensive touring schedule. His four albums released between 2000 and 2006, sealed Noah's status as a genuine pop star. His album sold well and topped European pop charts. His second album, the self-titled *Yannick Noah* went multiplatinum in France and earned his first Platinum Europe Award in 2004. His 2003 album *Pokhara* earned a Platinum Europe Award in 2004. The album included reggae-inspired pop music and featured a 40-page photo booklet of the Nepalese region from which the album takes its name. For his 2006 album *Charango,* Noah searched for inspiration in the Andes mountains of South America. There he found a traditional Latin American instrument called the charango, which he added to his reggae-inspired pop music for a new sound.

Aside from his thriving career as a popular musician, Noah continued to enjoy celebrity from his tennis days. In 2005 he was inducted into the International Tennis Hall of Fame. Noah also proved himself a generous philanthropist, starting the charities Les Enfants de la Terre, to help provide homes and support to needy children, and Fete le Mur, to promote tennis among underprivileged French children. He also started to enjoy the rise of fame in his own son, Joakim, who proved to be a leader on the college basketball court in Florida, leading the University of Florida to consecutive NCAA basketball championships in 2006 and 2007. Active and interested, Noah seemed far from finished reinventing himself.

Selected works

Albums

Black and What!, Welcome Records, 1991.
Yannick Noah, 2000.
Yannick Noah Live, 2002.
Pokhara, 2003.
Metisse, 2005.
Charango, 2006.

Sources

Periodicals

Jet, October 26, 1987; August 21, 1989; October 16, 1989; September 10, 1990; December 23, 1991; August 8, 2005.
New York Times, April 4, 1989; September 4, 1989; September 7, 1989; January 18, 1990; January 26, 1990; August 31, 1990; November 29, 1991; September 13, 1992, p. A10.
Sports Illustrated, June 6, 1991; April 13, 1992.
Sunday Times, January 26, 2003, p. 28.
Tennis, February 1992, p. 136.

On-line

Yannick Noah, www.yannicknoah.com (March 28, 2007).

—Marjorie Burgess and Sara Pendergast

Kimberly Oliver

1976—

Educator

In 2006, Maryland kindergarten teacher Kimberly Oliver won the prestigious National Teacher of the Year award after just a few years on the job. Oliver's work to prepare her students for a lifetime of learning had brought accolades from her fellow teachers as well as from parents and district administrators alike, and her school's vastly improved scores on state proficiency tests also were cited as a factor for her win. "I take it very seriously that parents have entrusted me with their most precious commodity, their children," she told Grace Rubenstein in an interview that appeared on the *Edutopia* Web site. "They have sent me the best that they have, and they want the best for them. My goal is really to bring out the best in each of my students each and every day, help them become a little smarter each and every day."

Born on October 20, 1976, Oliver grew up in Wilmington, Delaware, with an older brother in a household headed by their father, the pastor of a Baptist church, and mother who worked at a local community center. Her first day-care teacher, Oliver has said in several interviews, was a profound influence on her and the reason she decided to become a teacher. Though Oliver was occasionally discouraged from pursuing that choice of career, she remained settled upon it from an early age. "I remember having guidance counselors who told me 'You can be anything you want' and steering me toward other paths that might be more lucrative," she told Georgina Stark of the *Daily Press* of Newport News, Virginia, "but ultimately I've always wanted to be a teacher."

After graduating from William Penn High School, Oliver earned her undergraduate degree in English arts from Hampton University, a historically black school, in 1998. She went on to Wilmington College for a master's degree in elementary education, and had decided she wanted to work with younger children because, as she said in an interview with the *Washington Post*'s Lori Aratani, "they love to share. They are so eager to learn—and then share with you what they've learned." Her first teaching job was at an Elementary Workshop Montessori School in Wilmington, but after earning her master's degree in 2000 she was hired by the Montgomery County Public School system in Maryland.

Oliver was assigned to Broad Acres, an underperforming school with students from the lowest rung of the socio-economic ladder in the Washington, D.C., suburb. Fewer than 12 percent of its third graders were testing at the stipulated proficiency level on state tests when she came to work there. A year later President George W. Bush signed the No Child Left Behind Act, a sweeping package of federal legislation designed to improve the performance of primary and secondary public education in the United States. After Oliver's first year of full-time teaching, the staff at Broad Acres began adhering to a restructuring plan designed to improve student performance on the state-mandated tests that measured proficiency in reading and math.

Oliver was given a full-day kindergarten class that was smaller by several students than that of her first year. She and other teachers also began to meet regularly, and it was this new part of her job that helped her

At a Glance . . .

Born on October 20, 1976, in Wilmington, DE; daughter of Baptist pastor and a community-center worker. *Education:* Hampton University, BA, 1998; Wilmington College, MEd, 2000.

Career: Elementary Workshop Montessori School, Wilmington, DE, assistant teacher, 1999(?)-2000; Montgomery County Public Schools, Rockville, MD, kindergarten teacher, 2000–.

Awards: Council of Chief State School Officers (CCSSO), National Teacher of the Year, 2006.

Addresses: *Office*—c/o Montgomery County Public Schools, 850 Hungerford Dr., Rockville MD 20850.

immeasurably. Prior to the restructuring, "there was no set time for us to meet in the day, so I was doing a lot of things by myself," she told Rubenstein. "I was working late every night, staying at school till about six o'clock, planning each and every lesson, assessment, and activity, and it was very draining for me. The next year, we had time paid to work after school so that we could plan together, and it made a huge difference. It really helped me focus my lessons more because I wasn't reinventing the wheel."

One of the most challenging aspects of Oliver's job was the fact that nearly all of her students came from homes in which English was not the primary language; the kindergartners were the sons and daughters of immigrants from Africa, Vietnam, and Latin America. Oliver sought to build ties with the parents, many of whom had come out of less-than-ideal educational systems themselves, and engage them in an appropriate level of involvement with their children's learning. Her effort to secure grants to purchase bilingual books and books on tape materials for use at home was a success, as was the "Books and Supper Night" she initiated, a four-times-a-year event at Broad Acres that invited the students and parents for a communal evening meal and access to the school library.

Oliver was nominated by her peers for the state Teacher of the Year honor, and won the Maryland title in October of 2005. Six months later, she won the National Teacher of the Year award, administered by the Council of Chief State School Officers (CCSSO) since the early 1950s as the annual recognition for excellence in teaching. The impressive spike in test scores for her school was cited as one of the major factors in the selection of Oliver for the award: in the five years since she had been at Broad Acres, nearly 75 percent of third-graders were testing at their proficiency level in reading.

Unfortunately for Oliver, her state and national Teacher of the Year honors meant that she was away from her classroom for nearly two years in her temporary role as a national and international spokesperson for education. She began her national duties in that role in June of 2006, just two months after the award ceremony at the White House. On that day, President Bush and First Lady Laura Bush—a former elementary school librarian—commended Oliver for her dedication to her job and to the ideals embodied by universal access to education in America. A few months later, Oliver told Stark that she remembered feeling calm during the ceremony, but in retrospect it now seemed "surreal. When I look back at the pictures of it I'm like, 'I was standing that close to the president?'"

Sources

Periodicals

Daily Press (Newport News, VA) October 3, 2006.
Seattle Times, April 26, 2006, p. A7.
Washington Post, April 25, 2006, p. B1.

On-line

"A Conversation with Kimberly Oliver," *Edutopia,* www.edutopia.org/php/article.php?id=Art_1596 (February 21, 2007).

—Carol Brennan

Oguchi Onyewu

1982—

Professional soccer player

Onyewu, Oguchi, photograph. Ian Horrocks/Newcastle United via Getty Images.

Oguchi Onyewu is one of a handful of American soccer stars playing in professional European leagues. In 2004, he began an impressive run as a defense player with the Belgian club Standard de Liège, and in early 2007 moved over to England's Newcastle United. Onyewu also plays for the U.S. national team and was heralded as one of the sport's newest homegrown talents in the build-up to the 2006 FIFA World Cup. The U.S. national coach, Bruce Arena, told one reporter that Onyewu "has a rare combination of great physical qualities with the ability to play tactically, and he's a good one-on-one defender who reads the game very well," Arena asserted to *USA Today*'s Kelly Whiteside. "We've seen other players with these qualities, and I always said, 'When are we going to get an American player like that?'"

Born in 1982, Onyewu is the son of Nigerian parents, Peter and Dorothy, who came to the United States in the 1970s to study at Howard University in Washington, D.C. Their own names were selected around the time of their conversion to Roman Catholicism, but they gave each of their five children traditional Nigerian monikers: Onyewu's two sisters are Chi-Chi and Ogechi, and his brothers are called Uche and Nonye. His own name, Oguchialu, means "God fights for me."

Onyewu began playing soccer at the age of five on local kids' teams in the Maryland suburbs of the nation's capital, and by his teen years had proved such a promising talent that he had joined an elite junior team, F.C. Potomac, and was invited to participate in the U.S. Youth Soccer Olympic Development Program. That led to a berth on the U.S. Under-17 junior national team, and he was credited with helping them achieve a fourth-place finish—its best ever—during the 1999 Under-17 World Championships in New Zealand.

Onyewu graduated from Sherwood High School in Olney, Maryland, and enrolled in Clemson University of South Carolina. After playing two seasons with the Clemson Tigers' men's soccer team, he decided he was ready to seriously consider the regular offers that came from professional soccer clubs in Europe to sign him. In 2002, he inked a contract with F.C. Metz in France. The club was in France's first division at the time, but was ousted from top-tier Ligue 1 play and relegated to

At a Glance . . .

Born Oguchialu Chilioke Onyewu on May 13, 1982, in Washington, DC; son of Peter and Dorothy Onyewu. *Education:* Attended Clemson University, 2000-02. *Religion:* Roman Catholic.

Career: FC Metz, France, professional soccer player, 2002; La Louvière, Belgium, professional soccer player (on loan), 2003, Standard Liège, Belgium, professional soccer player, 2004; Newcastle United, England, professional soccer player, 2007; U.S. national team, player, 2004.

Awards: U.S. Soccer Athlete of the Year, United States Soccer Federation. 2006.

Addresses: *Office*—c/o Newcastle United Football Co. Ltd., St James' Park, Newcastle upon Tyne NE1 4ST, England.

Ligue 2 by the time that Onyewu arrived for training. This complicated the terms of his contract, and though he was paid he did not play for several months. Finally, the Metz management agreed to loan him out to a Belgian team, La Louvière, in 2003. He played one season with the team before moving on to another club in the Jupiler League, as the Belgian First Division league is known, in 2004.

Standard Liège was the home team of Liège, an industrial city in the French-speaking part of Belgium, and one of the country's most popular soccer teams. Onyewu quickly emerged as a player to watch, and Standard made him a permanent member on its roster in July of 2004. He enjoyed tremendous popularity in Liège for his defensive abilities throughout the next two seasons, and Standard even managed to finish in second place in the Jupiler League's 2005-06 season. He also continued to play for the U.S. national team after making his international senior-team debut in an October 2004 match against Panama.

Onyewu's West African heritage made him somewhat of a rarity in Belgium, where even in larger cities like Liège the slim minority population is generally of North African or Arabic descent. He admitted in an interview with Steven Goff of the *Washington Post* that there was some racism in the heated atmosphere of the arena, though. "One game, the fans were making monkey noises at some of our players," Onyewu told Goff, who noted that there were several players of African descent on the Liège team. "They just don't like foreigners. It's just ignorance. Some [opposing players] will say stupid stuff: 'You black this, black that.' And you think to yourself, 'Now what did you achieve by saying that?'"

Onyewu became a local celebrity in Liège and even throughout Belgium, and learned French quickly, which further endeared him to the country's ardent soccer fans. Newspapers called him the "Terminator," a reference to the American action-hero played in film by Arnold Schwarzenegger, because he towered above nearly everyone else, having reached a height of six feet, four inches, by the time he turned 23; he also weighed in at 210 pounds. In the history of the U.S. men's national team, only two other players were taller than Onyewu—and both were goalkeepers, making him the tallest player on the field in team history. Moreover, he was lean and muscular, with just seven percent body fat after having bulked himself up over the past few years via a weightlifting regimen. He did admit, however, that his physique could work against him at times, he explained to *New York Times* writer John Eligon. "A lot of times I get called for fouls when I barely do anything, just because of my size, I think," he said. "I just try to keep my hands to myself because I know as soon as I touch a player, they're going to fly, regardless, just because of my size advantage."

Onyewu's star rose even higher thanks to his brief but solid performance in the FIFA World Cup 2006 tournament. He started for the U.S. national team in each of its three games, but in the third one he was called on a foul by referees, which he protested. The replays seemed to show that Onyewu had not committed it, but the Ghanaian team was granted a penalty kick anyway, and scored a goal from it that gave them the lead. When the U.S. lost that game 2-1, they were ousted from World Cup play altogether. Nevertheless, Onyewu's talents earned him the U.S. Soccer Athlete of the Year award in 2006 from the United States Soccer Federation.

In January of 2007, after several weeks of rumors that Onyewu would sign with a club in England's first-tier league—known as the Premiership—the management of Newcastle United announced he would be joining their team for the last 13 games of the season. Technically, Onyewu remained under contract with Standard, but was likely to be signed permanently to the northern English city's team. "From the moment I signed up as a professional footballer, I always had my eye on the Premier League," Onyewu enthused to Paul Gilder, a sportswriter for city's *Journal* newspaper. "Because of my particular characteristics and abilities, I always wanted to play in England and I am happy to be able to realise that ambition. I feel lucky to have landed here and my dream has come true. Now it's up to me."

Sources

Periodicals

Journal (Newcastle, England), January 30, 2007, p. 50; January 31, 2007, p. 64; February 3, 2007, p. 104.

New York Times, July 24, 2005, p. 8.5.

USA Today, August 17, 2005, p. 3C.

Washington Post, April 11, 2006, p. E1.

On-line

Newcastle United, www.nufc.premiumtv.co.uk/page/ Welcome (April 9, 2007).

—Carol Brennan

William D. Payne

1932—

New Jersey State Assemblyman

With a long history of involvement in community politics, William D. Payne's career as New Jersey State Assemblyman began in 1998 when he was elected to represent the 29th legislative district. Prominent among the legislation he has championed are mentoring schemes for at-risk students, the incorporation of African American studies into New Jersey's public school curriculum, and the criminalization of racial profiling practices. The many committees on which Payne serves include the Regulatory Oversight Committee (as Chair), the Budget Committee (as Vice Chair) and the Federal Relations Committee. He has also served on the New Jersey Criminal Disposition Commission and since 2003 has been the Essex County Deputy Chief of Staff.

William D. Payne was born on July 8, 1932, in Newark, New Jersey. Educated at Rutgers University, he graduated with a bachelor's degree in political science in 1959. He then began a career in business consulting and in 1969 founded the firm of UrbanData Systems, Inc., where he held the position of president and CEO of the company until 1988. As he developed his public service career, Payne later maintained his own consulting company, William Payne and Associates, which specializes in public affairs and market development.

Although he was not elected to office until 1998, Payne's political career began much earlier. He has a long standing interest in community relations and in widening opportunity. Growing up in a family in which political engagement was considered important, Payne first became significantly involved in local politics in

1980 when he became commissioner and vice president of the Essex County Improvement Authority. At a time when traditionally industrial areas were struggling with difficult economic conditions the Authority's work included purchasing and redeveloping brownfield sites—polluted and abandoned industrial areas—to put them back to use. One project in particular during his time was the development of the Essex County Airport Business Park to attract companies requiring office space close to major transport links.

In 1986 Payne moved on to one of the biggest challenges of his career. As chairman of the Newark Housing Authority he helped plan and implement a radical revision of Newark's housing policy. Around one third of New Jersey's older high-rise housing projects were torn down to make room for new townhouses. Many of Newark's housing projects were uninhabitable and the cost of maintaining empty and semi-derelict buildings was a drain on the whole housing budget. Payne and his team set about developing new housing schemes and by 1989 when Payne moved on, most of the planning was complete. Unfortunately delays and legal problems meant that significant numbers of new housing units were not completed until the mid-1990s, almost a decade after the process began.

Payne's background in marketing led to several appointments as campaign manager, first for his brother Donald's New Jersey Congressional campaign in 1988, and for his nephew, Assemblyman Craig A. Stanley, in 1996. Payne ran unsuccessfully in the Newark mayoral race in 1994, but Payne won his bid

At a Glance . . .

Born William D. Payne on July 8, 1932, in New-ark, NJ; children: Eric, Lisa, Gina, Kristi. *Education:* Rutgers University, BA, Political Science, 1959. *Religion:* Christian.

Career: UrbanData Sys., Inc., founder, president and CEO, 1969-88; Essex County Improvement Authority, commissioner, vice chairman, 1980-86; Newark Housing Authority, commissioner, chairman, 1986-89; Congressman Donald M. Payne campaign, campaign manager, 1988; One to One/N.J. School-Centered Mentoring Organization, executive director, 1992-94; Assemblyman Craig Stanley campaign, Irvington, NJ, marketing development consultant, chief of staff, and campaign manager, 1996-97; NJ General Assembly, assemblyman, 1998; William Payne & Associates, principal; NJ Assembly, deputy majority conference leader, 2002–.

Memberships: NJ General Assembly, appropriations committee; NJ Congressional Award Council, 1995; NJ Tourism Advisory Council; Joint Committee on Mentoring; Small Business Advisory Council, NY Federal Reserve Bank.

Addresses: *District Office*—40 Clinton St, Suite 200, Newark, NJ, 07102; *Office*—125 W State St, Trenton, NJ 08608-1101; *Web*—www.njleg.state.nj.us/members/payne.asp.

for election to the New Jersey General Assembly in 1998. He continued to represent the 29th legislative district for the next decade.

Poverty and education were among the chief issues Payne championed as an assemblyman. His interest in poverty and its links with poor housing and education went back to his earliest days in politics. In 1992 he served New Jersey Council on Adult Literacy and has been a leading voice in a campaign to establish mentoring schemes in New Jersey schools to encourage and protect at risk students. A bill sponsored by Payne provided $750,000 to support mentoring schemes in New Jersey.

More recently, in 2006, Payne headed a campaign to improve the teaching of Black history in New Jersey's schools. Remembering his own experiences as a child Payne told the *New York Times* that he wanted to make Black history a more important part of the K-12 curriculum in order to change the "subliminal messages that everything good is white." Payne established the Amistad Commission in New Jersey to help promote education in Black history and was also successful in pushing through groundbreaking legislation to criminalize racial profiling in the recruitment of public employees.

Sources

Periodicals

New York Times, February 12, 1984; May 3, 1987; February 12, 2006, 14NJ, p. 7.

On-line

"Assemblyman William D. Payne," *New Jersey Legislature*, www.njleg.state.nj.us/members/payne.asp (February 19, 2007).

"William D. Payne," *Biography Resource Center*, www.galenet.com/servelet/BioRC (February 19, 2007).

—Chris Routledge

Rodney Peete

1966—

Professional football player, broadcaster

Peete, Rodney, photograph. John M. Heller/Getty Images.

Quarterback Rodney Peete enjoyed an unusually long career in the National Football League (NFL), playing for various teams between 1989 and 2004. Although hampered by injuries, Peete had several strong seasons that pointed to the gridiron great he could have been, thanks to his superb athletic abilities. One of the most appealing public representatives of the game of football, Peete also has gained publicity as one half of a successful celebrity marriage; his wife, Holly Robinson-Peete, has been a consistent presence in the top ranks of American television actresses. After his retirement, Peete moved easily into a broadcasting career as co-host of *The Best Damn Sports Show Period* on the Fox Sports Net cable television channel.

Rodney Peete was born in Mesa, Arizona, on March 16, 1966. His father, Willie Peete, was a football coach, an assistant at the University of Arizona when Rodney was born. But equally important as an athletic motivator was his mother, Edna. "Edna was the cornerstone of his upbringing," University of Southern California coach Larry Smith told Bruce Newman of *Sports Illustrated*. "Edna was a person who would never let her boys get too cocky. She was always there, at every game, but she was also critical. If Rodney didn't play a good game, Edna was the first person he had to face. She is very competitive."

The games Edna attended took place on baseball diamonds and basketball courts as well as football fields. Peete excelled at all three sports, and as a high school student he led basketball and baseball teams to state championships. He was most enthusiastic about football, but in that sport he faced discrimination in the predominantly white communities in which he grew up. Other black students told him there was no way he would win his chosen position of quarterback; they themselves had been encouraged to move to other positions, and the dearth of black quarterbacks at all levels of the game was no secret.

Nevertheless, coaches at Sahuaro High School in Tucson started Peete at quarterback and returned him to the position for his junior year after he moved to wide receiver as a sophomore. Their judgment was vindicated when Peete took the Sahuaro team to the state semifinals and was named Arizona High School Athlete of the Year. Peete moved to Shawnee Mission High School in Shawnee Mission, Kansas, for his

At a Glance . . .

Born on March 16, 1966, in Mesa, AZ; son of Willie Peete, a football coach, and Edna Peete; married Holly Robinson, 1995; children: four. *Education:* University of Southern California, BA, communications, 1989.

Career: Detroit Lions, professional football quarterback, 1989-93; Dallas Cowboys, professional football quarterback, 1994; Philadelphia Eagles, professional football quarterback, 1995-98; Washington Redskins, professional football quarterback, 1999; Oakland Raiders, professional football quarterback, 2000-01; Carolina Panthers, professional football quarterback, 2002-04; Fox Sports Net, *The Best Damn Sports Show Period,* co-host, 2004–.

Memberships: HollyRod Foundation, co-founder (with Holly Robinson-Peete), 1996–; HollyRod4Kids, co-founder (with Holly Robinson-Peete), 2004–.

Awards: Runner-Up for Heisman Trophy, 1989; named to All-Rookie NFL team by *Football Digest,* 1989.

Addresses: *Office*—Fox Sports Net, 1440 S. Sepulveda Blvd., Los Angeles, CA 90025; *Web*—www.rodneypeete.com.

senior year because his father had been hired by the NFL's Kansas City Chiefs, and he closed out his high school career with All-America honors. Though the Major League Baseball team the Toronto Blue Jays drafted Peete straight out of high school, college football programs also jockeyed to recruit Peete, and he chose to stick with that sport.

Peete made it clear to college football recruiters that he wanted to be a quarterback. His determination to be a quarterback made his enrollment at the University of Southern California in Los Angeles seem unusual because of that school's reputation for running-based offenses in its football program. Even Peete himself conceded, according to Newman, that "quarterbacks at USC won't set records or win the Heisman." But Peete went ahead to prove himself wrong. By the time he graduated from USC with a communications degree in 1989, he had set school records in numerous categories, including 8,225 yards gained passing over four seasons. He won the Johnny Unitas Golden Arm award in 1989 and was a runner-up for the coveted

Heisman. The USC Trojans went to the Rose Bowl in both of Peete's last two seasons.

Even as he notched these accomplishments, Peete also became a star on the baseball diamond as the Trojans' third baseman. He ended his three years on the team with a .297 average and 84 runs batted in. Peete's athletic ability drew the attention of professional teams in both baseball and football. The Oakland Athletics baseball team drafted Peete in the 13th round, and the Detroit Lions football team picked him in the sixth round in 1989. He chose the Lions and won the starting quarterback's job as a rookie that fall. Peete started eight games and was named to the NFL's All-Rookie team by *Football Digest* magazine. A powerful, six-feet-tall, 230-pound athlete, Peete was exciting to watch on the field.

It was only injuries that prevented Peete from emerging as a major star while playing for Detroit between 1989 and 1993. In a city whose sports fans were often merciless toward the quarterbacks of the struggling Lions, Peete was popular. His quarterback rating (or passer rating, a compilation of statistics relating to completion percentage, passing yardage, touchdowns, and interceptions) was fifth in the NFL in 1990, and in 1991, when Peete started the first eight games of the season, the Lions made a rare journey to the playoffs, losing to the Washington Redskins in the NFC championship game. He was troubled throughout his Lions career by a variety of knee and Achilles tendon problems, however, and after the 1993 season he was signed by the Dallas Cowboys as an unrestricted free agent.

In Dallas Peete served as backup to his former Heisman Trophy rival, Troy Aikman, starting one game during the 1994 season. He moved on to the Philadelphia Eagles in 1995, the Washington Redskins in 1999, and the Oakland Raiders in 2000. Throughout this period Peete gave strong performances while healthy, but he was often sidelined by injuries. His best year came in 1995, when he started 12 games for the Eagles and completed 215 of 375 passes for 2,326 yards, both personal bests; one highlight that season was a 58-37 victory over the Lions in which Peete completed 13 of 18 passes during the first half.

Coming off a disastrous 1-15 season, the Carolina Panthers signed Peete and made him a starting quarterback in 2002. By this time Peete was known as an intelligent analyst of the game, and the hope was that he could mentor younger players on a rebuilding club. He did more than that, starting 14 games at age 36 and improving the team's record to 7-9. During that season he made career highs in starts, passing attempts (381), pass completions (223), yards gained passing (2,630), and touchdown passes (15). The following year, when the Panthers went to the Super Bowl, he was replaced by younger quarterback Jake Delhomme after the team fell behind the Jacksonville Jaguars in its opening game. Delhomme credited Peete's influence, telling Joe Menzer of the *Winston-Salem Journal* that "I can't say enough good things about Rodney. He's seen a lot of football and he's someone I can lean on, someone who can give me tips."

Even during lean years, Peete enjoyed plenty of publicity thanks to his storybook romance with and subsequent marriage to television actress Holly Robinson. The two were introduced at a Los Angeles nightclub in 1993 by actress Lela Rochon, and the relationship flowered into marriage after Peete, in the fall of 1994, went down on one knee on the set of Robinson's situation comedy *Hangin' with Mr. Cooper* and proposed. They were married in 1995. Navigating the pitfalls of what was frequently a long-distance relationship, the couple had four children. Two of them, Rodney Jackson (R.J.) and Ryan Elizabeth Peete, were twins, born in 1998 with Peete in attendance after he was rushed with a police escort to the airport in Philadelphia. It was, he told Laura B. Randolph of *Ebony,* "the most amazing experience of my life."

In 1996 the Peetes formed the HollyRod Foundation to raise money for Parkinson's disease sufferers with financial difficulties. They then started HollyRod4Kids, an organization that benefited community programs aimed at children and organized shopping trips for underprivileged youngsters. The Peetes raised their children to pack toys and other gifts at holiday time and donate them to shelters for battered women and their families.

Peete officially retired from professional football after the 2004 season, in which he played two games with the Panthers. Over his career he appeared in 109 games, with 1,344 pass completions and 76 touchdown passes in 2,346 attempts. By April of 2005 he had landed a new job as full-time co-host of Fox's Best Damn Sports Show Period; he had already frequently appeared as a guest on the show. Peete provided commentary not only on football but also on the other sports he had played in high school and college. His broadcasting career enabled him to enjoy the chance to be closer to his family and to spend more time in their home in Los Angeles. He also supported his wife's new book, *Get Your Own Damn Beer, I'm Watching the Game: A Woman's Guide to Loving Pro Football.*

Sources

Periodicals

Cincinnati Post, December 5, 2002, p. B1.
Ebony, September 1995, p. 132; April 1998, p. 30; December 2002, p. 52; September 2005, p. 206.
Grand Rapids Press (Grand Rapids, MI), January 31, 2006, p. D2.
New York Times, September 19, 2002, p. D4.
Rocky Mountain News, January 7, 1996, p. B23.
Sports Illustrated, November 14, 1998, p. 44.
Winston-Salem Journal, September 15, 2002, p. C2; January 31, 2004, p. C5.

On-line

"Biography," *Rodney Peete,* www.rodneypeete.com (March 6, 2007).
"Rodney Peete," *Pro Football Reference,* www.pro-football-reference.com (March 6, 2007).
"The Scoop on Rodney Peete," *Fox Sports Net,* http://msn.foxsports.com/other/story/5322240 (March 6, 2007).

—James M. Manheim

Freddie Perren

1943-2004

Musician, music producer

Composer, arranger, and keyboardist Freddie Perren began producing records at the tail end of soul's funky domain and led the way to the glittering, wildly popular disco trend. His name may be unknown, but millions of people worldwide can cite the lyrics to songs such as "ABC," "Shake Your Groove Thing," and "If I Can't Have You"—all Perren productions. Perren worked with the biggest names in the music industry. For his production work, he shared a Grammy Award in 1978 for Album of the Year for the soundtrack to *Saturday Night Fever*, and he earned a Grammy Award in 1979 for best disco song: "I Will Survive." It was the only year the awards included this category. The disco era, for all its over-the-top glam, was short-lived. Perren's songs, however, live on.

Music on His Mind Led to Motown

Frederick James Perren was born on May 15, 1943 and raised in Englewood, New Jersey. From an early age he was destined for a career in music. "I asked him one time, 'How do you know what music to write?'" his sister Florence recalled to *The Star-Ledger*. "He said, 'I have tunes running in my head all the time.' That was so typical of him. He was interested in all kinds of music: He turned me on to opera." At Dwight Morrow High School, Perren was a member of the marching band, the orchestra, and sang in the chorus. He also became an accomplished piano player.

After graduation, Perren enrolled in the music program at Howard University in Washington, D.C. There he met many musicians with whom he would form lifelong collaborations including songwriter Fonce Mizell and record producer Larkin Arnold of Capital Records. Perren would later go on to establish a scholarship for financially needy music majors at the school. After earning a degree in music education in 1966, Perren taught music in Washington's public high schools and played keyboards for Chubby Checker. He also met songwriter Christine Yarian. The two would form a prolific pair, marrying, bearing two children, and collaborating on hundreds of songs, including "It's So Hard to Say Goodbye to Yesterday," a 1975 ballad that was revised as a number one R&B hit by Boyz II Men in 1991. "He was the most positive guy I ever met," Yarian recalled to *The Star-Ledger*. "He wouldn't let anybody tell him they had a problem. We had to use the word 'challenge' because, he said, we can always find an answer for a challenge."

In 1968, Perren and Yarian relocated to California to pursue musical careers. There he partnered with his college buddy Mizell and musician Deke Richards who had co-written "Love Child" for The Supremes. Together they wrote a song they were hoping to sell to Motown for an established group such as Gladys Knight and the Pips. Motown founder Berry Gordy had another act in mind—five young brothers from Indiana who had just signed with Motown as The Jackson Five. Under Gordy's direction, Perren and his collaborators reworked the tune as "I Want You Back." It became the quintet's first hit, capturing the number one spot on the both the R&B and pop charts.

Wrote Hits that Defined Disco

At a Glance . . .

Born Frederick James Perren on May 15, 1943, in New Jersey; died on December 16, 2004; married, Christine Yarian Perren; children: Derek and Amy. *Education:* Howard University, BA, music education, 1966.

Career: Motown Records, Los Angeles, CA, composer, producer, and studio musician, 1968-76; MVP Productions, founder and producer, 1978-8(?).

Awards: Grammy Award for Album of the Year, for *Saturday Night Fever*, 1978; Grammy Award for Best Disco Recording of the Year, for "I Will Survive," 1979.

Following the success of "I Want You Back," Perren, Mizell, and Richards joined Gordy under the ominous moniker of The Corporation and began churning out more hits, including The Jackson Five's chart-topper, "ABC." The catchy tune knocked The Beatles' "Let It Be" out of the number one spot on the *Billboard* charts. The Jackson Five sound, engineered by Perren and company, was quickly labeled "bubblegum soul" by the critics and struck a chord with a public weary from the social tumult in the country from the ongoing civil rights movement and the Vietnam War. The music was snappy, happy, and made you want to dance—a sound characteristic of Perren's personal style. "He was an up-tempo guy," his wife told *The Star-Ledger*. "He thought all the up-tempo songs should have the heartbeat of somebody who was dancing, and he always checked his rhythms to that."

With The Corporation, Perren co-wrote and/or produced several more songs for The Jackson Five including "The Love You Save," a number one on the charts in 1970 and "Mama's Pearl," number two in 1971. When Michael Jackson decided to go solo, The Corporation, co-produced his number five R&B hit "Ben." At the time, all songs produced or arranged by The Corporation were credited just that way; individual members were not listed on recordings. Persistent rumors have suggested that Gordy did this in order to prevent Perren, Mizell, and Richards from getting too famous and, thus, commanding higher pay. By 1972,

producer Hal Davis had taken charge of the Jacksons' work and The Corporation disbanded. Perren produced a few more projects for Motown including the soundtracks for the films *Hell Up in Harlem* from 1973 and *Cooley High* from 1975. In 1976, he produced the number one pop hit "Love Machine" for The Miracles.

After leaving Motown in 1976 Perren produced The Sylvers for Capital Records. With disco just hitting its stride, Perren wrote the group's number one hit "Boogie Fever." He also wrote and produced the disco chart-topper "Heaven Must Be Missing an Angel" for Tavares. For Polydor Records, he produced Peaches and Herbs, writing their two biggest hits–"Shake Your Groove Thing" and "Reunited." Perren also helped spread *Saturday Night Fever* by producing songs for the soundtrack, "If I Can't Have You" and "More Than a Woman." Perren shared in the soundtrack's Grammy Award for Album of the Year in 1978. In 1980, he produced and co-wrote Gloria Gaynor's "I Will Survive," one of the world's most recognizable songs. Part-feminist anthem, part-show tune, all-around infectious groove, the song soared up the charts, won the 1980 Grammy for Best Disco Recording, and become a world famous classic. However, it was one of Perren's last big hits. After working briefly with New Edition in the 1980s, he left the business. In 1993, he suffered a massive stroke from which he never quite recovered. On December 16, 2004, the 61-year-old Perren died at his home in California. Though his name has remained relatively unknown outside of the music industry, his music, like his best-known song, has survived in music clubs and discos worldwide.

Sources

Periodicals

Jet, January 17, 2005, p. 60.
The Star-Ledger (Newark, NJ), December 21, 2004, p. 33.

On-line

"Freddie Perren," *Disco Museum*, www.discomuseum.com/FreddiePerren.html (February 2, 2007).
"Freddie Perren, Biography," *All Music*, www.allmusic.com (February 2, 2007).

—Candace LaBalle

Charlotte E. Ray

1850-1911

Attorney, teacher

Charlotte E. Ray's courage, ability, and perseverance enabled her to break race and gender barriers to become the first African-American woman to graduate from an American law school, the first African-American women lawyer in the District of Columbia, and the third woman to be admitted to the U.S. bar. However, even those with the daring and the drive to break society's barriers may achieve success only to find themselves confronted with more obstacles.

From the accounts of those who knew, worked, and studied with her, Ray possessed the legal knowledge and skill that are the hallmarks of successful lawyers. Though Ray is known to have earned the respect of many of her colleagues and to have argued cases capably, she was not able to build a career as a lawyer. She could not surmount the widespread societal prejudice against her and was forced to return to teaching in order to earn a living. Nevertheless Ray's groundbreaking achievements paved the way for other women and people of color to enter the law and other professions that had once been reserved for white men only.

Charlotte E. Ray was born in New York City on January 12, 1850. Her parents, Charles Bennett Ray and Charlotte Augusta Burroughs Ray, had seven children, though two died as teenagers. The Ray household placed a high value on education and work for social justice. Charles Bennett Ray, a man of mixed African, Native American, and European heritage, was a minister at New York's Bethesda Congregational Church, and editor of the *Colored American*, an abolitionist newspaper. Charlotte Augusta Burroughs, Charles' second second wife, was also an anti-slavery activist who worked with her husband to help escaped slaves travel north to freedom on the underground railroad. The Rays believed strongly that African-American children needed education in order to improve their lives, and they worked hard to ensure that all of their children graduated from college, a most unusual achievement for a black family in the nineteenth century.

For her education, Ray had to move Washington, D.C., in the mid 1860s to attend the Institution for the Education of Colored Youth, one of the few schools where African Americans could obtain an academic education. The Institute had been founded in 1851 by a white educator named Myrtilla Miner, with the help of abolitionists Henry Ward Beecher and his cousin Harriet Beecher Stowe. Miner had taught school in Mississippi until she was refused permission to admit black children into her class. Moving to the nation's capitol, she opened the Normal School for Colored Girls, which in 1865 became the Institution for the Education of Colored Youth.

Upon completing her studies in 1869, Ray began to teach classes at Howard University's Normal and Preparatory Department, which trained students to become elementary school teachers and prepared them for classes in the Collegiate department. Howard had been founded by a group of social reformers in 1866 to provide quality education for the hundreds of new black citizens who had been freed from slavery and their descendents. From the moment of its founding, Howard University had a firm policy of non-discrimination, admitting both women and men of all races. The first students to enter the new college in 1867 were four white women, and the first graduates from its Normal and Preparatory Department were all women. In the forefront of women's education in the 1800s, Howard graduated a woman doctor in 1872, a woman pharmacist in 1887, and a woman dentist in 1896.

However, even in this atmosphere of relative tolerance, another African-American student, Mary Ann Shadd Carey, who entered Howard Law School during the early 1870s, was not permitted to graduate. Carey believed that the Howard administration discriminated against her because she was a woman. When Ray applied to enter Howard's newly established School of Law in 1872, she filed her application under the name "C.E. Ray." Some historians believe that she did this to conceal the fact that she was a woman, in case that might influence school administrators to refuse her application. However, others point out that many post-slavery blacks used only their initials because they did not want whites or others in authority to be tempted to call them by their first names, as they had during the era of slavery. There is no way to be sure why Ray to used her initials on her application, but she was accepted into Howard University's School of Law.

For the next three years, Ray pursued a demanding course of study, impressing her fellow students and teachers alike with her quick grasp of legal complexities. James C. Napier, a respected lawyer and one of Ray's Howard classmates, called her, "an apt scholar,"

and General Oliver O. Howard, one of the university's founders, described her as, "a colored woman who read us a thesis on corporations, not copied from the books but from her brain, a clear incisive analysis of one of the most delicate legal questions," according to Tonya Osborne of the Stanford University *Women's Legal History Biography Project.* Ray specialized in business law and became highly regarded as an expert in the legal issues of corporations. Her academic skill was recognized by her membership in the prestigious academic society, Phi Beta Kappa. When she graduated in 1872, Ray became the first African-American woman to graduate from a law school in the United States.

Upon finishing her law school program, Ray became the first black woman lawyer to enter the District of Columbia bar, which, not long before, had removed the requirement that applicants must be men. She was only the third woman in the entire nation to be admitted to the bar. She set up a business law practice, advertising in a local newspaper published by famous abolitionist Frederick Douglas, *New National Era and Citizen..* Soon she earned a reputation as a skilled and knowledgeable corporation lawyer. In addition to her commercial practice, she filed at least one suit in family law, a divorce petition on behalf of an abused wife.

However, though she was generally thought to be an excellent commercial and courtroom lawyer, Ray found herself, as a woman and an African American, unable to attract enough clients to support herself. White clients seldom chose a black attorney, and African Americans who could afford a lawyer were reluctant to hire a woman. A nationwide economic depression, ushered in by the Panic of 1873, also made it a difficult time to start a new business. After trying for several years to establish a legal practice, Ray was forced to give up. She returned to New York, where she joined her two surviving sisters working as a teacher in the Brooklyn public school system.

Little is known of Ray's later life. She continued to work for social change, attending the national convention the National Women's Suffrage Association and joining the National Association of Colored Women. During the late 1880s, she married a man with the last name of Fraim, and in 1897 she moved to the town of Woodside, New York, in the borough of Queens. She died there on January 4, 1911, from a severe case of bronchitis.

Though Ray was unable to continue her career as an attorney, her life still represents an enormous achievement. As the first African-American woman lawyer, and one of the first women lawyers in the nation, Ray opened a door for all the women of color who would come after her. The Greater Washington Area Chapter of the Women Lawyers Division of the National Bar

Association (GWAC), recognized Ray's contribution to the legal profession in 1989, when it established an annual "Charlotte Ray Award," to honor outstanding African-American women lawyers in the Washington area.

Sources

Books

"Charlotte Ray," in *Black Women in America: An Historical Encyclopedia,* Carlson Publishing, 1993, pp. 965-6.

Periodicals

Howard Law Journal, Winter 2000, p. 121-139.
Jet, April 24, 2006, p. 20.
Journal of Blacks in Higher Education. March 31, 1997, p. 134.
Journal of Women's History. Summer 2002, p. 207.
Louisiana Bar Journal, February 1993, p. 463.
Minnesota Lawyer, December 18, 2006.

On-line

"African American Heritage Trail," *Cultural Tourism DC,* www.culturaltourismdc.org/infourl3948/info-url.htm (January 20, 2007).
"Attorney Charlotte Ray Was Forced to Teach," *African American Registry,* www.aaregistry.com/african_american_history/24/Attorney_Charlotte_Ray_was_forced_to_teach (January 20, 2007).
"Charlotte E. Ray," *Biography Resource Center,* http://galenet.galegroup.com/servlet/BioRC (January 20, 2007).
"Celebrating Women's History Month: Government and Law, Charlotte Ray," *Women of Distinction 2006, New York State Senate,* www.senate.state.ny.us/sws/wod/gl_ray.html (January 20, 2007).
"Charlotte E. Ray: A Black Woman Lawyer," *Women's Legal History Biography Project, Stanford University,* http://womenslegalhistory.stanford.edu/papers/CharlotteRay.pdf (January 20, 2007).

—Tina Gianoulis

Eugene Booker Record

1940-2005

Vocalist, songwriter, producer

A triple talent as singer, songwriter, and producer, Eugene Record was the lead vocalist and principal creative talent of the R&B vocal group the Chi-Lites. In the early 1970s he composed and sang two of the classic ballads of contemporary popular music, "Have You Seen Her?" and "Oh Girl." Record's career traversed several distinct periods of African-American popular music in his native Chicago, Illinois, from doo-wop in the 1950s to disco and dance music in the early 1980s, and he devoted the last part of his life to gospel music. To each of these styles he brought something distinctive, a melancholy romanticism whose mature sense of loss stood in contrast to the youthful sensuality of much of the music that surrounded it on the radio and in record stores.

Eugene Booker Record was born on December 28, 1940, and lived his entire life in or near Chicago's South Side. He started playing the guitar when he was young, and his musical imagination was boosted by the classical piano pieces his sister practiced in the family home. By the time Record attended Englewood High School in the late 1950s he was singing the streetcorner harmony music known as doo-wop with friends, and along with Clarence Johnson and Robert "Squirrel" Lester he formed a trio, the Chanteurs.

Record recorded a pair of singles with the Chanteurs in 1959 for the local Renee label. With the addition of Creadel "Red" Jones and Marshall Thompson, the Chanteurs expanded to a quintet and became the Hi-Lites, contracting to a quartet lineup when Johnson left the group. Record worked as a taxi driver as the group recorded for small labels like Darin and Ja-Wes.

The group's most promising chances came when it recorded a few singles, including 1964's "I'm So Jealous," on the larger Mercury label. At that time, to avoid confusion with another Hi-Lites group connected with the label, the group added a "C" to the beginning of its name in honor of their native city. For a short time the group performed as Marshall and the Chi-Lites, with Thompson as lead vocalist.

"Our lifestyle revolved around singing," Record recalled, according to London's *Independent* newspaper. "I'd bring my guitar to rehearsals and play them my little songs, but the others would always tease me." Soon enough, however, Record emerged as the group's central talent. He married Barbara Acklin and started a family that grew to include five children: Eugene Jr., Bryan (Jerraine), Michelle, Angela, and Gena. Record and Acklin formed a successful songwriting team, collaborating on some of the Chi-Lites' biggest hits (including "Have You Seen Her?"). His plaintive lead vocals were heard on more and more of the Chi-Lites recordings, and it was his songwriting that caught the attention of producer Carl Davis at the new Chicago office of Brunswick Records when the Chi-Lites auditioned for him in 1967. Record was signed to a publishing contract by Davis, and he and Acklin turned out hits for other writers including Peaches and Herb's "Two Little Kids." In 1968, the Chi-Lites group was signed to Brunswick.

The group made an immediate impact with the ballad "Give It Away," which rose to the top 10 of what was then called the black singles chart in *Billboard* magazine and also dented the pop charts. By 1971 the

At a Glance . . .

Born on December 28, 1940, in Chicago, IL; died on July 22, 2005, in Hazel Crest, IL; married Barbara Acklin; married Jacqueline; children: Eugene Jr., Bryan, Michelle (Protho), Angela (Jones), Gena (Jones). *Education:* Attended Englewood High School, Chicago. *Religion:* Church of God in Christ.

Career: Chanteurs musical group (later known as Hi-Lites, and then Chi-Lites), founder and member, late 1950s-1975, 1980-88; Brunswick Records, songwriter, 1967; Warner Bros. label, solo artist, 1977-79; solo artist, 1990s-2005; ordained as minister, 1998.

Memberships: Crusaders Church, Chicago, IL.

Chi-Lites had three Brunswick albums under its belt, and Record was closely following wider songwriting trends; "For God's Sake (Give More Power to the People)" mirrored a trend toward funk-based protest songs on the part of such groups as the Temptations (with "Ball of Confusion"). The song was the title track of the Chi-Lites' third album and brought the group its biggest hit to date

Nothing prepared Record, however, for the success of the group's next album, *A Lonely Man,* with its two pop top-10 singles, "Have You Seen Her?" and "Oh Girl" (the latter a number-one pop hit). Record had actually written "Have You Seen Her?" several years earlier but had shelved it, convinced that its five-minute length and unconventional structure, weaving together sung and spoken reflections, doomed the song to radio oblivion. He changed his mind after the success of Isaac Hayes's *Hot Buttered Soul* release with its extended jams. A 1972 appearance on *The Flip Wilson Show* helped propel the song to hit status.

Record likewise failed to predict that success of "Oh Girl." When he brought the songs for the album to Davis, the producer responded that there was a number-one hit among the bunch. "I named them all before 'Oh Girl,'" Record remembered, according to the *Independent*, adding "I thought he was kidding." In the early 1970s Record was a major force in popular music, writing songs and producing recordings for such acts as Jackie Wilson. The Chi-Lites enjoyed a consistent presence on radio with such early 1970s hits as "Stoned Out of My Mind," "Homely Girl," and "There Will Never Be Any Peace (Until God Is Seated at the Conference Table)." Between 1969 and 1975, the Chi-Lites placed a total of 21 singles in *Billboard*'s top 100. By 1976, however, Brunswick was mired in tax difficulties, and the members of the group had pled guilty to tax evasion charges in order to put legal proceedings to rest.

The Chi-Lites temporarily disbanded that year, and Record launched a solo career just as the lush, mechanical disco sound was beginning to flower. He was signed to the Warner Bros. label. Record's three solo albums of the late 1970s, *The Eugene Record, Trying to Get to You,* and *Welcome to My Fantasy* were only moderately successful but continue to command the interest of collectors. The Chi-Lites re-formed in 1980 and issued several new albums in the early 1980s on the 20th Century label, scoring a moderate hit in 1982 with "Hot on a Thing (Called Love)."

In 1988 Record left the Chi-Lites after experiencing divine instructions to change the direction of his life and music. In 1992 he appeared on the evangelism-oriented television program *The 700 Club.* He began preaching, was ordained a minister, and became a member of the Crusaders Church on Chicago's far South Side. Record released a gospel album, *Let Him In,* in 1998. Record benefited financially from several covers and re-workings of his music. Rapper MC Hammer covered "Have You Seen Her?" in 1990, and gospel star BeBe Winans reworked it as "Do You Know Him?" In 2003 Beyonce's Grammy-winning hit "Crazy in Love" sampled the early Chi-Lites song "Are You My Woman?"; Record approved, telling *Jet* that "I would give her [Beyonce] a big hug and say thank you. And then I would commend her for a job well done." The Chi-Lites reunited for a documentary film, *Only the Strong Survive,* in 2002 and for a Public Broadcasting System special in 2004. Eugene Record died of cancer in Hazel Crest, Illinois, on July 22, 2005, at the home of his daughter, Gena Jones, with his second wife, Jacqueline, at his side. He left behind a catalog of more than 300 compositions.

Selected discography

Albums, solo

The Eugene Record, Warner Bros., 1977.
Trying to Get to You, Warner Bros., 1978.
Welcome to My Fantasy, Warner Bros., 1979.
Let Him In, Evergreen, 1998.

Albums with the Chi-Lites

Give It Away, Brunswick, 1969.
I Like Your Lovin' (Do You Like Mine?), Brunswick, 1970.
(For God's Sake) Give More Power to the People, Brunswick, 1971.
A Lonely Man, Brunswick, 1972.
A Letter to Myself, Brunswick, 1973.
Half a Love, Brunswick, 1974.
Chi-Litetime, London, 1976.
Happy Being Lonely, Mercury, 1976.
The Fantastic Chi-Lites, Mercury, 1977.

Heavenly Body, 20th Century, 1980.
Me & You, 20th Century, 1981.
Bottom's Up, Larc, 1983.
Just Say You Love Me, Ichiban, 1991.
20 Greatest Hits, Brunswick, 2001.

Sources

Periodicals

Daily Post (Liverpool, England), July 28, 2005, p. 13.
Daily Telegraph (London, England), July 26, 2005.
Independent (London, England), July 25, 2005, p. 51.
Jet, October 20, 2003, p. 40; August 8, 2005, p. 65.

New York Times, July 23, 2005, p. B20.
New York Times Magazine, December 25, 2005, p. 40.
Times (London, England), August 10, 2005, p. 55.

On-line

"The Chi-Lites," *Soulwalking,* www.soulwalking.co.uk/Chi-Lites.html (March 9, 2007).
"Chi-Lites," *All Music Guide,* www.allmusic.com (March 9, 2007).
"Eugene Record," *All Music Guide,* www.allmusic.com (March 9, 2007).
"Eugene Record," *SoulTracks,* www.soultracks.com/eugene_record.html (March 9, 2007).

—James M. Manheim

Constance LaMay Rice

1956—

Lawyer

Constance LaMay Rice has dedicated her career to protecting the legal, social, and economic rights of poor and marginalized people. As a co-director of the Los Angeles office of the National Association for the Advancement of Colored People (NAACP) Legal Defense and Education Fund and as co-founder of the public policy and legal action organization the Advancement Project, Rice has fought hard to change social systems that, in her view, deny justice and equality to large segments of the population. The aim of many of her legal cases, she explained in a feature in *Pasadena Weekly* magazine, has been "to help the poor end their own poverty."

A native of Washington, D.C., Rice was born on April 5, 1956, and grew up in a strong, supportive family. Her parents both worked; her mother, Anna L. Barnes Rice, as a science teacher; and her father, Phillip Leon Rice, as U.S. Air Force colonel. The family moved often when Rice was a girl, and she attended school in London, England, before completing high school in Texas in 1974. She went on to graduate from Harvard University in 1978 with a degree in government. Aside from her academic talents, Rice developed a strong physical education as well. Her commitment came after having been physically attacked by a man when she was in college. Rice had been unable to fight back against her assailant; as she explained in *Pasadena Weekly*, "it didn't occur to me because I hadn't been trained to fight." Rice determined to learn to protect herself. She succeeded, earning a first degree black belt in Tae Kwon Do in 1980. Rice was the first female student her respected Tae Kwon Do teacher had ever

accepted.

Rice continued her education in 1980 when she entered the New York University School of Law after being awarded the Root Tilden Public Interest Scholarship. As a student, she served as law clerk for the State of New York Department of Law and also worked under the mentorship of NAACP Legal Defense Fund attorney Lani Guinier. Completing her law degree in 1984, Rice served as law clerk for U.S. Court of Appeals for the Sixth Circuit judge Damon J. Keith in Detroit, Michigan.

Since 1986 Rice's career has been based in California. That year Rice joined the firm of Morrison and Foster, in San Francisco, as an associate attorney. In 1987 she accepted a position as special assistant to the associate vice chancellor of the University of California, Los Angeles. From 1990 to 1995 Rice served as president of the Los Angeles Department of Water and Power. After joining the Los Angeles office of the NAACP Legal Defense and Education Fund in 1990, Rice became involved in several prominent civil rights cases, including the 1996 challenge to California Proposition 209, which amended the California state constitution to prohibit public institutions from discriminating on the basis of race, gender, or ethnicity. Opponents of Proposition 209 argued that it would end affirmative action policies and contribute to increased inequality, but this argument did not succeed. Rice also played a part in the release from prison of Geronimo Pratt, a Black Panther convicted in 1972 of kidnapping and murder. Pratt served 27 years before his conviction was overturned in 1997 on the grounds that he had not

At a Glance . . .

Born on April 5, 1956, in Washington, DC. *Education:* Harvard University, BA, government, 1978; New York University, JD, 1984.

Career: U.S. 6th Circuit Court of Appeals, Detroit, MI, law clerk, 1984-86; Morrison and Foster, San Francisco, CA, associate attorney, 1986-87; University of California, Los Angeles, special assistant to the associate vice chancellor, 1987; Los Angeles Department of Water and Power, president, 1990-95; NAACP Legal Defense and Education Fund, Los Angeles, western regional counsel, 1990–; English, Munger and Rice, Los Angeles, CA, co-founder and partner, 1998–; Advancement Project, co-founder and co-director.

Memberships: NAACP.

Awards: NAACP Legal Defense and Education Fund, Civil Rights Lawyer of the Year, 1999; *California Law Business,* named among California's top 10 most influential lawyers, 2000; Los Angeles County, John Anson Ford Humanitarian Award, 2002; Women Lawyers of Los Angeles, Ernestine Stahlhut Award, 2004.

Addresses: *Office*—English, Munger and Rice, Suite 800, 1545 Wilshire Blvd., Los Angeles, CA 90017.

received a fair trial. After an embarrassing corruption scandal in the Los Angeles Police Department's Rampart Division in the late 1990s, the Police Commission appointed Rice to a blue-ribbon panel that investigated corruption charges and recommended reforms. Rice had made herself a vigorous career as an civil rights lawyer.

Rice's most important achievement, she explained in *Pasadena Weekly,* was getting three innocent men released from death row. Indeed, issues relating to imprisonment—including high incarceration rates, overcrowding, and denial of prisoners' rights—continue to inspire Rice's advocacy. She has spoken out about the dangers of intensifying racial violence in the country's prisons, and, during an episode of the PBS news program *Now,* suggested that abuse of prisoners is a significant problem in the United States. "Am I saying that our prisons are as bad as Abu Ghraib [in Iraq]? No," she said. "But do we have conditions that are illegal, unconstitutional and cruel and unusual? Yes."

Education reform is another subject about which Rice is passionate. In fact, she has called for nothing less than a complete dismantling and rebuilding of the nation's public schools. "Let's start a revolution here," she suggested during a seminar, reported in the *Washington Post,* to celebrate the landmark *Brown v. Board of Education* case of 1954 that desegregated U.S. public schools. "We need to celebrate the achievement of *Brown,*" Rice said, "but we have an obligation to change conditions we face today." Elaborating on this view to a reporter for *USA Today,* Rice added that just throwing money at the problem of poorly-performing schools is not enough to solve the problem. "Our system works for privileged kids of all races," she said, but it is a "devastating failure for poor kids of all races, including poor white children." Rice would like to see education reform begin with prenatal care, which would give every newborn the healthy environment necessary for early cognitive development. Schools, she believes, should focus on helping poor children move up the economic ladder. Indeed, building and protecting a healthy middle class is, for Rice, key to ensuring the viability of democratic society. Increased social mobility, she noted in *Pasadena Weekly,* is crucial because "the more prosperous an economic region is, the less friction, the less tension, the less crime, the less racial strife."

Since 1998 Rice has practiced law at English, Munger, and Rice, a firm that she co-founded and serves as partner. She has also devoted her energies to The Advancement Project, an organization she co-founded that is described on its Web site as a "democracy and justice action group." The Advancement Project works with local communities to obtain legal services, communication, technical support, and other needed services for poor communities. Among many issues that the organization is currently involved with is relief for victims of Hurricane Katrina, which hit the Gulf Coast in 2005 and destroyed much of the city of New Orleans.

Rice is a distant cousin to Condoleezza Rice, who served as an advisor to President George H. W. Bush and was National Security Advisor, and then Secretary of State, for President George W. Bush. Constance Rice has told interviewers that she admires her cousin, but not her politics.

Constance Rice has received numerous awards for her work promoting social reform. In 1999 she was named Civil Rights Lawyer of the Year by the NAACP Legal Defense and Education Fund. The following year she was named one of the Top 10 most influential lawyers in California by *California Law Business.* She received the John Anson Ford Humanitarian Award, Los Angeles County, in 2002 and the Women Lawyers of Los Angeles Ernestine Stahlhut Award in 2004. These accolades attest to her abilities, and in 2007 she had made no signal that she had even considered stopping her civic-minded work.

Sources

Periodicals

Pasadena Weekly, October 19, 2006.
USA Today, May 17, 2004.
Washington Post, May 16, 2004; November 11, 2006.

On-line

Advancement Project, www.advancementproject. org/index.html (February 12, 2007).
"Law Makers," *History Makers,* www.thehistorymak-ers.com (January 5, 2007).
"NOW: Politics & Economy, Income and Inequality; Constance Rice: Biography," *PBS,* www.pbs.org/ now/politics/rice.html (January 5, 2007).

—E. M. Shostak

Paul Rusesabagina

1954—

Hotel manager, author, humanitarian

Rusesabagina, Paul, photograph. Hubert Boesl/Landov.

For 76 days in 1994, as the central African nation of Rwanda seethed with genocidal fury, hotel manager Paul Rusesabagina sheltered 1,268 people who would otherwise probably have been hacked to death with machetes on the streets outside. His resources consisted of a telephone, a liquor cabinet, and an inborn ability to defuse confrontation through conversation. Though he faced likely death on numerous occasions as a result of his activities, Rusesabagina has declined the designation of hero. "A hero is someone who has done something that is miraculous," he pointed out to Robert Taylor of the *Contra Costa Times*. "When each and every person does what he is supposed to do, shall we call him a hero?"

The film *Hotel Rwanda* was based on Rusesabagina's story. It has been compared with *Schindler's List,* which told the true story of a German industrialist who saved the lives of a comparable number of Jews during World War II, but Rusesabagina rejects that comparison as well. "If Oskar Schindler had only had to stay strong for 100 days to save those people, as I did, I would agree with you," he told Clare Rudebeck of London's *Independent.* "But he went through it for five years.

He was a very brave man." In his autobiography, *An Ordinary Man,* Rusesabagina argued that "the individual's most potent weapon is a stubborn belief in the triumph of common decency. It is a simple belief, but it is not at all naïve. It is, in fact, the shrewdest attitude possible. It is the best way to sabotage evil."

Raised in Mud House

One of nine children in a rural Rwandan farm family, Paul Rusesabagina was born in 1954 near the village of Nkomero. His father, Thomas Rupfure, was a local elder whose authority in settling disputes was respected. Rwandan surnames are given by parents at birth, and Rusesabagina's, in his native Kinyarwanda language, means "warrior that disperses the enemies." His parents were illiterate, but he was sent to a school operated by the Seventh-Day Adventist Church in the nearby town of Gitwe, and by the time he was eight he had learned to read French. At 13 he added English on his way to eventual mastery of five languages.

In 1959 the young Rusesabagina had to sleep outside the house as his family provided shelter to refugees

At a Glance . . .

Born 1954 in Nkomero, Rwanda; married Esther (first marriage, divorced); Tatiana (second marriage); children: four. *Education:* Attended Faculty of Theology, Cameroon; training in hospitality industry with Sabena Corp. *Religion:* Seventh-Day Adventist.

Career: Mille Collines Hotel, Kigali, Rwanda, desk clerk, then advanced to management positions, 1979-1991; Diplomates Hotel, Kigali, general manager, 1992-1996; Belgium, taxi driver, 1996-?; trucking company, Zambia, founder; humanitarian lecturer, 2004–.

Awards: Presidential Medal of Freedom, 2005.

Addresses: *Publisher*—Penguin Group, 375 Hudson St., New York, NY 10014.

seeking shelter from one of the clashes that occurred periodically in Rwanda between the Hutu and Tutsi ethnic groups. Rusesabagina in his autobiography, backed by several scholars, contended that the Hutu-Tutsi split in Rwanda was intensified and manipulated by European colonial powers who sought to divide the Rwandan people and thus conquer them more easily; Hutus and Tutsis, unlike the ethnic groups that have come into conflict in other African countries, share a common culture and language. As the minority Tutsis were installed as hereditary rulers by Rwanda's Belgian overlords, the social distinctions between the two groups grew deeper. Hutus gained control in elections held in 1959, and hostilities flared several times after Rwanda obtained its independence from Belgium in 1962. Rusesabagina's father was a Hutu, and his mother was Tutsi.

More interested in getting an education than in becoming involved with ethnic politics, Rusesabagina aimed at first toward a career as a pastor, traveling in 1976 to the West African nation of Cameroon to attend a Seventh-Day Adventist school called the Faculty of Theology. But Rusesabagina found that he was drawn to the excitement of city life rather than to the spartan lifestyle of a small-town minister, and he began to question whether he was really cut out for the ministry. Back in Rwanda he moved with his new wife, Esther, to the capital city of Kigali at the end of 1978.

Entered Hotel Industry

The city was full of young men looking for work, but Rusesabagina had several advantages. He spoke French and English well, and giving practice sermons had turned him into an effective communicator. When a childhood friend alerted him to an opening at the posh Mille Collines hotel, he jumped at the chance. Working at the front desk, Rusesabagina quickly gained the attention of his superiors with his linguistic skills and service-oriented attitude. He was quickly promoted, and before long he was the hotel's assistant general manager. Along the way he learned that the hotel's poolside cafe and bar were frequented by Rwanda's movers and shakers as they talked of political affairs and made deals with European companies. Making careful mental note of their liquor preferences, he began to cultivate contacts among the Rwandan elite.

Rusesabagina's marriage suffered and ended in divorce as he worked long hours at each new job, but in 1987 he met a woman named Tatiana, a nurse from a small village in northern Rwanda. She was Tutsi, but that didn't matter to Rusesabagina at the time. Thanks to his newfound contacts in the government, he was able to arrange her transfer to Kigali, and the two were married two years later. They had a son, Tresor, and then three more children, Lys, Roger, and Diane. In 1992 Rusesabagina received another promotion, becoming general manager of the Diplomates Hotel, a sister property of the Mille Collines. Both hotels were owned by the Swiss-Belgian Sabena conglomerate.

The company flew Rusesabagina to Switzerland and to Brussels, Belgium, for training sessions in which he learned the fine points of European wine appreciation and hotel service. But meanwhile, in Rwanda, the Hutu-dominated government of President Juvenal Habyarimana was facing pressure from a Tutsi-led rebel force and was attempting to hold onto power by whipping up ethnic hatreds against Tutsis. The purportedly independent radio station RTLM, actually under Habyarimana's control, referred to Tutsis as cockroaches and alleged that they were planning to kill Hutus. Huge shipments of machetes flowed into the capital and were distributed to government-affiliated youth gangs called *Interahamwe,* meaning "those who stick together."

Presidential Plane Shot Down

On April 6, 1994, a plane carrying Habyarimana was shot down by a shoulder-fired missile—by whom remains unclear—as it approached Kigali Airport, killing both Habyarimana and Burundian president Cyprien Ntaryamira. "Do your work," RTLM announcers exhorted the Hutu populace (as Rusesabagina recalled in *An Ordinary Man*). "Clean your neighborhood of brush. Clear the tall trees" (Tutsis were thought to be taller than Hutus). Within hours, Rwanda erupted in genocidal violence. United Nations troops stationed in Rwanda, had they acted as the genocide began, could likely have halted the worst of the killing, but did not act; their superiors were intimidated in part by the experience of United States peacekeepers in the disastrous Battle of Mogadishu in Somalia the previous year. Over the next three months, an estimated 800,000 Tutsis were killed in Rwanda.

As he rode through Kigali's streets a few days after the assassination, Rusesabagina recalled in *An Ordinary Man*, "Surrounding us on every side were the bodies of people who had been freshly murdered. They had been pushed out of the roadway. A few of the lucky ones had been shot, but most had been hacked apart by machetes. Some were missing their heads. I saw the intestines of one man coming out of his belly like pink snakes." Rusesabagina's own son went next door and found that his boyhood friend had been slaughtered. He did not speak for days.

By that time, Rusesabagina's humanitarian odyssey had already begun. Although he himself was a suspect figure for the organizers of the genocide and was in danger of being killed at any time, his Tutsi neighbors sought out his protection as chaos engulfed the city—he was never sure exactly why. Indeed, as he took a group of 26 people, including his own family, to the Diplomates Hotel, an army captain gave him a Kalashnikov rifle and indicated that he should kill the whole group. Rusesabagina searched for any words that would keep the conversation going and prolong their lives for a few moments more. First he said he did not know how to use a gun. Then he told the captain that the group, which included elderly people and children, was not worthy of the captain's time. Finally, and successfully, he offered a bribe, saying that he would have to get the money from the hotel safe.

Hotel Became Refuge

Many of the next 76 days unfolded the same way. The Diplomates Hotel was seized by combatants, but Rusesabagina, frantically making phone calls and sending faxes, persuaded Sabena to appoint him manager of his old place of employment, the Mille Collines Hotel, and moved his family and friends there. Other Tutsis and moderate Hutus heard that the hotel was a place of refuge, and soon the building, designed for 300 guests, held 1,268 people. All survived the carnage outside, although militiamen were almost at the hotel's door during the entire period and several times approached with orders to enter and kill everyone inside.

Their survival was due to Rusesabagina's calm and resourcefulness under pressure. "If there is a secret to how I succeeded in keeping those people safe, it was that I did not change in any way," he told Rudebeck. "I remained the hotel manager. I went to my office every day. I made sure there were enough supplies. That helped me to stay calm in that madness." Many of his challenges were logistical. Electricity and water were cut off, which could have quickly created a sanitation crisis with fatal results. Rusesabagina solved that problem by rationing water from the hotel's 78,000-gallon swimming pool, where just days before Rwandan generals had hobnobbed with European guests. Food was smuggled in as Rusesabagina cut deals with merchants at a nearby market.

Phones were cut off as well, but one fax line was missed. Rusesabagina spent his evenings sending pleas for help to international governments, including that of the United States, trying to alert the world to the carnage in Rwanda. He had no success. "Maybe the world didn't think Rwanda was worth an intervention," Rusesabagina told Oprah Winfrey in an *O, The Oprah Magazine* interview. "Maybe that's because Africa is far away from America and Europe. Perhaps it happened because Rwanda did not have oil. Or maybe it's because people were focused on South Africa," where the decades-old apartheid system was ending.

Plied Militiamen with Liquor

On many occasions Rusesabagina had to make quick decisions to save the lives of individual guests or of the entire group. That he himself was an ethnic Hutu, and that the hotel was a European-owned luxury property, bought him very little time. Rusesabagina called in favors from every name in his address book, often inviting cold-blooded killers into his office to partake of his stock of fine cognac and scotch when they entered the hotel demanding that guests be turned over to them; he found that the longer he kept talking, the greater were his chances of success. "In Rwandan culture, we say that two men can never sit down and deal without a drink," he told Winfrey. "So I'd always bring a drink to sit and talk. And certainly, any person who came to talk with me arrived at a positive conclusion."

At one point Rusesabagina was given the chance to leave the hotel in a United Nations truck but refused to desert those he was protecting. After discussion with them, he did send his wife and family—one of the small details in which the film *Hotel Rwanda* differed from actual events was that in the film, he sends them away without telling them what is happening. In any event, his attempt to arrange their departure from Rwanda was unsuccessful; the truck was stopped, and his wife was beaten and nearly killed.

The genocide in Rwanda finally stopped when Tutsi rebels overran the country, but Rusesabagina's problems were not over. He heard of death threats against himself and his family, and he continues to be regarded with suspicion both by Hutus and by Tutsis who point to his close contacts with highly placed Hutu commanders during the massacres. Finally, in 1996, Rusesabagina and his family fled Rwanda for Belgium. At this point his story was unknown to the outside world. He found a job as a taxi driver, eventually saving enough money to buy several motor vehicles and open a small trucking company in the African nation of Zambia.

Rusesabagina's path to world renown began in 2000, when American screenwriter Keir Pearson heard his story from a friend who had lived in Tanzania; the friend in turn had heard from Rwandan refugees about the hotel manager who had single-handedly saved hundreds of lives. The result was *Hotel Rwanda,* which appeared in 2004 with actor Don Cheadle in the role of Rusesabagina and Sophie Okonedo as Tatiana. "I like Don …," Rusesabagina told Martyn Palmer of the London *Times.* "I am very happy to have such a handsome fellow play me in this film…. They have changed one or two things because it is a movie. And you know, really, it is not possible to capture the full horror of what happened. How can you do that?"

Though Rusesabagina declined the title of hero, *Hotel Rwanda* director Terry George was one of many who would argue that the word was appropriate. "Paul had a number of choices," George told Robert Taylor. "He could have gone with the mob. He could have fled. And probably gotten his wife and children out as well. There is a monumental amount of courage behind Paul's decision to stay." Among those who agreed was U.S. President George W. Bush, who awarded Rusesabagina the Presidential Medal of Freedom in 2005. Rusesabagina's autobiography, *An Ordinary Man,* appeared in 2006, by which time he was giving speeches around the world, attempting to use his newfound fame to raise the world's consciousness of Africa's prob-lems—including the unfolding genocide in the Sudanese region of Darfur.

Selected works

Books

(With Tom Zoellner) *An Ordinary Man* (autobiography), Penguin, 2006.

Sources

Books

Rusesabagina, Paul, with Tom Zoellner, *An Ordinary Man,* Penguin, 2006.

Periodicals

Contra Costa Times (Walnut Creek, CA), January 10, 2005.
Houston Chronicle, December 7, 2006, p. 7.
Independent (London, England), February 21, 2005, p. 9.
Jet, November 28, 2005, p. 4.
O, The Oprah Magazine, March 2006, p. 222.
People, January 24, 2005, p. 113.
Sacramento Bee, March 7, 2007.
Star Ledger (Newark, NJ), October 18, 2005, p. 55.
Star Tribune (Minneapolis, MN), April 13, 2006, p. A19.
Times (London, England), February 19, 2005, p. 40.

—James M. Manheim

James Stewart Jr.

1985—

Motorcycle racer

James Stewart Jr. has been called the Tiger Woods of motorcycle racing. But even Woods didn't have a boatload of sponsors and a collection of fancy sportscars by the time he was 16. Stewart has emerged as the dominant force in motocross (outdoor, dirt-track motorbike racing, usually in a rural setting) and supercross (motocross's indoor cousin, usually found in large stadiums in metropolitan areas). By his early twenties, Stewart had already logged enough victories and series championships to place him among the sport's all-time leaders. Moreover, in the sport pursued by an overwhelming majority of white participants, Stewart has achieved far more than any other African American in history. By the time he is done racing, he may well have achieved more than anyone of any race or ethnicity.

James Stewart Jr. was born on December 21, 1985, in Bartow, Florida. His father was a professional motocross racer in Central Florida, so James Jr. was exposed to motorcycles and racing practically from birth. When he was just days old, James Sr. took him for his first ride, and as a toddler he would climb around on the bike, under the close supervision of his father. James Jr. started riding motorcycles when he was three years old. He was given his first bike on his fourth birthday, and that year he entered his first race. By the time he was seven, Stewart had won his first national amateur championship and picked up his first sponsor. The Stewart clan traveled the country in a motorhome so that young James could compete on the national circuit. James and his younger brother Malcolm were homeschooled by their mother, Sonya, in order to accommodate the family's itinerant lifestyle.

As Stewart rose through the amateur ranks, he picked up the nickname Bubba, which may have been a variant of his family's preferred pet name for him: Boogie. In 1993, Stewart's racing idol, Tony Haynes—one of the few African-American standouts in a sport dominated by Caucasians—broke his neck in a crash and was paralyzed from the waist down, ending his motocross career. Stewart asked Haynes if he could have his racing number, 259. Haynes agreed, and Stewart vowed to take the number to the top of the profession.

In his early teens, Stewart rose to unprecedented heights in motocross/supercross for someone so young. He developed a successful style that featured not only high speed, but an ability to capture "big air" on his jumps. In 1997 the Stewarts bought 40 acres of land in Haines City, Florida, so they could build their own motocross track to practice on. They also built a home on the site.

Stewart continued to bring home trophies in prodigious numbers. He won an unprecedented 11 national amateur championships in all, assembling what has been called the most impressive amateur career in the history of American motocross racing. In January of 2002, having just turned 16, Stewart turned professional—though the distinction between amateur and professional becomes rather murky when one considers the number of sponsorship and endorsement deals he had already racked up by that time. In his first pro race at Edison International Field in Anaheim, California, he placed a respectable third. Competing in the 125cc class, he went on to win nine national titles in his

At a Glance . . .

Born on December 21, 1985, in Bartow, FL.

Career: Amateur motorbike racer, 1990-2001; professional motorbike racer, 2002–.

Awards: AMA (American Motorcyclist Association) Lites National Motocross Championship, 2002, 2004; AMA Rookie of the Year, 2002; "20 Teens Who Will Change the World," *Teen People,* 2003.

Addresses: *Team Office*—c/o Kawasaki Motors Corp. USA, 9950 Jeronimo Rd., Irvine, CA, 92618.

rookie season, good for the AMA (American Motorcyclist Association) Lites National Motocross Championship, making him the youngest rider ever to claim the title. He was also named AMA Rookie of the Year.

Coming off of his spectacular rookie season, Stewart was named one of "20 Teens Who Will Change the World" in the April 2003 issue of *Teen People.* That year, he claimed the AMA Supercross Lites West Championship by winning seven out of the eight rounds that make up the series. He was slowed down, however, by a big crash at a race in Las Vegas, in which he broke his collarbone. The injury forced him to miss several important races. Once recovered, however, Stewart quickly returned to his dominant form. He won every remaining race of the AMA Lites National Championship Series, good enough for a third-place overall finish in the series, despite missing four of the 11 races. Stewart's domination of the 125cc class was partly the result of his innovative riding style. His most unique move was what he called "the Bubba Scrub," which involves taking jumps at a lower-than-normal trajectory and turning the bike so that it is nearly parallel to the ground. The move both saves time and looks good to spectators. In addition, Stewart is aggressive on turns, taking a sharper angle than many other racers are willing to attempt.

2004 brought Stewart's career to even greater heights. So thorough was his mastery of the 125cc division that some writers took to calling him the Tiger Woods of motorbike racing, a nod to both his superlative skill and his success in a sport with few minorities among its elite

participants. Stewart entered 12 races in 2004, and won 11 of them, earning him another AMA Lites National Motocross Championship. At 18 years old, Stewart finished the 2004 season with four AMA series titles and a record 47 AMA Lites race victories.

Following his amazing 2004 season, Stewart "graduated" to the bigger, faster 250cc class in 2005. Unfortunately, his first season in that division was marred by a series of injuries. He broke his arm practicing for the second round of the championship series, forcing him to miss nine races. In his return race, he placed third, and then went on to win two of the next three rounds. However, a broken thumb and a bacterial infection in his digestive tract later in the season further hampered his performance.

Entering the 2006 season, Stewart was determined to establish a "new beginning." He shed the number 259 he had worn throughout his career to honor Tony Haynes, and donned the number 7. He also decided to dump his longtime nickname "Bubba," though not all of his fans got the message right away. Stewart's new beginning has been an auspicious one. He enjoyed a solid season in 2006, winning a number of big races and finishing second only to superstar Ricky Carmichael in the overall AMA standings. As the 2006-07 season began, a passing of the torch appeared to be taking place. Carmichael, who had dominated the 250cc division for several years, announced that he was leaving the circuit after the season. Stewart, through his performance—which included five consecutive victories as of mid-February 2007—announced that he was more than ready to bear that torch for years to come.

Sources

Periodicals

Arizona Republic, January 14, 2007.
Boys' Life, October 2003, p. 8.
Cincinnati Post, July 24, 2004.
Columbian (Vancouver, WA), July 26, 2002, p. B1.
Cycle World, April 2002, p. 116.
Dirt Rider, August 2000.
Orlando Sentinel, March 7, 2003.
Seattle Times, April 29, 2006.
Sports Illustrated, April 11, 2005.
Sports Illustrated for Kids, March 1, 2004, p. 34.
St. Petersburg Times, December 18, 2004. On-line
"The New Beginning," *James Stewart Jr.,* www. jamesstewartonline.com (March 26, 2007).

—Bob Jacobson

Sun Ra

1914-1993

Jazz musician

Legendary jazz pianist, composer, and orchestra leader Sun Ra was one of the most original figures in twentieth-century American music. For over 40 years he led a group of musicians, dancers, and singers—known by dozens of names including the Cosmocentric, Heliocentric, Myth Science, and Omniverse Arkestras—in wild performances across the planet. At least 1,000 of his compositions could be heard on hundreds of recordings. In addition to the piano and organ, Sun Ra played percussion and various electronic instruments, synthesizers, and invented instruments. He was the first big-band leader to break down the conventional sectioning of brass and reeds and to introduce performance art into jazz. His musical influence extended beyond jazz to alternative rock.

Came From Saturn

As an adult Sun Ra claimed to have come from the planet Saturn. In fact Herman Poole "Sonny" Blount was born in Birmingham, Alabama, on May 22, 1914, one of numerous children of Cary and Ida (Jones) Blount. His father was a railroad worker and his mother worked in the restaurant of the Birmingham train station where young Blount would eat his meals and listen to the player piano. He was raised in the Baptist Church by his maternal grandmother Margaret Jones and great-aunt Ida Howard, although even as a young child he questioned the scriptures. Each week his great-aunt took him to the black theater and he heard every band that came through Birmingham. For his 11th birthday Ida Howard bought him a piano. Blount

played by ear and taught himself to sight-read. He wrote poetry and began composing songs. Soon he was playing in the city's black social clubs. As a teenager Blount developed testicular cryptorchidism—a severe type of hernia in which the testes fail to descend into the scrotum. Some sources link the ongoing physical pain from this development with Blount's increasing social isolation.

Blount excelled at Industrial High School where he played in the school orchestra under the legendary John T. "Fess" Whatley. As a senior he played his first professional gig in Whatley's Sax-o-Society Orchestra. After graduation in 1932 Blount went on tour with the Society Troubadours, formed his own group, The Nighthawks of Harmony, and played as a sideman. He led a Whatley band that enrolled as the school band with full scholarships at the Alabama State Agricultural and Mechanical Institute for Negroes. Blount entered the teacher-training program and began his first formal classical piano study with Lula Hopkins Randall.

Blount left the school after one year. He told Bert Primack of *Down Beat* in 1978 that "since I was making such good marks, there wasn't no need being an intellectual if I couldn't do something that hadn't been done before, so I decided I would tackle the most difficult problem on the planet...finding out the real meaning of the Bible." Returning to Birmingham Blount formed a rehearsal band at his great-aunt's house and began experimenting with new musical forms, as well as with the first tape recorders and electronic keyboards.

At a Glance . . .

Born Herman Poole Blount on May 22, 1914, in Birmingham, AL; changed his name to Le Sony'r Ra, abbreviated as Sun Ra, 1952; died on May 30, 1993, in Birmingham, AL. *Education:* Alabama State A&M Institute for Negroes, teacher-training program, 1935. *Military Service:* conscientious objector, Civilian Public Service Camp, PA, 1941.

Career: jazz keyboardist, composer, arranger, band and orchestra leader, poet, Birmingham, AL, 1932-46, Chicago, IL, 1946-61, Montreal, Quebec, 1961, New York City, 1961-68, Philadelphia, PA, 1968-93; Sun Ra and His Arkestra (musical group), leader early 1950s-93; El Saturn Research, Chicago, IL, founder and principal, 1956-88; Ihnfiniti, Inc., founder and principal, 1967-?; University of California, Berkeley, instructor, 1971.

Memberships: Indiana University Black Music Center, Honorary Advisory Committee.

Selected awards: *Down Beat* magazine, numerous awards, Hall of Fame; National Endowment for the Arts, American Jazz Master Award, 1982; State of Alabama, Alabama Hall of Fame, 1988; City of Philadelphia, Liberty Bell citizenship award, 1990; Germantown Historical Society, Hall of Fame, 1998.

Reborn as Sun Ra

With the outbreak of World War II, Blount was drafted but claimed conscientious objector status. After being jailed briefly, he was sent to a Civilian Public Service Camp in Pennsylvania to do forestry work, but was quickly discharged due to his physical disabilities. He returned to Birmingham to teach and lead his band. Early in 1946 after the death of his great-aunt Blount left for Chicago.

For the next 15 years Blount worked in Chicago as a pianist, arranger, and composer. He played with Fletcher Henderson's band at the famous Club DeLisa and, after Henderson left in 1947, Blount spent the next five years as the rehearsal pianist and copyist for the DeLisa house band. He continued his musical experiments, moving further away from conventional jazz. He also studied ancient Egypt and taught himself hieroglyphics.

Together with Alton Abraham, his patron and later his business manager, Blount formed an informal group called Thmei Research. He preached his reinterpretations of black history and the Bible on Chicago street corners and wrote leaflets and broadsheets that were signed "Ra", "Sun," or "El." In 1952 Blount legally changed his name to Le Sony'r Ra, abbreviated as Sun Ra.

Formed the Arkestra

By the early 1950s Ra was building a rehearsal band that would eventually become the Arkestra. His goal was to rehearse for 10 years before performing. Although they were soon playing in clubs most nights, one musician estimated that they rehearsed 180 hours for every hour of performance. In his biography of Sun Ra, John F. Szwed wrote: "Rehearsals were exhausting but exhilarating ordeals, half musical instruction, the other half teaching, prognostication, and spiritual and practical advice...he nonetheless lectured them on personal discipline; on the history of black people and their role in the creation of civilization; on the use of music in changing the world; and on etymology and numerology, on astronomy and astrology...spiked with jokes, wordplay, biblical interpretation, and anecdotes about famous jazz musicians." Sun Ra fed and lodged his musicians and demanded abstinence from drugs and alcohol. Involvement with women was discouraged. Infractions were punished by taking away a solo.

Sun Ra took an unusual approach to marketing his music. In 1956 Sun Ra formed El Saturn Research. Between 1956 and 1988 Saturn released 71 albums, most of which were sold at concerts with hand-painted covers. Sun Ra designed increasingly outrageous costumes for the band and his choreography became more complex. Szwed quoted from a 1993 Robert L. Campbell interview with musician Lucious Randolph: "Sun Ra was going through a change: we started jumping around...not like jumping jacks, straight up and down; and it had to be in a specific place.... We started wearing beanies with propellers that lit up. Sun Ra wore a space hat with a light on it.... We did space chants." Szwed quoted from a 1968 Bert Vuijsje interview with Sun Ra: "Some people may not be able to accept this music or know what it is, but in fact they don't need to listen to the music; they just need to look at our clothes because I have incorporated music in them too."

In 1961 the Arkestra moved to New York City, settling into the "Sun Palace" in the East Village, which had become the new center for black creative arts. Sun Ra joined Amiri Baraka (LeRoi Jones) at the Black Arts Repertory Theater/School in Harlem and in 1966 the Arkestra provided the music for Baraka's play *A Black Mass*.

Filmed Space Is the Place

By 1965 Sun Ra's music had become wilder and more complex. The Arkestra's performances grew longer, sometimes lasting five or six hours. With Abraham and others, Sun Ra incorporated a business, Ihnfinity, Inc., in 1967. The company's purpose, as Szwed quoted from its statement of purpose, was "To perform spiritual-cosmic-intergalactic-infinity research works relative to worlds-dimensions-planes in galaxies and universes beyond the present now known used imagination of mankind, beyond the intergalactic central sun and works relative to spiritual and spiritual advancement of our presently known world."

In 1968 after being evicted for nonpayment of rent, Sun Ra moved his commune of musicians to Philadelphia into an East Germantown house owned by the father of alto saxophonist Marshall Allen. In 1971 the Arkestra briefly lived in an Oakland, California, house owned by the Black Panther Party while Sun Ra taught a course entitled "The Black Man in the Cosmos" at the University of California at Berkeley.

Sun Ra's 1974 film *Space Is the Place* became a cult classic. With its tacky special effects, the film paid homage to the science-fiction movies of the 1950s and 1960s. Sun Ra wrote all his own lines for the film, in which he returns to Earth to lead blacks to a utopian planet.

From 1973 on Sun Ra and the Arkestra toured constantly, playing concerts and festivals around the world. The performances became spectacles. Sun Ra added fire-eaters, muscle men, and midgets to his performances. His performances opened them with a single thunder drum, and other instruments joined in one-by-one. Singer June Tyson entered singing "Along Came Ra," who followed in with the dancers. Complex group improvisations preceded pop songs or swing arrangements, works by Henderson, Jelly Roll Morton, Duke Ellington, Thelonious Monk, even doo-wop and disco, Chopin and Rachmaninoff. Then came the space hymns such as "Love in Outer Space" or "The Satellites Are Spinning," accompanied by light shows and slides or films. However no two performances were ever the same and each composition might have 15 different arrangements. Soon other space bands such as George Clinton's Parliament-Funkadelic were modeling themselves after the Arkestra. However the Arkestra was perpetually broke and the musicians often found themselves stranded penniless at the end of a tour.

The Arkestra Lived On

By 1986 the Arkestra was sometimes giving classic big-band performances of standards, pop tunes, or Disney music, interspersed with intergalactic spectacles. Despite his reputation as reclusive and secretive, Sun Ra appeared on *Saturday Night Live,* the *Today Show,* and MTV. He spoke out against nuclear energy, the dangers of nuclear war, and pollution.

Sun Ra's music was opened to a new generation when Evidence Records began reissuing the Saturn singles

and albums, as well as previously unreleased recordings, in the early 1990s. Sun Ra's music became more widely appreciated and, during the following decade, his writings were republished.

Sun Ra continued to perform and record even after a 1990 stroke left him partially paralyzed. However with the Arkestra on tour, Sun Ra was sent to Birmingham to be cared for by his sister. There the hernia which had helped define his life was surgically corrected. Sun Ra died on May 30, 1993, after months in a Birmingham hospital. The Arkestra played at his funeral and the mourners left singing "Space is the Place." Honoring Sun Ra's dying request, the Arkestra continued under the direction of saxophonist John Gilmore until his death in 1995. As of 2007 the Sun Ra Arkestra was touring under Marshall Allen and rehearsing at the Sun Ra house in Philadelphia, which had become a music school. In addition to the music of the Sun Ra Arkestra, Sun Ra left a legacy that included approximately 200 albums, several films, and published poetry.

Selected works

Albums

Jazz by Sun Ra, Transition, 1956; as *Sun Song,* Delmark, 1993.
Super-Sonic Jazz, Saturn, 1956.
Jazz in Silhouette, Saturn, 1958.
The Heliocentric Worlds of Sun Ra, Vols. I and *II,* ESP-Disk, 1965.
The Magic City, Saturn, 1965.
Strange Strings, Thoth Intergalactic, 1966.
A Black Mass, Jihad, 1968.
Soundtrack to the Film "Space is the Place" (includes "The Satellites are Spinning," "Love in Outer Space") Blue Thumb, 1972.
Concert for the Comet Kohoutek, ESP, 1973.
Solo Piano, Vol. 1, Improvising Artists, 1977.
Lanquidity, Philly Jazz, 1978.
Nuclear War, Y Ra, 1982.
John Cage Meets Sun Ra, Meltdown, 1986.
Second Star to the Right (Salute to Walt Disney), Leo, 1989.
The Singles, Evidence, 1996.
Greatest Hits: Easy Listening For Intergalactic Travel, Evidence, 2000.
Live at Club Lingerie, Transparency, 2006.

Books

The Immeasurable Equation, Vol. I, Ihnfinity, Inc./ Saturn Research, 1972.
Extensions Out: The Immeasurable Equation, Vol. II, Ihnfinity, Inc./Saturn Research, 1972.
Sun Ra: The Immeasurable Equation. The Collected Poetry and Prose, BoD, 2006.
The Wisdom of Sun Ra: Sun Ra's Polemical Broadsheets and Streetcorner Leaflets, compiled and introduced by John Corbett, WhiteWalls, 2006.

Films

The Cry of Jazz, 1956.
Space Is the Place, 1974.
Sun Ra: A Joyful Noise, 1980.
The Magic Sun, 2005.

Sources

Books

Campbell, Robert L. and Christopher Trent, *The Earthly Recordings of Sun Ra,* Cadence Jazz, 2000.

Kapsalis, Terry, John Corbett, and Anthony Elms (Eds.), *Pathways to Unknown Worlds: Sun Ra, El Saturn and Chicago's Afro-Futurist Underground, 1954-68,* WhiteWalls, 2007.

Lock, Graham, *Blutopia: Visions of the Future and Revisions of the Past in the Work of Sun Ra, Duke Ellington, and Anthony Braxton,* Duke University Press, 1999.

Szwed, John F. *Space is the Place: The Life and Times of Sun Ra,* Pantheon, 1997.

Periodicals

African American Review, Summer 1995, pp. 253-255.

Austin American-Statesman (TX), October 10, 1996, p. 12.

Billboard, June 12, 1993, pp. 12-13; August 19, 2000, p. 78.

Down Beat, May 4, 1978, p. 15.

Guardian (London), October 22, 2005, p. 8.

Philadelphia Inquirer, December 28, 2005.

On-line

"Sun Ra—Space is the Place," *Perfect Sound Forever,* www.furious.com/perfect/sunra2.html (February 12, 2007).

—Margaret Alic

Jermain Taylor

1978—

Professional boxer

From the time he was a small boy helping to raise his younger sisters, Jermain Taylor has responded to challenges with a fierce determination to overcome them. Whether it was training himself to speak without a stutter or convincing his mother to allow him to learn to box, the soft-spoken Taylor simply set a goal and worked persistently to achieve it. In his boxing career, this has meant a relentless drive for success that has led him first to an Olympic bronze medal, then to a world middleweight championship in all four of the organizations that sanction professional boxing. The first Arkansas-born boxing champion, Taylor has become a hero in his home state and has repaid his home state fans with his very public loyalty and pride to be an Arkansan.

Taylor was born in Little Rock, Arkansas, on August 11, 1978. When he was five years old, his father abandoned the family, leaving Taylor's mother Carlois to raise her four children alone. While his mother worked as a nurse's assistant to support the family, Taylor learned to care for his three younger sisters, taking on an adult role in the family while still a child himself. As the family struggled financially, he also contributed by taking part-time jobs, such as working as a bus boy in a local restaurant.

During his boyhood, Taylor developed a severe stutter. The difficulty in speaking made social interactions stressful and embarrassing. In school he was frequently teased by his classmates, and speaking in front of the class became a humiliating and terrifying ordeal for him. Taylor responded to the harassment he received from other children with anger, frequently got into fights, and became isolated and withdrawn.

Boxed to Stay Out of Trouble

Fearing that Taylor was on his way to trouble in his teenage years, his uncle took him to a neighborhood boxing gym run by a brick mason named Ozell Nelson. Taylor's uncle had been a boxer and knew that the ring could provide a constructive and disciplined outlet for the anger and frustration felt by many young people of color growing up in urban poverty. However, when Taylor got into the ring to spar with Nelson's son, he was badly beaten. Though his mother was horrified to see Taylor's injuries and forbade him to box again, Taylor took his defeat as a challenge and was determined to go back. Nelson saw potential in the 13 year old. "He wasn't afraid and he was willing to take a punch," he told Brian Iole of *Review-Journal*, "I told him, 'Jermain, if you keep working, in six months, you'll destroy my son.'"

Between them, Taylor and Nelson convinced Carlois Taylor to relent and allow her son to learn to box. Nelson became not only Taylor's coach and teacher, but also his mentor and father figure. Taylor proved Nelson right by learning to win as they drove Nelson's old pickup truck to amateur bouts all over Arkansas. Under Nelson's instruction, Taylor developed a relentless jabbing style and powerful right and left hooks. He was so ferocious, even in practice, that a sparring partner gave him the nickname he would keep throughout his career, "Bad Intentions."

At a Glance . . .

Born on August 11, 1978, in Little Rock, AR; married Erica Smith, 2003; children: Nia.

Career: Olympic Boxing Team, 2000; professional boxer, 2001–; International Boxing Federation, middleweight champion, 2005; World Boxing Association, middleweight champion, 2005–; World Boxing Council, middleweight champion, 2005–; World Boxing Organization, middleweight champion, 2005–.

Selected awards: *Ring Magazine,* Most Improved Fighter Award, 2003; Arkansas Department of Human and Health Services Community Service Awards, Distinguished Citizen, 2006; Arkansas Broadcasters Association, Arkansan of the Year, 2006; Arkansas Sports Hall of Fame, 2007.

Addresses: *Agent*—c/o Andrew Meadors, Meadors Adams & Lee, Inc., P.O. Box 3456, Little Rock, AR 72203.

Soon Taylor began establishing an impressive record of wins as a light middleweight, both inside and outside the borders of his home state. In 1996, he graduated from McClellan Magnet High School in Little Rock and came to national attention as a boxer, winning the Under 19 National Championship, followed by two Police Athletic League (PAL) National Championships. In 1997, he placed second, and in 1998 he placed third in the U.S. Nationals. He earned a bronze medal in the 1998 Goodwill Games and, in 1998 and 1999, won the National Golden Gloves championship. The next year, he easily won a place on the U.S. Olympic boxing team.

Fought for World Championship

At the 2000 Olympics in Sydney, Australia, Taylor won the bronze medal in boxing, becoming the first Arkansas athlete to earn Olympic honors. However, he was disappointed to win only third place, and soon set his sights on another goal—to box professionally and become world champion. On January 27, 2001, Jermain Taylor, now a middleweight, fought his first professional bout, part of an evening billed as the "Night of the Olympians." He defeated veteran boxer Chris Walsh with a technical knockout (TKO).

As Taylor launched his professional boxing career, he assembled a crew of trusted support people, including his old friend and first coach Ozell Nelson and his Olympic boxing coach Patrick Burns. His promoter,

Lou DiBella, helped steer him through the matches that would advance his career and earn him the most money. A 2003 win against Marcos Primera, an experienced Venezuelan middleweight with a national reputation, finally earned Taylor recognition throughout the world of boxing.

Taylor directed his boxing career much as he executed his fights, with patience, persistence, and timing. With the help of his management team, he did not rush his fights, but planned his approach to the championship carefully, winning 22 bouts, 17 with knockouts. A February 19, 2005, TKO against Daniel Edouard earned him the right to fight champion Bernard Hopkins, who held all four possible world middleweight titles.

Taylor fought Hopkins on July 16, 2005 in Las Vegas. As he often did, he came on strong at the beginning, earning points in early rounds. The older Hopkins grew more aggressive towards the end of the match, but many observers believed he grew overconfident by the 12th round. Taylor won in a controversial split decision, with two judges giving the match to Taylor and one to Hopkins. Jermain Taylor had fulfilled his ambition to become world middleweight champion four times over: he was champion of the International Boxing Federation, the World Boxing Association, the World Boxing Council, and the World Boxing Organization.

Many fans and Hopkins himself complained about the close decision in the championship fight. Taylor had previously signed a contract agreeing to a rematch and he was eager to prove that he could keep his newly-won championships. Due to the complex rules of the organization, in order to fight an immediate rematch, he had to give up the International Boxing Federation title, and he agreed to do this. His next fight with Hopkins took place in Las Vegas on December 2, 2005. Once more, Taylor prevailed, this time with a unanimous decision from the judges.

An Arkansas Hero

Between 2005 and 2007, Taylor successfully defended his titles twice: June 17, 2006 against Ronald "Winky" Wright, and December 9, 2006 against Kassim Ouma. For his fight with Ouma, Taylor returned to Little Rock, billing the bout "Home for the Holidays" and sharing his success with his hometown fans.

Indeed, Taylor's loyalty to his home state and his Arkansan fans has become one of his trademarks. He has a razorback hog, the University of Arkansas mascot, embroidered on the back of his robe, the word Arkansas on his trunks, and traditionally ends any interview by yelling, "I love you Arkansas!" His pride in his Arkansas heritage, his polite and unassuming manner, and his relentless determination to win have made him beloved by his fans. He has been given keys to four

Arkansas cities, was named "Arkansan of the Year" in 2006, and was honored by state Governor Mike Huckabee, who named July 22, 2005, "Jermain Taylor Day." Taylor has responded to his fans' affection by remaining friendly and accessible and taking time to sign autographs. He has shared his childhood experiences with young people at a Little Rock stuttering clinic. His own stuttering had been largely conquered with speech therapy and hours of practicing in front of a mirror, just in time for the hundreds of press interviews required of the world middleweight champion.

In 2003, Taylor married another professional athlete, Erica Smith, who played basketball for the Women's National Basketball Association's Washington Mystics. On December 10, 2004, the two had a daughter, Nia. Though he has a demanding career with a busy travel schedule, Taylor is a devoted parent, determined to avoid the mistakes his own father made. The family lives on a large suburban estate near Little Rock.

Sources

Periodicals

Arkansas Business, August 8, 2005, pp. 1-3; November 21, 2005, pp. 26-7.
Jet, January 8, 2001, p. 49; August 8, 2005, p. 50; December 19, 2005, p. 62. *Sports Illustrated,* July 25, 2005, p. 87; December 12, 2005, p. 134; June 26, 2006, p. 93.

On-line

"Jermain Bad Intentions Taylor," *Jermain Taylor,* http://jermaintaylor.com/ (March 2, 2007).
"Jermain Taylor," *HBO,* www.hbo.com/boxing/fighters/taylor_jermain/bio.html (March 3, 2007).
"Jermain Taylor: Persistence Pays Off," *Review-Journal,* www.reviewjournal.com/lvrj_home/2005/Jul-13-Wed-2005/sports/26873472.html (March 3, 2007).
"Jermain Taylor," *Ringwork: Boxing's Best News and Gear,* www.ringwork.com/Bios.aspx?BioBoxer=58 (March 2, 2007).
"Larry Merchant Post Fight Interview: Jermain Taylor," *HBO,* www.hbo.com/boxing/events/2006/0617_taylor_wright/columns/merchant_interview_taylor.html (March 2, 2007).
"Stuttering Clinic Hosts Boxing Great Jermain Taylor," *Medical News of Arkansas,* http://arkansas.medicalnewsinc.com/news.php?viewStory=385 (March 3, 2007).
"Taylor Made: Jermain 'Bad Intentions' Taylor," *Everlast,* www.everlastboxing.com/articles/jermain-taylor-interview.html (March 3, 2007).

—Tina Gianoulis

Mose Tolliver

1915(?)-2006

Artist

Alabama folk artist Mose Tolliver spent the final 40 years of his life creating images that won him international renown. Tolliver, who signed his work Mose T., painted on simple wood boards, using ordinary house paint, and these "stylized figurative paintings were instrumental in gaining international recognition for Outsider artists of the American South," asserted David Ebony, a critic for *Art in America.* Of his career that began only after a work accident in his late 40s left him permanently disabled, Tolliver took a more easygoing view. "I ain't interested in no art," he once told an interviewer, according to *Atlanta Journal-Constitution* writer Howard Pousner. "I just like to do my pictures."

Tolliver was born in Pike Road, Alabama on July 4, but sources report varying dates for the year of his birth that range from 1915 to 1920. His parents were sharecroppers. Tolliver had limited formal schooling, and was diagnosed with dyslexia, the learning disability, later in life. His family moved to the Alabama state capital, Montgomery, where in 1930 he took a job with a local furniture company. For the next 35 years, he worked as a mover for McClendon Furniture to support the family of 12 children he had with his wife, Willie Mae, whom he married in 1941.

One day in 1965, Tolliver was sweeping the floor in the shipping department at McClendon's when a box of marble slid off a forklift and onto him. Both of his feet were crushed, and he spent the remainder of his life on crutches. A few years later, an executive at the com-

pany who was an amateur painter took him to an art exhibition, and encouraged Tolliver—who had painted tree stumps as a creative outlet during his teen years—to take some art classes. Tolliver decided to teach himself to paint instead, and by the mid-1970s the front lawn and porch of his Montgomery home were often decorated with his art, which he sold to passers-by for a dollar or two.

Tolliver painted on masonite and plywood panels that his sons cut for him to a size that he could place on his lap, and he used ordinary household paint to create images of animals, flowers, and fruit. Word soon spread of his talent and ever-growing collection of paintings—some days he finished as many as ten—and art aficionados began paying visits to his home. In 1981, he was offered a solo exhibition at the Montgomery Museum of Art, and the honor made him one of the first African-American folk artists of his generation to have a major museum show. That event, wrote Sue Steward, a journalist with London's *Guardian* newspaper, "registered both Tolliver and African-American folk art on mainstream radar, and, as a result, his home drew collectors from afar."

A year later, Tolliver's work was included in *Black Folk Art in America: 1930-1980* at the Corcoran Gallery of Art in Washington. The exhibition, which also toured several U.S. cities, was a landmark event for the recognition of black folk artists and Outsider Art in the mainstream art world. Sometimes called vernacular art, Outsider Art is a genre of art that comes from entirely

---

At a Glance . . .

Born on July 4, 1915 (some sources say 1919 or 1920) in Pike Road, AL; died of pneumonia, October 30, 2006, in Montgomery, AL; son of share-croppers; married Willie Mae 1941 (died 1992); children: 12.

Career: McClendon Furniture, mover, 1930-65; self-employed gardener, 1930-65; artist, 1973(?)–.

---

self-taught artists working "outside" the influences of prevailing artistic currents. Artists like Tolliver painted the world they knew, and scholars of the movement consider Outsider Art some of the clearest representations of a deep-seated human desire to depict the visual world.

Of the hundreds of images Tolliver painted, his rather risqué female figures became a favorite of collectors. These depicted a woman, with the characteristic over-sized head that was a hallmark of his portraits, with her legs extended over the head; sometimes the women sat atop scooters. His more conventional figurative works "were more challenging and edgy," noted Pousner in the *Atlanta Journal-Constitution*, with "characters frequently staring directly at viewers with ambiguously cool expressions and straight-lined lips. Yet around these haunting countenances often would swirl gorgeous patterns and dabs of paint, applied in wet-on-wet coats that added depth and variations of color."

Other works from Tolliver's bedroom studio—where paintings were stored under the bed and in a closet in which a collector once sprinkled with rat poison to make art-buying visits less fearful—had political overtones. His "Freedom Bus" paintings, for example, referenced the 1955 Montgomery bus boycott that was prompted by the arrest of civil rights hero Rosa Parks and the organized boycott that is considered the start of the civil rights movement in America. Tolliver's fellow blacks in Montgomery relied heavily on public transport for their jobs, but the bus company refused to bow to pressure to desegregate seating, and empty buses ran along the routes along for more than a year; Tolliver's paintings depicted these passenger-free buses.

Tolliver enjoyed immense recognition for his work during the last quarter-century of his life. His paintings were sold in galleries for five-figure sums, and he was honored with solo exhibitions at the Museum of American Folk Art in New York City and several group shows, including *Testimony: Vernacular Art of the African-American South,* which originated at the Kalamazoo Institute of Arts in Michigan and toured

several American cities. Collectors still came to his Montgomery home, and "depending on his level of inebriation and whether Willie Mae was around, they would leave with paintings as gifts or having paid realistic prices," wrote Steward in the *Guardian*. After Willie Mae died in the early 1990s, the "relatively wealthy local celebrity...let his passion for nightclubs and cars run free," Steward added.

Tolliver encouraged his children to pursue their own artistic talents, and his daughter Annie emerged as a respected folk artist in her own right. Other relatives sometimes painted images, which he signed himself with his distinctive "Mose T" signature with its reverse "s"—a rather worrisome issue for private collectors and museums, who wish for authentic works by an artist's hand. In his final years, he was disabled by a stroke and stopped painting altogether when his vision declined. He died of pneumonia on October 30, 2006, in Montgomery. He had been the last living artist among the 20 included in the *Black Folk Art in America* exhibition at the Corcoran Gallery back in 1982. "His death perhaps marks the end of an era that we may well look back on as a golden age of self-taught art," Susan Crawley, associate folk art curator at Atlanta's High Museum of Art, told the *Atlanta Journal-Constitution*. "Now that the market for work by self-taught artists is established, it is less and less likely that we will find artists like Mose Tolliver whose style was developed without any influence from the marketplace."

Selected works

Solo exhibitions

Montgomery Museum of Fine Art, Alabama, 1981.
Museum of American Folk Art, New York, NY, 1993.

Group exhibitions

Corcoran Gallery of Fine Art, Washington, D.C., 1982.
Anton Haardt Gallery, Montgomery, Alabama, 1992.
New Orleans Museum of Fine Art, 1994.
Testimony: Vernacular Art of the African-American South, Kalamazoo Institute of Arts, Kalamazoo, MI, 2000.

Collections

African American Museum, Dallas, TX.
Montgomery Museum of Fine Art, Montgomery, AL.
Museum of American Folk Art, New York, NY.
National Museum of American Art, Washington, DC.
Philadelphia College of Art, Philadelphia, PA.
High Museum of Art, Atlanta, GA.
Milwaukee Art Museum, Milwaukee, WI.
Smithsonian Institution, Washington, DC.

New Orleans Museum of Art, New Orleans, LA.
American Visionary Art Museum, Baltimore, MD.

Sources

Books

St. James Guide to Black Artists, St. James Press, 1997. Periodicals *Art in America,* January 2007, p. 174.

Atlanta Journal-Constitution, October 14, 1998, p. B2; August 13, 2006, p. K1; November 1, 2006), p. E1.
Guardian (London, England), December 12, 2006, p. 32.
New York Times, November 3, 2006, p. B8.

—Carol Brennan

Allen Toussaint

1938—

Musician, music producer

Allen Toussaint made a name for himself in the music industry with such diverse talents as songwriter, singer, pianist, arranger, composer, producer, studio head, and talent scout. In a career spanning four decades, the New Orleans native has penned classics such as "Working in the Coal Mine" and "Southern Nights" and produced chart-toppers including funk's "Right Place Wrong Time" and disco's "Lady Marmalade." He has worked with artists from Fats Domino to Paul Simon to Elvis Costello and recorded several albums showcasing his funky vocals and fiery piano playing. In 1998, he was inducted into the Rock and Roll Hall of Fame. Those who know him—fellow musicians, music junkies, musicologists—hail him as a musical treasure not only for his ability to mine the riches of R&B, blues, country, pop, and jazz to create soul-stirring, toe-tapping, feel-good music, but also for never forgetting his roots. Since the 1960s, Toussaint has a been a major force in creating, producing, and bringing the New Orleans sound to the national stage.

Found Early Calling as Piano Player

Allen Toussaint was born on January 14, 1938, in New Orleans, Louisiana. He first laid his eyes on a piano about six years later when an aunt sent an old upright to Toussaint's home for his sister. At that time, playing the piano was considered essential training for a young lady. Though his sister ended up in piano lessons, it was Toussaint who fell in love with the instrument. He told Keyboard. "For some reason, days [after the piano arrived], I understood the black keys and the white keys, and saw the structure." He learned to play by listening to records and picking out the melodies he heard. Nothing was off-limits and he avidly played anyone from Ray Charles to Liberace. However, he soon found his true inspiration in Professor Longhair, a New Orleans piano legend famous for his funky, unfettered style. "That just shocked me, to hear the piano go like that," Toussaint told Keyboard. "Of course, many of the old blues guitar players did that, but I was listening to piano players, and they usually stuck pretty straight to it. Professor Longhair had another reason and rhyme for everything. His language, his speed of operation, his mobility—everything was just totally different."

In 1955, after playing around town with local groups, 17-year-old Toussaint got his big break when he was asked to fill in for Huey "Piano" Smith in Earl King's band for a show in Alabama. Back in New Orleans, more high-profile appearances followed including several gigs at the legendary Dew Drop Inn. This led to a stint playing piano on several recording sessions for Fats Domino. In 1958, Toussaint recorded his first solo album, The Wild Sound of New Orleans, under the alias "Tousan" for RCA Records. The instrumental song "Java" was later re-released by Dixieland trumpeter Al Hirt who took the song to number one on the Billboard charts. Another early Toussaint instrumental, "Whipped Cream" became a Herb Alpert hit and then the theme music for the 1960s television show The Dating Game.

Toussaint moved behind the scenes in 1960 when he was hired to handle A&R (artist and repertoire) for New

At a Glance . . .

Born on January 14, 1938, in New Orleans, LA; children: Alison and Clarence "Reggie". *Military Service:* U.S. Army, 1963-65.

Career: Minit Records, A&R, New Orleans, LA, musician, songwriter, producer, 1960-63; Sansu Enterprises, New Orleans, LA, producer and co-founder, 1965-73; Sea Saint Recording Studios, New Orleans, LA, co-founder and producer, 1973–; NYNO Records, New Orleans, LA, and New York, NY, founder and producer, 1996–.

Memberships: New Orleans Artists Against Hunger and Homelessness, co-founder.

Awards: Rock and Roll Hall of Fame, inductee, 1998; Louisiana Lifetime Achievement Award, State of Louisiana; Louisiana Legend Award, Friends of Louisiana Public Broadcasting; Entertainer of the Year, Big Easy Awards; Walk of Fame, Tipitina's New Orleans.

Addresses: *Office—*NYNO Records, 1230 Avenue Of The Americas, New York, NY 10020; *Web—*www. nynorecords.com.

Orleans' Minit record label. Toussaint produced, wrote, arranged, and played piano on dozens of tracks released by a stable of top New Orleans talent including Ernie K-Doe, Irma Thomas, Jessie Hill, and Lee Dorsey. In 1961, Ernie K-Doe took Toussaint's "Mother-in-Law" to the top of the charts. In 1963, Toussaint's producing career was briefly interrupted when he was drafted into the Army. He served two years and by 1966 was back in New Orleans making music. He and buddy Marshall Sehorn formed the production company Sansu Enterprises and oversaw a string of hits for R&B singer Dorsey, including 1966's "Working in the Coal Mine," which Toussaint wrote, and which went to *Billboard's* number five spot, and which has been recorded over the years by groups as diverse as Devo and The Judds.

Became Synonymous with New Orleans Music

At Sansu, Toussaint began one of the most prolific partnerships of his career when he signed The Meters as the label's house band. The quartet has since become synonymous with the distinctive, bass-driven sound of New Orleans-style funk. Under Toussaint's

production, they released a string of early hits including "Sophisticated Cissy," "Cissy Strut," and "Ease Back." On working with them, Toussaint told *Keyboard,* "With The Meters, you'd open the door and let them in, and close the door... the stuff that they were writing and putting together was so good, you didn't want to touch it." Though the group followed Toussaint when he and Sehorn opened the state-of-the-art Sea Saint Studios in 1973, a few years later amid rumors of creative clashing, Toussaint and the group went their separate ways. Meanwhile, Toussaint hit music gold when the song he produced for Dr. John, "Right Place Wrong Time," exploded onto the 1973 charts, instantly becoming a funk classic. Two years later, the Toussaint touch struck again with "Lady Marmalade," a mega hit for disco group Labelle. The spectacular success of these and other Toussaint hits made the studio a Mecca for top musicians from Paul Simon to Paul McCartney.

Toussaint's work as a producer kept him from pursuing his own musical career. "With so many other great New Orleans artists around," he explained on the *NYNO Records* Web site, "I've felt obliged to put my own projects on the back burner." Nonetheless, he found time to release a string of critically acclaimed albums including *From a Whisper to a Scream, Love, Life and Faith,* and *Motion.* The title track of his 1975 release, *Southern Nights,* later became a chart-topping country hit for Glen Campbell and was ranked as the "The Most Performed Song of the Year" in 1977. Despite appearing on dozens of compilations and concerts, it was not until 1996 that Toussaint released his next album, *Connected.* A funky cocktail of New Orleans piano and R&B, the album was the first for Toussaint's new label NYNO Records. Two years later, Toussaint was inducted into the Rock and Roll Hall of Fame. He was honored as a non-performer which prompted musician Elvis Costello to tell *Esquire,* "I'd argue with that definition. If you listen to the records that Allen's produced...he's all over them. His piano is really, really dominant on most of those records. And as an arranger and songwriter, he's someone who knocks me out every time."

In August of 2005, Hurricane Katrina hit New Orleans. Toussaint had stayed home to ride out the storm, but after seeing the destruction the storm left in its wake, he walked through knee-high water, hopped a bus to Baton Rouge, and caught a plane to New York. His house and studio had been destroyed. Long a supporter of community causes in his hometown, Toussaint wasted no time participating in several concerts to benefit the hurricane victims. At one, he and Costello bonded and the result was 2007's *The River in Reverse.* The pair had worked together before, but the album marked a highpoint for both of their careers. A collection of 13 songs, ranging from poignant to bluesy to R&B, the album rings with an undercurrent of protest for the wrongs New Orleans has suffered and a shimmering hope that they can be made right. The album received a 2007 Grammy nomination for Best

Pop Vocal Album. Though it didn't win, *The River in Reverse* has proven that Toussaint, who has often been described as the embodiment of New Orleans music, is like the city and the music he loves so much, unforgettable and unstoppable.

Selected discography

Albums

The Wild Sounds of New Orleans, (as Tousan), RCA Victor, 1958.
Touissaint (From a Whisper to a Scream), Tiffany/Sceptor Records, 1971.
Life, Love and Faith, Warner Brothers/Reprise Records, 1972.
Southern Nights, Warner Brothers/Reprise Records, 1975.

Motion, Warner Brothers/Reprise Records, 1978.
Connected, NYNO Records, 1996.
The River in Reverse, with Elvis Costello, Verve Records, 2006.

Sources

Periodicals

Entertainment Weekly, June 9, 2006, p. 37.
Esquire, June 2006, p. 44.
Keyboard, November 1, 2006, p. 20.

On-line

"Allen Toussaint," *NYNO Records,* www.nynorecords.com/allen.shtml (February 11, 2007).

—Candace LaBalle

Walter J. Turnbull

1944–2007

Founder, executive director, singer

As the leader of the Boys Choir of Harlem, Walter Turnbull specialized not only in cultivating the love of music in children, but in turning lives around. His work with the choir—which toured the world, appeared on film soundtracks, and released recordings—as well as with the Choir Academy that choristers attend—helped to highlight what inner-city kids can achieve under the right circumstances. "We try to provide an entire environment that encourages discipline, hard work, and self-respect," he once told the *Los Angeles Times*. "Everything in terms of their academic and artistic work is based on mutual respect and hard work." Turnbull's own life story was an example of the rewards of discipline and faith. After overcoming numerous obstacles in his youth, he achieved advanced degrees in music, sang in operas around the world, and transformed the Harlem choir from a church-basement dream to an international success.

Found Joy in Music

Turnbull was born in 1944 in Greenville, Mississippi. His father, Jake Turnbull, Jr. "found inspiration in the bottom of a liquor bottle," Walter wrote in his autobiography *Lift Every Voice: Expecting the Most and Getting the Best from All of God's Children*. His parents thus split up early in Walter's life, and he and his siblings were raised by their mother, Lena. Her devout faith was a life-long inspiration to her son, and even when she abruptly switched her allegiance to the Seventh Day Adventist Church—one reason for her marriage's collapse—he was guided by her strong spirituality.

Reflecting back on his youth, Turnbull noted in his autobiography that "Music had begun to grab my heart." He took piano lessons and sang in the church choir, though the Seventh Day Adventists ironically took a hard line on music, considering most forms of popular music—even gospel—as "sinful." Young Turnbull found the hymns and other sacred music of the church satisfying. "It was very beautiful and moving when the congregation and the choir raised their voices," he recalled, and such memories no doubt played a part in his future vocation.

Equally influential, however, was the authority of Turnbull's choir director. "Miss Jones was tough," he remembered in *Lift Every Voice*. "She would do anything for you, but she was not afraid to ridicule you or your family if you messed up." While Miss Jones's heavy-handed approach often relied on tactics that might be considered abusive, she shepherded her singers to glory; they became the finest school choir in the state. And her young charges were so desperate for her affirmation that they would sometimes gather hours before school began so as to greet her with demonstrations of their progress.

Turnbull's successful years in the choir resulted in a number of scholarship offers. He elected to attend Mississippi's Tougaloo College, and soon excelled in the choir there. Chosen as a soloist during his freshman year—a rarity—he became increasingly interested in opera. During his junior year he made the decision to become an opera singer. He graduated cum laude from

At a Glance . . .

Born July 19, 1944, Greenville, MS, son of Jake Turnbull, Jr. and Lena Green; died on March 23, 2007, in New York, NY. *Education*: Tougaloo College, BA, 1966; Manhattan School of Music, MA, 1968, DM, 1984; attended Columbia University School of Business Institute for Non-Profit Management.

Career: Professional singer appearing in numerous operas and musical performances, 1960s–. Boys Choir of Harlem, founder and executive director, 1968-2006; New York Public Schools, teacher, 1970s-80s; New York City, taxi driver, 1970s-80s.

Awards: President Ronald Reagan, Volunteer Action Award, 1986; State of New York and National Association of Negro Musicians, William M. Sullivan Award; President Bill Clinton, National Medal of Arts, 1997; numerous honorary degrees.

Tougaloo, and, subsequently, attended summer sessions at Chatauqua, New York, which he described in his book as a "totally musical world."

Turnbull worked hard, cleaning toilets for a living, and was ultimately accepted for graduate study at the Manhattan School of Music. He characterized the institution as "small and a joy to attend. I knew on the first day that I had made the right choice." His choir experience stood him in good stead, since his knowledge in this area exceeded that of his classmates. He became an operatic apprentice at Lake George during the summers, and thanks to the occasional illnesses that befell members of the casts, sang in productions of such operas as *La Traviata* and *Die Zauberflote*. He ultimately earned both Master of Music and Doctor of Musical Arts degrees from the Manhattan School.

Started Choir to Help Children

Turnbull sought a place of worship in New York City and found it in Harlem's Ephesus Church. But it was while working as a singer at the Trinity Episcopalian Church in Connecticut that he became newly interested in boys choirs; the Trinity choir was noteworthy and suggested new possibilities to him. Soon he found himself proposing a boys choir at Ephesus; in 1968, 20 boys gathered in the Ephesus Church basement for the very first rehearsals. "The rehearsal wasn't memorable musically," he recalled in his memoir, "but I was satisfied that they could sing, and more important, that they wanted to do something other than hang out on the streets."

Turnbull's enthusiasm was infectious, and his dedication and relentless enforcement of discipline had dividends. The choir—with its repertoire of Bach chorales, Mozart pieces, hymns and some original songs by friends of Turnbull's—was soon the pride of the area, and other churches began requesting performances. Though Turnbull was able to raise funds to maintain the choir, he continued to struggle to gather the funds needed to keep it operating even after it achieved international fame years later.

Turnbull worked as a teacher in a public school, where he witnessed first-hand the lack of compassion and discipline that he worked so strenuously to correct as leader of the boys choir. He also observed a bitter teachers' strike, which affected not only life in the classrooms but life in the community. Increased racial strife and social tension took its toll on choir enrollment. Ultimately, Turnbull and his allies decided that the choir should incorporate as a nonprofit organization. His decision to call it the Boys Choir of Harlem, however, had a surprisingly negative impact on many members of the congregation; they wanted nothing to do with the name Harlem, since for them it suggested to them all the negative attributes of the inner city.

The choir found a new home at the Marcus Garvey Community Center, and Turnbull continued to pursue his dream of a world-class chorale that at once interpreted great classical works and maintained the "unique and warm" qualities of the African American singing style that pervaded pop, jazz, and gospel. In *Lift Every Voice* he explained, "No one had developed a standard for black voices. Though a certain amount of flexibility is afforded the voices of soloists, choral music styles are largely measured by a Western European yardstick. I needed to expand those limits and define our sound within the context of the black experience, where hallelujah has a different ring, a soul of its own." In the midst of this high-minded pursuit, however, he was still subject to harsh economic realities and had to drive a cab to supplement his income.

The choir moved to yet another headquarters, the Church of the Intercession, in 1975. Four years later, a girls choir was founded. And though his labor of love continued amassing fans, Turnbull also confronted—as he related in *Lift Every Voice*—the difficulty of trying "to reverse generations of urban pathologies." Many students were unable to handle the rigors of choir membership, sidetracked by the lure of the streets and unstable home lives. "I thought that I could save every child that I taught," he reflected ruefully. "I was naive."

Even so, the creation of a summer program and the choir's first European tour—which took them to Harlem's sister city, Haarlem, Holland—helped inspire Turnbull's students. A made-for-television movie was made from one child's experience on the tour, which encompassed performances in London and at Notre Dame cathedral in Paris. The choir's first national tour took place in 1983. Yet even audiences who cheered the chorale's mastery of difficult compositions had little inkling of the hard work required to keep students motivated. "Our effort is to help a child have a better lifestyle, to help navigate a very difficult period of growing up in a major urban environment," Turnbull told the *Los Angeles Times* at the time. "Many of these children—90 percent of them—are from single-parent homes. It is extremely important for them to be part of something positive and exciting."

Established Academy to Do More

Keeping it exciting required great patience from both students and teachers; Turnbull repeatedly emphasized that teachers who give up on students have themselves failed. Still, it became increasingly obvious that the choir needed its own school. "The defining moment was when we realized we needed to do more for the children's lives," he told the *Los Angeles Times*. "Were we really going to be able to have a school, or just a choir and only be concerned about singing and making music? We had to do more. We work with their families. That's what we do. It's more than a choir. Lives have been saved."

Thus, in 1986, the Choir Academy of Harlem was established. (That year Turnbull received the Volunteer Action Award from President Ronald Reagan.) Starting with elementary school students, the institution added grades as the students got older, graduating its first 12th grade class in 1996. In the Academy coursework the same exacting standards apply as in the choir itself, and students must achieve at least a B average in order to stay in the choir. Turnbull realized impressive results from his demanding regimen: 98 percent of his students went on to college, and many continued on to graduate study and careers in music. He wrote movingly in his book of watching a performance by a choir alumnus: "His artistry was excellent, and my chest almost exploded with pride."

Yet the challenges faced by the choir staff were immense. Paramount among them was helping kids overcome the taunts of their peers who might consider choir singing unmanly and helping them to learn to avoid solving problems with violence. "I'm sure they're teased by their friends," Turnbull once told the *Los Angeles Times*. "But how many kids can look at their friends and say, 'Have you ever been to Japan, to the Caribbean, or California?' Most kids in our city don't even have the chance to get out of the borough, even in a lifetime." Meanwhile, the choristers' families had to be educated, too, about the necessity for patience and steadfast involvement; some simply expected to deposit an unruly child and collect a disciplined one.

A 1989 story on the television news magazine *60 Minutes* told the choir's uplifting story so effectively that it drew in scores of new fans. When asked by the program's reporter Morley Safer how his kids were different from the victims of urban decay who dominated the news, Turnbull pointedly replied, "My kids are no different. They come from the same projects. They come from the same kinds of families. The difference is that there is somebody here willing to do something for them, and they are willing to do something. There is an opportunity here."

Turnbull's ensemble contributed to a number of film soundtracks, notably *Glory* (1989), *Jungle Fever* (1991), and *Malcolm X* (1992). The choir recorded its first full-length album in 1994, but had already made guest appearances on recordings by Quincy Jones, Mandy Patinkin, Kathleen Battle, and Alvin and the Chipmunks. 1994 also saw them perform a smash two-week run on Broadway headlining *The Boys Choir of Harlem and Friends, Live on Broadway.* Turnbull was even named one of the "15 Greatest Men on Earth" by *McCall's* magazine. By the 2000s, the choir had recorded 16 albums.

Enjoyed Students' Success

But for Turnbull, none of these laurels could compare to the testimony of his students, whose letters are collected at the end of *Lift Every Voice.* "In my eight years at the choir," reported student Jimmie K. Kimbrough, "Turnbull has been my mentor, a father and someone that you can talk to about anything. Like myself, a lot of members have single parents, and Dr. Turnbull fills that gap. He's on you 24-7 (24 hours and seven days a week) and always brings the best out of someone." Tyree Marcus referred to Turnbull as "a father figure, a role model, and someone to look up to. If it wasn't for him and some of the other teachers," he added, "I don't know what I'd be doing." Keron Nixon reported that Turnbull numbers among the many "caring people that are willing to improve the lives of people," but is "greater than all of them because he is like the hardest worker of them all, and I give my respects."

In 1995 Turnbull published *Lift Every Voice,* which he co-wrote with Howard Manly. *Emerge* magazine noted that while it takes a while "before Turnbull finds his path and follows it," the volume "leads the reader to an enchanting place." Marian Wright Edelman wrote in the *Los Angeles Times* that the book would help readers in an embattled era to "remember the strength of innocence." As Turnbull himself noted in the *Chicago Tribune,* "It's not just about the choir, it's about discipline. It's about feeling good about yourself—that's hope."

The success of his former students remained the greatest pride of Turnbull to the end of his life. Yet the last years before his death were difficult and left the future of his life's work in question. The trouble started in the late 1990s. Turnbull was criticized for "turning a deaf ear to repeated reports of allegation that a music instructor had sexually molested one of the male students," according to the *Los Angeles Times*. The academic rigor of the school also started to slip, with two-thirds of the school's seniors in peril of not graduating in 2006, according to the *New York Amsterdam News*. Furthermore, controversy over Turnbull's financial management of the Academy led to the eviction of the Choir from its rent-free Madison Avenue address and intense pressure from the New York State Department of Education to replace Turnbull as director. The school closed and the 50-member choir was maintained by mostly volunteer staff. Turnbull suffered a stroke in early 2007, and died from complications related to cancer on March 23, 2007, in New York.

Though the future of the Choir remained in peril at the time, Turnbull's admirable efforts on behalf of urban youth remained worthy of note. Throughout the troubles he had maintained his good reputation among his admirers. "Turnbull not only sought to reach out and make sure our young people were educated well, but also had cultural values—of our culture and the culture of others," Rev. Edward Johnson, vice chairman of the Harlem Congregations for Community Improvement told the *Los Angeles Times*. "Walter Turnbull made our children the ambassadors to the world," ex-Mayor David Dinkins said at Turnbull's memorial service, according to *The Black World Today*, "He did his best to keep them out of harm's way." Turnbull's brother Horace added that, though he had built a program that earned international acclaim, "Walter's life was not about the music. It was always about the children." The successes of those hundreds of children are Walter Turnbull's legacy.

Sources

Books

Turnbull, Walter, with Howard Manly, *Lift Every Voice: Expecting the Most and Getting the Best from All of God's Children*, Hyperion, 1995.

Periodicals

Buffalo News (NY), March 24, 2007, p. D5.
Chicago Tribune, March 19, 1989; January 27, 1995.
Essence, December 1995, p. 78.
Los Angeles Times, April 27, 1990, p. F1; December 3, 1995, p. 2; February 10, 1996, p. F1; January 20, 2004, p. A8; January 30, 2004, p. E1; January 30, 2006, p. A9; March 24, 2007, p. B11.
New York Amsterdam News, January 12-18, 2006, p. 1.

On-line

"Walter Turnbull Joins the Ancestors," *The Black World Today,* www.tbwt.org/index.php?option=content&task=view&id=900&Itemid=2 (April 11, 2007).

—Simon Glickman and Sara Pendergast

Courtney B. Vance

1960—

Actor

Courtney B. Vance has risen to become one of black Hollywood's most respected actors. After making a powerful Broadway debut in the Pulitzer Prize-winning drama *Fences* in 1987, Courtney B. Vance has enjoyed a busy career in theater, film, and television. His breakthrough film role came in the 1996 hit *The Preacher's Wife*; Vance, as a problem-plagued inner-city minister, shared the screen with Whitney Houston, Denzel Washington, and Gregory Hines. Yet he laid a firm foundation for his continuing career starting in 2001, with his five years portraying an assistant district attorney on *Law and Order: Criminal Intent*. A talented actor, Vance has furthered his career aspirations to include film production.

Focused on Education, Discipline

Vance was born in Detroit in 1960. His father, Conroy Vance, held a variety of occupations, including grocery store manager, and benefits administrator for the Chrysler Corporation. His mother, Leslie Vance, was a former librarian. The family included Vance's older sister, Cecilie. Detroit was a turbulent place during Vance's childhood years in the 1960s, as urban unrest broke out across the nation. "The Detroit riots went right by my house, the tanks and soldiers. I remember I went up to one of them to shake his hand and he turned his bayonet on me. I was about 8," Vance told Henry Sheehan of the *Orange County Register*.

Vance's parents had high expectations for their children. Television was forbidden and bedtime was early. "The focus had to stay on school," Vance told *People*.

Both sports and academics loomed large in Vance's youth. While attending the posh Detroit Country Day School on a scholarship, he was captain of the school's football, basketball, and track teams. Excellence as a scholar-athlete got him into Harvard University, where he majored in history. It was at Harvard that Vance acted on stage for the first time. As a lonely freshman, he joined a theatrical group in order to meet people. "After I got into it, I found I had an affinity for it. I felt I had found my gift," he told *People*.

By the time he graduated from Harvard in 1982, Vance had decided to pursue a career as an actor. "My parents were shocked, they said, 'What are you talking about, boy?'" Vance told the *Amsterdam News*. To further hone his acting skills, he attended the school of drama at Yale University, which has been the training ground for many prominent performers, including Meryl Streep, Sigourney Weaver, Holly Hunter, and Frances McDormand. While at Yale, Vance acted in the works of Shakespeare and other master playwrights. One modern classic in which he appeared was Lorraine Hansberry's *A Raisin in the Sun*. Mel Gussow of the *New York Times* said the 1983 Yale Repertory Theatre production revealed Hansberry's play as "an enduring work of contemporary theater," adding that the entire cast was "exceptional" from its leads Beah Richards, Mary Alice, and Delroy Lindo, to "three young Yale drama students who play representatives of a forthcoming generation."

Headed to Broadway with Fences

During his last months at Yale, Vance became involved with August Wilson's drama *Fences*, which was having its first staging at the Yale Repertory Theatre in the spring of 1985. Vance played the supporting role of Cory Maxson, a star high school athlete in 1950s Pittsburgh whose dreams of glory on the collegiate gridiron are crushed by his embittered father, Troy, a garbage collector and former player in the Negro baseball leagues. Troy refuses to let Cory accept a football scholarship and Cory ends up joining the Marines. Frank Rich of the *New York Times* had mixed feelings about *Fences* in its original incarnation, finding August Wilson's "extraordinary voice…too tidily fenced in by his generic dramatic carpentry." Rich called Vance's Cory "as formidable a foil as his etiolated role will allow."

Fences reached Broadway in March 1987, with most of its Yale cast intact, including Vance as Cory, James Earl Jones as the angry father Troy, and Mary Alice as Troy's long-suffering wife, Rose. John Simon of *New York* praised *Fences* as "dignified, understatedly eloquent, elegant…a work that tries to make sense of a predicament in which race is subsumed by humanity, in which black color is no more defining than the blue collar, and whose ultimate pigmentation is the black and blue of bruises—not so much on the body as on the soul." Simon added that "Courtney B. Vance gives a remarkably calibrated and compelling performance." Frank Rich thought *Fences* had improved since he first saw it at Yale two years earlier. Rich wrote in the *New York Times* that "it speaks of the power of the play—and of the cast assembled by the director Lloyd

Richards—that Mr. Jones's patriarch doesn't devour the rest of *Fences* so much as become the life force that at once nurtures and stunts the characters who share his blood…Courtney B. Vance is not only formidable in challenging Mr. Jones to a psychological (and sometimes physical) kill-or-be-killed battle for supremacy but also seems to grow into Troy's vocal timbre and visage by the final scene."

In 1988, Vance played Mercutio in *Romeo and Juliet* at off Broadway's Public Theater. The production, which featured Peter MacNichol and Cynthia Nixon as the title characters, was poorly received. "The one bravura performer who makes it worth seeing: Courtney B. Vance…in Mercutio's death scene, he literally spits out his 'plague a' both your houses' line—an electrifying reading that makes all that follows seem paler than it is," wrote David Blum in *New York*. Vance explained to Blum that he "simplified" his flamboyant performance during previews so by opening night he was not getting such extreme reactions, including big laughs, from audiences.

Earned Praise for Stage, Film Roles

Vance won the off-Broadway honor, the Obie Award, for his work in *My Children! My Africa!*, written and directed by the white South African playwright Athol Fugard. In the play, which was staged at the Perry Street Theatre in the winter of 1989-1990, Vance portrayed Thami, a black South African high school student teamed with a white female student, Isabel, for a nationwide literary quiz. They are coached by Thami's schoolmaster/mentor, Mr. M. The three characters represent differing views on how to deal with the racial problems in their country. Mr. M believes learning is the way to freedom; Isabel seeks openness and goodwill; Thami advocates more aggressive measures. Edith Oliver of *The New Yorker* said Vance "gives a remarkable performance as Thami; at one point, when Isabel invites Thami to her house to tea to meet her mother and father, the complexity of his silence and the turbulence of his emotions are as riveting as any of his speeches."

In 1990 Vance landed a high profile role on the New York stage in *Six Degrees of Separation* by John Guare. In this comedy-tinged drama, which opened at the Vivian Beaumont Theatre at Lincoln Center in November 1990, Vance played a young New York con man, calling himself Paul, who convinces a wealthy Upper East Side white couple that he is the son of actor Sidney Poitier. Paul moves in with the couple and vanishes as soon as his deception is found out. Stockard Channing co-starred with Vance as Ouisa Kittredge, the Manhattan matron whose life is changed by the event. Vance was not with the play when it began off-Broadway. Frank Rich of the *New York Times*, said that "Mr. Vance, younger than James McDaniel, his predecessor as Paul, proves a fine addition to the company…if Mr. Vance alters the chemistry of *Six*

Degrees slightly, it is to accentuate the bond that inexorably develops between Paul and Ouisa...The real if buried plot of *Six Degrees* deals not with Paul's fraudulent identity but with the authenticity of spirit that allows him and Ouisa to break through those degrees of separation that isolate people in a dehumanizing metropolis overpopulated by all kinds of phonies." Vance was somewhat cynical about his nomination for a Tony Award for best actor for his performance in *Six Degrees*. "This is political. I assume it was my turn to win. It's all political," he told the *Orange County Register*. Apparently, it wasn't Vance's turn to win. He lost the award to Nigel Hawthorne in *Shadowlands*. Vance was disappointed but not devastated when the role of Paul in the 1993 film version of *Six Degrees* went to Will "Fresh Prince" Smith.

Vance made his first feature film appearance in *Hamburger Hill* in 1987. A drama about battle-weary American troops trying to capture and defend territory in Vietnam, Vance was part of an ensemble cast including Dylan McDermott. "Courtney B. Vance is outstanding as a black medic. His death, in the embrace of two white soldiers to the chattering requiem of a helicopter, is one of the most powerful scenes in the film," wrote Jack Kroll of *Newsweek*.

Portrayed Characters with Dignity

One of Vance's most noteworthy film projects was a screen version of Mark Twain's novel *The Adventures of Huckleberry Finn*. Vance played the pivotal role of Jim, the runaway slave. "My feeling is that if Jim is not right, the movie will fall apart," Vance told Henry Sheehan of the *Orange County Register*. Vance joined the list of actors who have essayed the controversial role, including Rex Ingram, retired boxer Archie Moore, Paul Winfield, Brock Peters, and Samm-Art Williams. "It's so delicate, it's life walking through a minefield...One of the toeholds I found is dignity. That had to be one of the major concerns and major focuses of doing it," Vance explained to Sheehan about portraying Jim. Released in 1993, the Disney-produced film, which co-starred Elijah Wood as Huck, was generally panned by critics, many of whom thought Vance looked too young for the part of Jim.

Another important role in a little-seen film was Vance's portrayal of Bobby Seale in 1995's *Panther*. A dramatization of the history of the Black Panthers, the film was directed by Mario Van Peebles and written by Melvin Van Peebles. "I didn't know much about the Panthers. I went to prep school. But I really wanted to do this movie. With the Panthers so much has been under the carpet for years. With many of the people involved characterized as radicals, Communists and militants, it's time to actually look at them, to bring out the classified documents, to actually see what was the real story," Vance told the *Amsterdam News*. *Pan-*

ther, which also featured Kadeem Hardison, received many good reviews but failed at the box office.

The Preacher's Wife gave Vance the opportunity to appear in a lighthearted, big-budget screen project. Though given a mediocre reception by critics, the film was a crowd pleaser during the 1996 Christmas season. The Penny Marshall directed film, an urbanized remake of the 1947 movie *The Bishop's Wife*, told the story of a human-looking angel (Denzel Washington) sent to help out a beleaguered inner-city minister, Henry Biggs (Vance), and his wife, Julia (Whitney Houston). "The background of the story is familiar to me. The church is like the one I attended growing up in Detroit. I know people like Reverend Biggs and Julia. I felt I had something special to bring to the film," Vance told *Jet*. "Courtney Vance adds a serious note to the colorful ensemble as the conflicted Reverend Biggs," wrote Deborah Gregory in *Essence*.

Relied on Faith in Work, in Life

To prepare for the role of Reverend Biggs, Vance visited the Abyssinian Baptist Church in Harlem. He was baptized there in December 1995, shortly before production on the film began. "I'd been trying to find a spiritual outlet for awhile. When I got this role, it was an excuse to do what I've always wanted to do. I didn't have to get baptized to do this film, but I decided it was time," Vance told *Jet*. It was his religious faith that helped Vance cope with the 1990 suicide of his father. "It devastated our family," he told *People*.

On a happier note, Vance announced his engagement to actress Angela Bassett in December 1996. Vance and Bassett were longtime acquaintances who began a more serious relationship after running into each other at a play in Los Angeles in 1996. "We're like old friends who all of a sudden looked up and said, 'Hmmmm ...' Gradually it dawned on us that we like each other," Vance told *People*. The couple married in 1997, and had twin children in 2006 through a surrogate.

Vance prefers to play parts that mean something to him. He noted during a Sidewalk TV interview with Cindy Rhodes that he was drawn to stories with "drama." He found plenty in film and television, playing such roles as a police office in *Naked City*, a hitman in *Love and Action in Chicago*, and Martin Luther King in *Parting Waters*. His most prominent role in the new millennium came on the popular television series *Law and Order: Criminal Intent*, which he joined in 2001. His portrayal of an assistant district attorney on the series prompted theater and film professor Steven Vineberg wrote in the *New York Times* to praise Vance as a "gifted" actor. After five years on the show, Vance turned his attentions toward home. With his wife, he penned the first nonfiction book from Harlequin publishers, *Friends: A Love Story,* which chronicled the longtime friendship and then decade-long marriage of Bassett and Vance. The book published in time for Valentine's day in 2007, but Vance had no intentions of abandoning film for a writing career; he had already begun work producing a new film entitled *Erasure.*

Selected works

Plays

The Comedy of Errors, Shakespeare and Company, Lenox, MA, 1982.
A Raisin in the Sun, Yale Repertory Theatre, New Haven, CT, 1983.
Fences, Yale Repertory Theatre, 1985.
Fences, Goodman Theatre, Chicago, IL, 1986.
Fences, 46th Street Theatre, NY, 1987.
Romeo and Juliet, Public Theatre, NY, 1988.
My Children! My Africa!, Perry Street Theatre, NY, 1989-1990.
Six Degrees of Separation, Lincoln Center, NY, 1990-1991.

Films

Hamburger Hill, 1987.
Hunt for Red October, 1990.
In the Line of Duty: Street War, TV, 1992.
The Adventures of Huckleberry Finn, 1993.
Percy and Thunder, TV, 1993.
Race to Freedom: The Underground Railroad, TV, 1994.
The Affair, I and II, TV, 1995.
Dangerous Minds, 1995.
The Last Supper, 1995.
Panther, 1995.
The Piano Lesson, TV, 1995.
The Tuskegee Airmen, TV, 1995.
The Preacher's Wife, 1996.
The Boys Next Door, TV, 1996.
Twelve Angry Men, TV, 1997.
Naked City, TV, 1998.
Love and Action in Chicago, 1999.
Space Cowboys, 2000.
Whitewash: The Charles Brandley Story, 2002.

Television

Thirtysomething, 1989.
Picket Fences and *Law and Order,* 1995.
Law and Order: Criminal Intent, 2001-2006.

Sources

Periodicals

Amsterdam News (New York), May 6, 1995, p.23.
Cincinnati Call and Post, May 11, 1995, p.1B.
Ebony Man, January 1997, p. 36.
Essence, December 1996, p.40.
Jet, December 16, 1996, p.58-62; January 13, 1997, p.33.
Michigan Chronicle, May 9, 1995, p.1B.
Nation, December 17, 1990, p.783.
New York, April 6, 1987, p.92; May 30, 1988, p.24.
New York Beacon, May 10, 1995, p.35; October 11, 1995, p.35.
New York Times, November 9, 1983, p.C23; May 7, 1985, p.C17; March 27, 1987, p.C3; April 10, 1987, p.C1,4; May 24, 1988, p.C15; December 19, 1989, p.C19; November 9, 1990, p.C5; February 3, 1995, p.D16; August 11, 1995, p.C3; August 21, 1995, p.C11; April 5, 1996, p.C12; December 13, 1996, p.C8.
New Yorker, April 6, 1987, p.81; January 15, 1990, p.80.
Newsweek, April 6, 1987, p.70; September 14, 1987, p.83.
New York Times, March 3, 2002, p. 2.37.
Orange County Register, May 18, 1991, p.F2; April 1, 1993, p.F4; April 2, 1993, p.16; February 18, 1994, p.42; May 3, 1995, p.F5; August 11, 1995, p.6; October 13, 1995, p.83.
People, January 20, 1997, p.96-97.
Pride, November 30, 1995, p.68.
Voice, November 28, 1995, p.33.
Wall Street Journal, August 28, 1995, p.11; December 13, 1996, p.12.
Washington Post, February 4, 1995, p.D1; May 3, 1995, p.C1; August 11, 1995, p.F1; August 20, 1995 (television supplement), p.7; February 4, 1996, p.G1; April 27, 1996, p.C7; December 13, 1996, p.C1.
Weekly Journal, November 16, 1995, p.12.

On-line

"Courtney and Angela: Sweet Love," *Upscale Magazine,* www.upscalemagazine.com/portal/view.asp?chanID=2&id=98 (April 9, 2007). "Sidewalk TV: Angela Bassett and Courtney B. Vance," *Sidewalks Entertainment,* http://sidewalkstv.com/webclips/v/bassett-vance.html (April 9, 2007).

—By Mary Kalfatovic and Sara Pendergast

Mal Whitfield

1924—

Olympic athlete, sports ambassador

Mal Whitfield was one of the heroes of American track and field during the 1940s and 1950s, winning three gold medals, a silver, and a bronze in the 1948 and 1952 Olympic Games. His preferred discipline was the 800 meter race, the distance at which he dominated international athletics from 1946 to 1955, but he was also an outstanding 400 meter runner. Since retiring from the track, Whitfield has worked in Africa, training African athletes and becoming one of sport's most influential advocates. He has won many awards and has been inducted into the National Track and Field Hall of Fame, the Ohio State Sports Hall of Fame, the Olympic Hall of Fame, and the New York Sports Museum Hall of Fame.

Mal Whitfield was born Malvin Greston Whitfield on October 11, 1924, in Bay City, Texas. He moved with his family to Watts, Los Angeles while he was still a baby and by the age of 12 both his father and mother had died. From then on he was raised by his sister Betty. He left Thomas Jefferson High School in 1943 to join the Army Air Force (the branch of the military that became the U.S. Air Force.) He attended Ohio State University before a tour of duty in Korea which included 27 combat missions as a rear gunner. Among his many achievements is to have become the first American serviceman on active duty to win an Olympic gold medal.

Whitfield established himself as one of the all-time great American athletes at the 1948 London Olympics. Running swiftly on a sodden Olympic track, Whitfield took the lead in the closing 100 meters of the 800 meter race to set a new Olympic record of 1:49.2

minutes and win a gold medal. He followed up the victory with another gold medal as part of the USA's 4 x 400 meter relay team and a bronze in the individual 400 m, picking up the nickname "Marvelous Mal" along the way. Commenting at the time he said "the Olympic medal alone will keep a winner warm for a lifetime. Winning the gold for my country as well as for myself was a thrill I shall never forget!"

After the 1948 Games Whitfield went back to active service but was allowed to continue training. He won the National Collegiate Athletic Association (NCAA) title at 800 meters in 1948 and held the Amateur Athletic Union (AAU) title from 1949 to 1951. At the 1951 Pan American games in Buenos Aires, Argentina, he again won the 800 meter race, cementing his reputation as one of the finest runners of his generation at that distance. Yet Whitfield remained an Army Air Force serviceman and while serving in Korea he prepared for the 1952 Helsinki Olympics by training on the base's airstrip in between bombing missions. The Helsinki Games were to be his last, but he again won gold in the 800 meter race, equaling his 1948 Olympic record, and collecting a silver medal as part of the 4 x 400 meter relay team. He set a world 880-yard record of 1:49.2 in 1950 and again in 1952 when he brought it down to 1:48.6. An indication of Whitfield's stamina and ability came at a meet in Eskilstuna, Sweden, when he set a world record for the 1000 meter of 2:20.80 and then followed it up an hour later with a personal best of 4.62 in the 440 yards. In 1954 Whitfield became the first black athlete to win the James E.

At a Glance . . .

Born Malvin Greston Whitfield on October 11, 1924, in Bay City, Texas; children: four. *Education:* Ohio State University and Los Angeles State University, BS, 1956. *Military Service:* US Army Air Force, 1943-52.

Career: Track and field athlete, 1945-54; U.S. State Department, goodwill ambassador, 1955-89; Whitfield Foundation, founder, 1989–.

Memberships: Ohio State Alumni Sports Association, 1946; President's People-to-People Sports Committee, 1954; President's Physical Fitness Program, 1955; Los Angeles State University Alumni Sports Association, 1956; U.S. Track and Field Coaches Association; Veteran of Foreign Wars, US Legionnaire; US Foreign Service Association.

Awards: Olympic Gold Medals, for 800 m and 4x400 m, 1948, and for 800 m, 1952; Olympic Silver Medal, for 4x400 m, 1952; Olympic Bronze Medal, for 4x400 m, 1948; John E. Sullivan Award, 1954; Ohio State University Alumni Award; Helms World's Trophy; National Track and Field Hall of Fame, 1974; Ohio State University Sports Hall of Fame; Los Angeles State University Hall of Fame, 1986; Olympic Hall of Fame, 1988; New York Sports Museum Hall of Fame; National Track and Field Hall of Fame, 1992.

Addresses: *Office*—Whitfield Foundation, PO Box 10387, Washington, DC 20020-0687.

Sullivan Award as the outstanding American athlete of the year.

By the time he retired from competition in 1955 Whitfield had dominated the 800 meter distance for nine years, winning 66 of the 69 major middle-distance races in that time. But he had also been developing coaching skills, first in Japan as far back as the late 1940s, when he coached Japanese athletes in the run-up to the London Olympics and later in Africa, where he was to develop a second career as a sports ambassador.

Whitfield received an honorable discharge from the military in 1952 and in 1955 took up his first post for the Department of State, as Sports Goodwill Ambassador for the Educational Exchange program. He toured Europe and the Middle East before returning to Los Angeles State University to complete his BS degree. Then after four years advising African countries such as Liberia and Nigeria he joined the United States Foreign Service, where he served for the following 34 years. Over the course of his career he visited 132 countries advising and inspiring athletes and acting as a goodwill ambassador promoting international sports and the Olympic ideals.

To further promote sports and continue the work he had done as a sports ambassador for the United States, Whitfield started a foundation in 1989. The Whitfield Foundation provides scholarships, equipment, and training for young athletes and is responsible for founding the Senior Citizens' International Olympics. He also remained active in promoting and supporting athletes in Africa. Moreover, Whitfield donated one of his gold medals to be on display at the National Track Hall of Fame in 2002, so that "I could encourage young people by letting them see what a gold medal looks like" he said according to the *New York Times.*

Whitfield has received many honours besides his medals and records, including being inducted into the National Track and Field Hall of Fame in 1974 and the U.S. Olympic Hall of Fame in 1988. President Ronald Reagan said of Whitfield, as quoted on the Whitfield Foundation Web site: "Whether flying combat missions over Korea or winning Gold Medal after Gold Medal at the Olympics, or serving as an ambassador of goodwill, Mal Whitfield gave his all. This country is proud of you and grateful to you."

Selected works

Books

Learning to Run, East African Pub. House, 1967.

Sources

Periodicals

Jet, July 19, 2004, p. 10; August 8, 2005, p. 14; November 7, 2005, p. 8.
New York Times, February 24, 2002, p. B11.

On-line

"About Mal Whitfield," *Whitfield Foundation,* www.whitfieldfoundation.org/about/index.html (February 23, 2007).
"Mal (Marvelous Mal) Whitfield," *USATF Hall of Fame,* www.usatf.org/HallOfFame/TF/showBio.asp?HOFIDs=181 (February 23, 2007).
"U.S. Olympic Committee Class of 1988," *U.S. Olympic Committee,* www.usoc.org/62_12068.htm (February 23, 2007).

—Chris Routledge

Dudley Williams

1938—

Dancer

Dudley Williams has danced professionally for more than four decades. One of the primary dancers in the preeminent modern dance company with an African-American orientation—the Alvin Ailey American Dance Theater—Dudley Williams has been identified in the minds of dancegoers with several of Ailey's most famous dance solos, including a lengthy solo segment called "I Want to Be Ready," from Ailey's *Revelations* (1960). Williams's career has been remarkable as well for its longevity; joining the Ailey company in 1964, he did not retire until 2005, when he continued to dance in a unique company, oriented toward older dancers, that he co-founded. According to Susan Q. Stranahan of the AARP *Bulletin,* Williams has been "one of the longest active professional dancers anywhere."

Dudley Williams was born in New York City on August 18, 1938. He grew up in Harlem's East River housing projects, which, as he told Robert Tracy of *Dance Magazine,* were "a melting pot of everything." His father Ivan was a carpenter, his mother Austra a homemaker who cared for Williams's developmentally disabled younger sister and pushed her children toward the study of classical piano, buying a spinet instrument for the family's small apartment. But Williams gravitated toward dance even though he did not take to the tap dancing lessons to which he was sent at age six.

In between piano lessons, he and a friend would watch movie musicals and then go outside and try to imitate the routines on the street—while wearing roller skates. They were razzed by neighborhood youngsters, but "[i]t didn't bother me at all," Williams recalled to Robin Pogrebin of the *New York Times.* "I would say, 'So? So?' I was having a wonderful time. Small things for small minds." Williams enrolled at Manhattan's High School of Performing Arts after missing the school's music auditions but passing the dance test. His mother was initially angry about the switch, but both his parents eventually came around to support his dance career.

Williams graduated from the High School of the Performing Arts in 1958 and won a scholarship to the city's prestigious Juilliard School of music and dance. His career had already begun while he was in high school; he and a fellow student, Eleo Pomare, performed at community centers and even formed a small company called the Corybantes. His first appearance as a professional was in the musical *Show Boat,* performed at New York's Jones Beach in the summer of 1959. At Juilliard he alternated periods of dance classes with performances in the companies of Talley Beatty, Donald McKayle, and May O'Donnell, whom he cited as a special influence. "May coaxed us to go and see what was going on out there in the dance world, and that is why I love that woman to death," Williams told Tracy. She also arranged for Williams to join the studio of modern dance pioneer Martha Graham, and he became part of the Martha Graham Dance Company in 1961.

Alvin Ailey, who occasionally took classes with Graham during this period, was another influence. "I was absolutely in awe of Alvin because he was gay and such a beautiful man," Williams told Tracy. But, although Ailey had spotted Williams near the beginning of his career and even cast him in a small role, he thought of

At a Glance . . .

Born on August 18, 1938, in New York, NY; son of Ivan (a carpenter) and Austra Williams. *Education:* High School of the Performing Arts, New York, 1958; attended Juilliard School, New York; studied dance in studio of Martha Graham.

Career: Dancer, 1959–; Martha Graham Dance Company, New York, dancer, 1961; Alvin Ailey American Dance Theater, dancer, 1963-2005; Paradigm Dance Company, co-founder (with Gus Solomons Jr. and Carmen de Lavallade), 2005–.

Awards: *Dance Magazine* Award, 1997.

Addresses: *Booking Agent*—c/o Ken Maldonado, Zia Artists, 506 Fort Washington Avenue, 1H, New York, NY 10033; *Web*—www.paradigm-nyc.org.

Williams as a dancer more oriented toward ballet and turned him down several times when Williams applied to audition with the Ailey company. Williams's chance came in 1963, when Ailey needed a replacement dancer for an upcoming tour of Europe. Williams enthusiastically signed on and was flabbergasted when Ailey, in Paris, told the young dancer that he was going to learn *Reflections in D,* one of the signature dances usually performed by Ailey himself.

Always troubled by stage fright (he told the *New Yorker* that "I sweat in the palms of my hands—I wish the theatre would burn down") Williams nevertheless not only survived that first performance but also made *Reflections in D* his own after Ailey retired from performing. He continued to perform with the Graham company for several more years, but by 1968 he had devoted himself completely to Ailey. "I chose Alvin because his works were more human," he told Pogrebin. "Hercules I wasn't." In the late 1960s Williams suffered a knee injury; told by doctors that he would never walk again, he not only walked but danced on stage within two weeks. He credited Pilates exercises for his recovery and continued to do them through his entire career.

Williams had a peculiar position within the Alvin Ailey American Dance Theater in that he always danced solo. "I don't partner," he told Ailey early in his career, and as a result "I never got a lot to dance because he always had to create something special for me. I didn't grow up picking up women—that wasn't my cup of tea. I was a dancer." Ailey not only assented to this prefer-

ence but also developed a memorable series of solos for Williams. Among them were the role of Lazarus rising from the dead in *Mary Lou's Mass* (1971, to a religious piece by jazz composer Mary Lou Williams) and that of South African anti-apartheid activist Nelson Mandela in 1986's *Survivors.* His most famous Ailey dance, however, was another that he took over and made his own: in "I Want to Be Ready," from *Revelations,* he danced to a spiritual about laying sin aside. "Williams's specialty is contained emotion, and that was perfect for this soul-testing dance," noted the *New Yorker.*

Dance is a physically punishing profession that frequently forces its practitioners to end their careers in their 30s or 40s, but Williams's slender, five-feet-eight, 130-pound frame seemed indestructible. He continued to dance with the Ailey company after Ailey's death in 1989, and eventually he and the new director, Ailey protégé Judith Jamison, were the only remaining veterans of the company's early days. When he retired in 2005 after 44 years of dancing, he knew of no other dancer in the United States with a longer career, and he was certainly among the most durable dancers in the entire world. A special Ailey company concert, performed at the end of 2004 to a packed City Center auditorium, paid tribute to his contributions.

Williams's retirement from the company did not mark the end of his dance career. With dancers Gus Solomons Jr. and Carmen de Lavallade, both over 60, he formed Paradigm Dance Company. The company grew, he told Stranahan, as "an accident" after a one-time appearance by the three on a program mounted by a company called Dancers Over Forty, but the concept took hold. *New York Times* critic Jennifer Dunning noted after a 2006 Paradigm performance at New York's Symphony Space that the company "sought to use the seasoned gifts of mature dance artists who may no longer be able to whip off a double pirouette but know nuance like nobody's business." Williams remained active as a teacher as well, and he had lost none of his enthusiasm for dancing. "Good Lord. I love it," he told Stranahan. "I absolutely love it. I think God gave me a talent and if I don't use it, shame on me. That's the way I look at it. I love dancing, I love performing, and I can still do it, why not? Why not?"

Selected works

Dances

Congo Tango Palace, Talley Beatty.
Love Songs, Alvin Ailey.
Mary Lou's Mass, Alvin Ailey.
Reflections in D, Alvin Ailey.
Revelations, Alvin Ailey (includes Williams solo "I Want to Be Ready").
A Song for You, Alvin Ailey.

Survivors, Alvin Ailey.
Three Black Kings, Alvin Ailey.

Sources

Books

International Dictionary of Modern Dance, St. James, 1998.

Periodicals

Dance Magazine, December 1997.
New Yorker, May 9, 2005, p. 34.
New York Times, December 13, 1984, p. C22; December 22, 2003, p. E1; December 31, 2004, p. E2; April 22, 2006, p. B11.

On-line

"Dudley Williams, A Life Spent Onstage," *National Public Radio,* www.npr.org/templates/story/story.php?storyId=4249143 (March 20, 2007).
"Free to Dance: Dudley Williams," *Public Broadcasting System,* www.pbs.org/wnet/freetodance/biographies/dwilliams.htm. (March 13, 2007).
"I Can Still Do It," AARP *Bulletin,* www.aarp.org/bulletin/yourlife/i_can_still_do_it.html (March 13, 2007).

—James M. Manheim

Jackie Wilson

1934-1984

Vocalist

Jackie Wilson was "a gifted singer of considerable range and an athletic showman who commanded a stage like few before or since," according to his Rock and Roll Hall of Fame biography. Wilson was a key figure of the late 1950s and early 1960s in American popular music, the singer of "Lonely Teardrops" and other numbers that have won places for decades in the playlists of oldies radio stations. His chilling long falsettos exerted an influence on the vocal acrobatics of the soul singers who followed him. Wilson enjoyed only intermittent success dur-

Wilson, Jackie, photograph. Frank Driggs Collection/Getty Images.

ing his own career, sometimes failing to anticipate new trends in African-American music, but a busy schedule of reissues that followed his untimely death in 1984 has attested to his influence and enduring popularity.

Jack Leroy Wilson Jr. was born in Detroit on June 9, 1934. His parents, Jack and Eliza Wilson, had come to Detroit from Mississippi, and he grew up in Highland Park, Michigan, an auto-manufacturing enclave surrounded by the city of Detroit. By age six he was singing, and even before reaching adolescence he found that he could fit in with musicians singing blues or gospel music in the streets and storefront churches of Detroit. At 12 he joined a group called the Ever Ready

Gospel Singers.

The influence of gospel did not keep Wilson out of trouble, however (and as an adult he converted to the Jewish faith). He attended Highland Park High School but kept missing class and eventually dropped out. Sent to the Lansing Correctional Institute, he took boxing lessons and fought in Golden Gloves matches back in Detroit. He considered becoming a professional boxer. After marrying Freda Hood as a 16-year-old in 1951 and starting a family, he tried to buckle down to work at a Ford Motor Company foundry but lasted only two weeks. From then on, his income came exclusively from performing music.

Fortunately, Wilson quickly made his mark on the music scene. He started performing in nightclubs at age 15 and worked with a group called the Royals that also included future Four Tops lead vocalist Levi Stubbs. Wilson's career took a step up in 1953 when he won an audition to join the rhythm-and-blues vocal group Billy Ward and the Dominoes after one of its members joined the military. He got another break when the group's lead singer, Clyde McPhatter, departed to form the Drifters; Wilson was chosen as his replacement. Although the Dominoes did not match the commercial success they had experienced in the early 1950s with such songs as "Sixty Minute Man," Wilson's talents received national exposure. The Dominoes appeared in Las Vegas, and a young Elvis Presley became a lifelong admirer of Wilson after hearing him cover his hit "Don't Be Cruel."

After the Dominoes scored a pop top-ten hit with "St. Therese of the Roses" in 1956, Wilson decided to launch a solo career. He was signed to the Brunswick label by executive Nat Tarnopol, who became his manager. In Detroit, Wilson worked at rounding up new material. He met the young songwriters Berry Gordy Jr. and Roquel Davis at the Flame Show Bar, a nightspot that incubated much of the talent later showcased on the Motown label, and the pair gave him the novelty number "Reet Petite." Wilson released the song as a single in September of 1957 and scored a moderate hit in Britain as well as the United States.

The following year Wilson reached the pop top ten with another Gordy composition, "Lonely Teardrops"; the single was a major hit in African-American markets and became the vocalist's first million-seller. Through the late 1950s, Wilson was a major chart presence with such singles as "To Be Loved," "That's Why (I Love You So)," "Doggin' Around," and "I'll Be Satisfied," many of them composed or co-composed by Gordy. Part of his success was due to his ability to appeal equally to black and white audiences, and part of it was reportedly due to the spectacular choreography and raw energy of his stage shows; fans dubbed him "Mr. Excitement." Unfortunately, Wilson was active during the period just before the invention of videotape, and few visual records of his performances exist.

Gordy used some of the money he earned from the hits he wrote for Wilson to launch the Motown label, and Wilson's fusion of smooth pop styles with African-

American idioms influenced many of that label's early successes. In retrospect, Wilson would likely have been a perfect fit at Motown, but he remained at Brunswick and was steered toward popular styles by Tarnopol. Many of his recordings of the 1960s featured string stylings by longtime Decca-label arranger Dick Jacobs, and he appeared at such pop clubs as New York's Copacabana and at various Las Vegas hotels. With African-American music moving in a rootsier direction in both Detroit and Memphis, Wilson hit top chart levels only intermittently in the early 1960s. He scored major hits with "Night" (1960), the upbeat "Baby Workout" (1963), and the socially relevant "No Pity (In the Naked City)" (1965). He released a flood of albums on the Brunswick label, but few sold in large numbers.

Nevertheless, Williams remained a strong concert draw. Tension surrounded his performances in the segregated South, and he was beaten by New Orleans police after a disagreement on one occasion. Female fans flocked to his shows; women, it is said, would rip his clothes off after he jumped into a crowd, and one of them shot and wounded him in 1961; a romantic triangle may have been involved. In the late 1960s Wilson enjoyed a string of hits recorded with Chicago soul producer Carl Davis, including "Whispers" (1966) and the top-ten hit "Higher and Higher." By 1970, however, his releases languished in the lower reaches of *Billboard* magazine's black-music charts. In all he landed 24 recordings in the magazine's top 40.

Wilson toured with the Dick Clark Revue and performed at other oldies-oriented venues in the early 1970s. Headlining the Dick Clark show in Cherry Hill, New Jersey, on September 25, 1975, Wilson was stricken by a massive heart attack. He hit his head while falling, and the resultant brain damage left him in a coma from which he never awakened. Prior to his own death in 1977, Elvis Presley helped pay Wilson's medical bills. Wilson died in Mount Holly, New Jersey, on January 19, 1984. In 1987 he was inducted into the Rock and Roll Hall of Fame. An 11-disc collection of Wilson's recordings was issued in 1999 by the Edsel label in Britain, where the singer had always maintained strong popularity, and by the early 2000s he was recognized as a classic figure of rhythm and blues. A play about Wilson's life, *The Jackie Wilson Story (My Heart Is Crying…Crying),* was written by Jackie Taylor and staged by the Black Ensemble Theater of Chicago.

Selected works

Singles (on Brunswick label)

"Reet Petite," 1957.
"To Be Loved," 1958.
"We Have Love," 1958.
"Lonely Teardrops," 1958.
"That's Why," 1959.
"I'll Be Satisfied," 1959.

"You Better Know It," 1959.
"Talk That Talk," 1959.
"Night," 1960.
"Doggin' Around," 1960.
"All My Love," 1960.
"A Woman, A Lover, A Friend," 1960.
"Alone At Last," 1960.
"Am I the Man?" 1960.
"My Empty Arms," 1961.
"Please Tell Me Why," 1961.
"I'm Comin' On Back to You," 1961.
"Years from Now," 1961.
"The Way I Am," 1961.
"The Greatest Hurt," 1961.
"Hearts," 1962.
"I Just Can't Help It," 1962.
"Baby Workout," 1963.
"Shake, Shake, Shake," 1963.
"Baby Get It," 1963.
"Squeeze Her—Tease Her," 1964.
"Danny Boy," 1965.
"No Pity (In the Naked City)," 1965.
"Whispers," 1966.
"I Don't Want To Lose You," 1967.
"(Your Love Keeps Lifting Me) Higher and Higher," 1967.
"Since You Showed Me How To Be Happy," 1967.
"I Get the Sweetest Feeling," 1968.
"For Once in My Life," 1968.
"Let This Be a Letter (To My Baby)," 1970.
"This Love Is Real," 1970.
"Love Is Funny That Way," 1971.

Albums

Lonely Teardrops, Brunswick, 1958 (reissued Diablo, 1998).
Doggin' Around, Brunswick, 1959.
So Much, Brunswick, 1960 (reissued Diablo, 1999).
Jackie Wilson Sings the Blues, Brunswick, 1960 (reissued Diablo, 1999).
My Golden Favorites, Brunswick, 1960.
A Woman, A Lover, A Friend, Brunswick, 1960 (reissued Edsel, 1999).
You Ain't Heard Nothin' Yet, Brunswick, 1961.
By Special Request, Brunswick, 1961.
Body & Soul, Brunswick, 1962 (reissued Edsel, 1999).
Jackie Wilson at the Copa, Brunswick, 1962 (reissued Edsel, 1999).
Baby Workout, Brunswick, 1962 (reissued Edsel, 1999).

Shake a Hand, Brunswick, 1962 (reissued Diablo, 1999).
Somethin' Else!, Brunswick, 1964 (reissued Edsel, 1999).
Spotlight, Brunswick, 1965.
Soul Galore, Brunswick, 1966 (reissued Diablo, 1999).
Whispers, Brunswick, 1966 (reissued Diablo, 1999).
Higher and Higher, Brunswick, 1967 (reissued Diablo, 1999).
I Get the Sweetest Feeling, Brunswick, 1968 (reissued Edsel, 1999).
It's All a Part of Love, Brunswick, 1971.
You Got Me Walking, Brunswick, 1973 (reissued Edsel, 1999).
Nowstalgia, Brunswick, 1974.
Jackie Wilson's Greatest Hits, Brunswick, 1973.
This Love Is Real, Brunswick, 1973 (reissued Edsel, 1999).
Nobody But You, Brunswick, 1977 (reissued Edsel, 1999).
The Very Best of Jackie Wilson, Rhino, 1994.
The Jackie Wilson Story (4 vols.), Charly, 1999.
Best of Jackie Wilson (2 vols.), Collectables, 2003.
The Essential Masters with Billy Ward and His Dominoes, Varese Sarabande, 2004.
Jackie Wilson Live, Collectables, 2006.
History of Jackie Wilson (3 vols.), Edsel, 2006.

Sources

Books

Contemporary Musicians, vol. 3, Gale, 1990.

Periodicals

Times (London, England), September 14, 1999, p. 39.
Winston-Salem Journal (Winston-Salem, NC), July 31, 2001, p. B6.

On-line

"Jackie Wilson," *All Music Guide,* www.allmusic.com (March 17, 2007).
"Jackie Wilson," *Rock and Roll Hall of Fame,* www.rockhall.com (March 17, 2007).
Jackie Wilson—Mr. Excitement, www.jackiewilson.net (March 17, 2007).

—James M. Manheim

Bobby Womack

1944—

Vocalist, songwriter

With a career stretching back to the early 1960s and forward into the 2000s, vocalist Bobby Womack has been a mainstay of the classic soul sound, a performer whose distinctively gritty style and instinct for strong material have never deserted him through numerous ups and downs in his personal life and professional career. The composer and creator of several classic rock hits, Womack has received critical recognition of his talents but never the superstar status those talents would merit. "His is one of the great voices," noted Phil Johnson of London's *Independent* newspaper. "It influenced the young Mick Jagger of the Rolling Stones—whose first Number One record Womack wrote—and also Rod Stewart, who made a rather better attempt at copying it."

Five Blind Boys Visited Home

Bobby Dwayne Womack was born in Cleveland, Ohio, on March 4, 1944, the one son of steelworker and part-time gospel singer Friendly Womack. The elder Womack organized Bobby and his brothers, Cecil, Curtis, Harris, and Friendly Jr., into a quintet called the Womack Brothers. Despite the extreme youth of some of its members, the group quickly gained a reputation beyond Cleveland, touring as an opening act with such performers as the Five Blind Boys of Alabama, who often dropped by the Womack household for some home cooking from Womack's mother, Naomi, when they were in Cleveland. In 1953 the group opened for the leading gospel group of the day, the Soul Stirrers,

and a few years later Roscoe Robinson of the Blind Boys suggested to the lead singer of that group, Sam Cooke, that he sign the brothers to his new label, SAR.

At the time the Womack Brothers believed that performers who sang secular music were going to hell, and they told Cooke so. Cooke, who was planning his successful move in a secular direction, suggested a compromise, as Womack recalled to Charlie Melvin of England's *Birmingham Post*: "I'll tell you what, if you cut a gospel record and it don't hit, would y'all cut me a pop song?" A few Womack Brothers gospel releases met with little success, and the brothers kept up their end of the bargain and renamed themselves the Valentinos. Friendly Womack Sr. exiled them from the house after this decision, and Bobby Womack remained estranged from his father until just before Friendly Womack's death in 1981.

In 1960 Cooke wired the group $3,000 to buy a new car and drive to Los Angeles, but, Womack recalled to John Soeder of the Cleveland *Plain Dealer,* "I noticed that all of the pimps and gangsters and hustlers drove Cadillacs. So instead of getting a new car like Sam told us, I bought a used Cadillac." The decision was a bad one. "It took us three weeks to get to California. The tires blew out, the engine went out, the gas tank had a hole in it, and the windshield wipers, the first time we put them on, they went clean across, looky yonder. We never saw 'em again." The brothers drove while leaning out the window to avoid the exhaust fumes that accumulated in the passenger compartment.

At a Glance . . .

Born on March 4, 1944, in Cleveland, OH; son of Friendly Womack (a steelworker and gospel singer) and Naomi Womack; married Barbara Cooke, 1964 (divorced 1970); married and divorced a second time; children: Truth, Vincent. *Education:* Attended East Tech High School, Cleveland, OH.

Career: Womack Brothers, gospel group member (with siblings), early 1950s; Valentinos (new name for Womack Brothers when group turned to secular music), late 1950s-60s; Memphis, TN, and Muscle Shoals, AL, songwriter and session guitarist, mid-1960s; solo artist, 1968–; United Artists, label artist, 1971-75; Columbia, label artist, 1976-78; Arista, label artist, 1979-80; Beverly Glen, label artist, 1981-84; MCA, label artist, 1985-?.**Addresses:** *Agent*—Universal Attractions, 145 West 57th Street 15th Floor, New York, NY 10019.

Rolling Stones Recorded Song

When Womack arrived in Los Angeles, however, he was hired by Cooke as a guitarist, and the Valentinos began drawing good nightclub crowds. They recorded several moderately successful singles, two of which, "It's All Over Now" and "Lookin' for a Love," later became major rock hits for the Rolling Stones and the J. Geils Band, respectively. At first, Womack recalled to Melvin, he resisted the idea of giving "It's All Over Now" to the Rolling Stones, telling Cooke, "Man, I could care less. Let them get their own song, this is our record." He changed his mind when the Rolling Stones' version went to Number One in the United Kingdom and Cooke began bringing him royalty checks. Whatever problems he faced later in his career, financial instability was rarely among them (although he did hit a low point in the early 1990s). "It's All Over Now" made Womack a rich man.

That was fortunate, because Womack's expanding career soon took a nosedive. He married Barbara Cooke, Sam Cooke's widow, after Cooke's death in a 1964 shooting incident, and audiences assumed he was trying to take advantage of Cooke's death. Womack maintained that he was trying to support a troubled woman who had been close to his mentor (the marriage ended in divorce in 1970), but buyers ignored some fine recordings he and the Valentinos made for Chicago's Chess label and its Checker subsidiary. Womack headed south and found work as a studio guitarist in Memphis, Tennessee, and Muscle Shoals, Alabama, with soul producer Chips Moman. He backed such artists as Aretha Franklin and Joe Tex as a guitarist, and

he also flourished as a songwriter; 17 of his compositions, including "Ninety-Nine and a Half (Won't Do)," were recorded by Memphis soul vocalist Wilson Pickett.

These successes rehabilitated Womack's image, and he decided to relaunch his solo career. In 1968 he had a minor hit on the Minit label with the Moman-produced "What Is This," but most of his strongest original material had been given to Pickett. As a result, Womack turned to a procedure that became one of his trademarks—thoroughly reimagined cover versions of rock and pop songs. His recording of the Mamas and the Papas hit "California Dreamin'" cracked *Billboard* magazine's black singles top 20 (and was revived for a Saab auto commercial in Britain in 2004), and several more successful singles followed as Womack formed a songwriting partnership with Moman's studio assistant Darryl Carter.

As Minit and then its parent Liberty were absorbed into the large United Artists label, Womack's career achieved a higher profile. The albums he recorded for United Artists in the early and middle 1970s are considered classics of soul music. *Communication* (1971) spawned the hit "That's the Way I Feel About 'Cha," and the black music chart-topping "Woman's Gotta Have It" came from *Understanding* (1972). "Harry Hippie" (1972) was a tribute to Womack's brother Harris, who had been murdered by a jealous girlfriend. In 1974 Womack enjoyed his biggest hit with a remake of "Lookin' for a Love," originally modeled on the country gospel song "Couldn't Hear Nobody Pray." The song topped black music charts and reached the pop top ten.

Troubled by Substance Abuse

Womack grieved for his lost brother, yet his grief was compounded by the loss of two of his sons: his four-month-old son Truth died in his crib in 1978 and later another son committed suicide. Womack fought against his own depression. He struggled with drug and alcohol abuse, and after the failure of his country album *BW Goes C&W* in 1976, his productivity and his commercial fortunes declined. Womack continued to work, however. He recorded several albums for the Columbia and Arista labels in the late 1970s, with limited success. In 1980 he contributed vocals to "Inherit the Wind," a release by Wilton Felder of the jazz group the Crusaders.

Despite a reputation as a party animal who could be difficult to work with, Womack was recognized for his talents by industry insiders even during the low points in his career. In 1981 he signed with the independent Beverly Glen label in Los Angeles and released one of his most critically acclaimed albums, *The Poet.* He followed it up with *The Poet II* despite wrangling with Beverly Glen over payments, and the two albums became major successes in the United Kingdom and made Womack a star there. Womack signed with MCA in 1985 and released several successful singles, including "I Wish He Didn't Trust Me So Much" and "Let Me Kiss It Where It Hurts." He joined the Rolling Stones in 1986 to sing a duet with Mick Jagger on "Harlem Shuffle."

Although African-American music had been affected by synthesizer-pop trends in the 1980s, Womack unapologetically stuck with classic soul styles through a series of albums on the MCA label. His voice, noted Phil Johnson, had distinctive "pitted, sandpaper textures," and his singing, interspersed with spoken interjections, drew heavily on his gospel roots. Womack's periodic tours remained strong draws in both America and the United Kingdom, and he continued to release new recordings occasionally; 1994's *Resurrection*, recorded for the Slide label headed by Rolling Stones member Ron Wood, referred to some of the singer's personal tragedies. He returned with the gospel collection *Back to My Roots* in 1999 and *Left Handed, Upside Down* in 2001. Although hip-hop starts frequently sampled the soul music of Womack's era, Womack resisted many of their attempts to use his own music. "Me being from the old school, I would not say 'bitch' on a record," he pointed out to Johnson. "I couldn't face my mother if I did." Still performing in the mid-2000s, Womack had seen much of his earlier work reissued in CD compilations.

Selected discography

Albums

Fly Me to the Moon, Minit, 1968.
How I Miss You, Baby, Minit, 1969.
More Than I Can Stand, Minit, 1970.
That's The Way I Feel about You, United Artists, 1971.
Communication, United Artists, 1971.
Understanding, United Artists, 1972.
A Woman's Got To Have It, United Artists, 1972.
Sweet Caroline, United Artists, 1972.
Harry Hippie, United Artists, 1972.
Facts of Life, United Artists, 1973.
Across 110th Street (film soundtrack), United Artists, 1973.
Nobody Wants You When You're Down and Out, United Artists, 1973.
Lookin' for a Love, United Artists, 1974.
Bobby Womack's Greatest Hits, United Artists, 1974.
You're Welcome, Stop on By, United Artists, 1974.
Check It Out, United Artists, 1975.
BW Goes C & W, United Artists, 1976.

Safety Zone, United Artists, 1976.
Home Is Where the Heart Is, CBS, 1976.
Pieces, CBS, 1977.
Roads of Life, Arista, 1979.
The Poet, Beverly Glen, 1981.
The Poet II, MCA, 1984.
Bobby Womack and the Valentinos, Beverly Glen, 1984.
So Many Rivers, MCA, 1985.
Womagic, MCA, 1986.
Soul Survivor, EMI America, 1987.
The Last Soul Man, MCA, 1988.
Greatest Hits of Bobby Womack, Liberty, 1989.
Save the Children, Epic, 1990.
Resurrection, Slide, 1994.
Only Survivor: The MCA Years, MCA, 1996.
Back to My Roots, 1999.
The Best of "The Poet" Trilogy, Empire Music, 2001.
Left Handed, Upside Down, 2001.
Ultimate Collection, Charly, 2001.
Best of Bobby Womack, Collectables, 2003.
Lookin' for a Love: The Best of Bobby Womack 1968-1976, EMI, 2003.
The Preacher, 2004.
The Definitive Collection, Mastercuts, 2006.

Sources

Books

Contemporary Musicians, volume 5, Gale, 1991.
Stambler, Irwin, *Encyclopedia of Pop, Rock & Soul,* St. Martin's, 1989.

Periodicals

Birmingham Post (Birmingham, England), May 27, 2004, p. 14.
Boston Herald, September 20, 2001, p. 64.
Independent on Sunday (London, England), June 6, 2004, p. 10.
Jet, September 12, 1994, p. 17; November 28, 1994, p. 23.
Plain Dealer (Cleveland, OH), August 23, 1999, p. E1.

On-line

"Bobby Womack," *All Music Guide,* www.allmusic.com (March 17, 2007).

—James M. Manheim

Antoinette Wright

195(?)—

Museum administrator

In the late 1980s, Antoinette Wright combined her study of business management with an interest in history and the arts to become one of the few African American museum administrators. By 1990, she was able to combine her museum work with a deep commitment to preserving the history and accomplishments of her own people as deputy director of Chicago's DuSable Museum of African American History. In 1997, she became president and chief executive officer of the museum, a position from which she would guide the institution through an exciting period of expansion and growth.

Born in Chicago, Illinois, during the 1950s, Wright grew up on the city's South Side where her family operated a shop called Her Vel's Unlimited Ceramics, Arts, and Crafts. Working in the family business, Wright began to develop a lifelong interest in art, mythology, and history. She also loved math and earned extra money as an algebra tutor in high school.

Wright attended both DePaul University and Mundelein College in Chicago, earning her bachelor's degree in business administration from Mundelein in 1989. During the mid-1980s, she worked at an accounting firm that had close ties with both the civil rights organization Operation PUSH (People United to Serve Humanity), and with the office of Harold Washington, who, in 1983, had become the first African American mayor of Chicago.

Wright continued her studies at the Kellogg School of Nonprofit Management at Chicago's Northwestern University. She was awarded an Arts Administration Fellowship by Arts Midwest, a Minneapolis-based organization whose purpose is to support artists and the arts in communities throughout the Midwestern states. Arts Midwest's Arts Administration Fellowship is a scholarship program that provides grants for study and internship programs with the goal of encouraging people of color to enter the field of art and museum administration.

While an Arts Administration Fellow, Wright began learning the fundamentals of museum management by working at the Columbus Museum of Art and the Cincinnati Museum of Natural History, both in Ohio. In 1990, she was hired as deputy director of the DuSable Museum of African American History, where she brought her management skills to the nation's oldest institution for the preservation and study of black history.

The DuSable Museum was founded in 1961, as the American civil rights movement was introducing a new pride in black identity and an interest in African American history. A group of artists and educators in Chicago established the Ebony Museum of Negro History and Art in a former boarding house on the city's South Side. In 1968, the name of the museum was changed to honor Jean Baptiste Pointe DuSable, a mixed race explorer who had been the first permanent settler in the area that would become the city of Chicago. Born in Haiti, DuSable had been the son of a white French father and a black Haitian mother, and the administrators of the museum wished to acknowledge their city's African roots. In 1971, the museum

At a Glance . . .

Born Antoinette D. Wright in 195? in Chicago, IL; *Education:* Mundelein College, BA, business administration, 1989.

Career: DuSable Museum of African American History, deputy director, 1990-93; Donors Forum of Chicago, director of finance and administration, 1993-97; DuSable Museum of African American History, president and chief executive officer, 2005–.

Selected memberships: Association of African American Museums, board of directors; After School Matters, board of directors; Economic Club; American Association of Museums; Illinois Association of Museum.

Selected awards: Phenomenal Woman Award, 2004.

Addresses: *Office*—DuSable Museum, 740 E 56th Pl, Chicago, IL 60637.

achieved its first expansion when the Chicago park department donated an unused building in the city's Washington Park for use by the DuSable.

Antoinette Wright worked as deputy director of the DuSable Museum for three years, then left to take a job with the Donors Forum of Chicago. The Donors Forum is a nonprofit group that aims to connect grantmaking organizations and individual donors with advisors. The goal of the forum is to promote diversity by helping those who wish to donate money direct grants towards the communities that need them the most. Wright directed the Forum's financial operations and coordinated the organization's membership from 1993 through 1997. During that time, she developed her management skills and her business vision by supervising the handling of a $45.9 million Chicago Annenberg Challenge Grant, a five-year matching grant which had been awarded to the Chicago public school system.

In 1997, Wright returned to the DuSable Museum, this time to take the job of president and chief executive officer. The museum was in somewhat unstable financial condition, and Wright devoted her skills and energy to improving the business side of the institution. "We pulled in the reins," she told *Chicago* magazine interviewer Shia Kapos in February 2006, describing how, under her leadership, the museum streamlined its operations and increased fundraising. In fewer than 10 years, the museum had doubled its annual budget.

Part of Wright's leadership philosophy for the DuSable Museum has included bringing the community into closer contact with the museum by organizing large fundraising events that invited citizen participation, such as the Annual Arts and Crafts Festival. She has also helped initiate and plan large public events that dramatize the importance of African American history, such as a celebration to welcome the Freedom Schooner Amistad to Chicago's Navy Pier in 2003. The Freedom Schooner is a recreation of the famous slave ship that was the scene of a historic slave rebellion in 1839. Wright has also developed partnerships with other organizations and businesses to promote black history awareness, such as an African American Inventors calendar published by the museum in conjunction with Chandler-White Publishing. In 2005, Wright began to guide the DuSable through its most ambitious venture yet—a $25 million expansion project to enlarge and develop the museum. The new, expanded DuSable Museum is expected to be complete in 2007.

In 2003, an event occurred that brought tremendous satisfaction to those, like Antoinette Wright, who have worked to emphasize the importance of African American history. That year, Congress authorized the construction of a National Museum of African American History and Culture, to be built on the national mall in Washington, D.C., Wright spoke with Danielle Dawkins on the *Black College View* Web site about the importance of the new museum, which is scheduled for completion in 2013:

"When the DuSable Museum was founded, 45 years ago, we were the first and only museum telling the stories of African-Americans. Now, there are more than 100 African-American history museums around the country. The more our stories are told, the longer they will stay alive.... There is an African Proverb, which states, 'Until the lion writes his own story, the tale will always glorify the hunter.'"

Sources

Periodicals

Ebony, February 2005, p. 12.
Jet, October 1, 2001, p. 24; January 13, 2003, p. 20; August 18, 2003, p. 32.
Chicago, February 2006, p. 2.
Chicago Defender, July 15, 2003, p. 9; March 10, 2004, p. 15.
Chicago Weekend, October 10, 2002, p. 3.
Westside Gazette (Ft. Lauderdale, FL), December 31, 2003, p. 6B.

On-line

"African-American History at the Smithsonian," *Black College View,* http://media.www.blackcollegeview.

com/media/storage/paper928/news/2006/01/
30/NationalAndInternational/AfricanAmerican.His-
tory.At.The.Smithsonian-2473286.shtml (January
26, 2007).

"Antoinette D. Wright," *Biography Resource Center*,
http://galenet.galegroup.com/servlet/BioRC
(March 20, 2007).

DuSable Museum of African American History,
www.dusablemuseum.org/ (January 26, 2007).

"Antoinette Wright." *Women's Networking Community,* www.womensnetworkingcommunity.org/html
/2005_dinner_speakers/wright05_bio.htm (January
26, 2007).

"Museum to Grow in 2007," *Hyde Park Herald,*
www.hydepark.org/historicpres/histpresindepth.
htm (January 26, 2007).

"Who's Who in Cultural Institutions," *Chicago Business,* http://chicagobusiness.com/cgi-bin/article.pl?
portal_id=155&page_id=1784 (January 26, 2007).

—Tina Gianoulis

Cumulative Nationality Index

Volume numbers appear in **bold**

American

Aaliyah **30**
Aaron, Hank **5**
Abbott, Robert Sengstacke **27**
Abdul-Jabbar, Kareem **8**
Abdur-Rahim, Shareef **28**
Abele, Julian **55**
Abernathy, Ralph David **1**
Abu-Jamal, Mumia **15**
Ace, Johnny **36**
Adams Earley, Charity **13, 34**
Adams, Eula L. **39**
Adams, Floyd, Jr. **12**
Adams, Jenoyne **60**
Adams, Johnny **39**
Adams, Leslie **39**
Adams, Oleta **18**
Adams, Osceola Macarthy **31**
Adams, Sheila J. **25**
Adams, Yolanda **17**
Adams-Campbell, Lucille L. **60**
Adams-Ender, Clara **40**
Adderley, Julian "Cannonball" **30**
Adderley, Nat **29**
Adkins, Rod **41**
Adkins, Rutherford H. **21**
Agyeman, Jaramogi Abebe **10**
Ailey, Alvin **8**
Akil, Mara Brock **60**
Al-Amin, Jamil Abdullah **6**
Albright, Gerald **23**
Alcorn, George Edward, Jr. **59**
Alert, Kool DJ Red **33**
Alexander, Archie Alphonso **14**
Alexander, Clifford **26**
Alexander, Joyce London **18**
Alexander, Khandi **43**
Alexander, Margaret Walker **22**
Alexander, Sadie Tanner Mossell **22**
Alexander, Shaun **58**
Ali, Hana Yasmeen **52**
Ali, Laila **27**
Ali, Muhammad **2, 16, 52**
Allain, Stephanie **49**
Allen, Byron **3, 24**
Allen, Debbie **13, 42**
Allen, Ethel D. **13**
Allen, Marcus **20**
Allen, Robert L. **38**
Allen, Samuel W. **38**
Allen, Tina **22**
Allen-Buillard, Melba **55**
Alston, Charles **33**

Amerie **52**
Ames, Wilmer **27**
Amos, John **8**
Amos, Wally **9**
Anderson, Anthony **51**
Anderson, Carl **48**
Anderson, Charles Edward **37**
Anderson, Eddie "Rochester" **30**
Anderson, Elmer **25**
Anderson, Jamal **22**
Anderson, Marian **2, 33**
Anderson, Michael P. **40**
Anderson, Norman B. **45**
Anderson, William G(ilchrist), D.O. **57**
Andrews, Benny **22, 59**
Andrews, Bert **13**
Andrews, Raymond **4**
Angelou, Maya **1, 15**
Ansa, Tina McElroy **14**
Anthony, Carmelo **46**
Anthony, Wendell **25**
Archer, Dennis **7, 36**
Archie-Hudson, Marguerite **44**
Arkadie, Kevin **17**
Armstrong, Louis **2**
Armstrong, Robb **15**
Armstrong, Vanessa Bell **24**
Arnez J. **53**
Arnwine, Barbara **28**
Arrington, Richard **24**
Arroyo, Martina **30**
Artest, Ron **52**
Asante, Molefi Kete **3**
Ashanti **37**
Ashe, Arthur **1, 18**
Ashford, Emmett **22**
Ashford, Nickolas **21**
Ashley-Ward, Amelia **23**
Atkins, Cholly **40**
Atkins, Erica **34**
Atkins, Juan **50**
Atkins, Russell **45**
Atkins, Tina **34**
Aubert, Alvin **41**
Auguste, Donna **29**
Austin, Junius C. **44**
Austin, Lovie **40**
Austin, Patti **24**
Avant, Clarence **19**
Ayers, Roy **16**
Babatunde, Obba **35**
Bacon-Bercey, June **38**
Badu, Erykah **22**

Bahati, Wambui **60**
Bailey, Buster **38**
Bailey, Clyde **45**
Bailey, DeFord **33**
Bailey, Radcliffe **19**
Bailey, Xenobia **11**
Baines, Harold **32**
Baiocchi, Regina Harris **41**
Baisden, Michael **25**
Baker, Anita **21, 48**
Baker, Augusta **38**
Baker, Dusty **8, 43**
Baker, Ella **5**
Baker, Gwendolyn Calvert **9**
Baker, Houston A., Jr. **6**
Baker, Josephine **3**
Baker, LaVern **26**
Baker, Maxine B. **28**
Baker, Thurbert **22**
Baldwin, James **1**
Ballance, Frank W. **41**
Ballard, Allen Butler, Jr. **40**
Ballard, Hank **41**
Bambaataa, Afrika **34**
Bambara, Toni Cade **10**
Bandele, Asha **36**
Banks, Ernie **33**
Banks, Jeffrey **17**
Banks, Michelle **59**
Banks, Tyra **11, 50**
Banks, William **11**
Banner, David **55**
Baraka, Amiri **1, 38**
Barber, Ronde **41**
Barber, Tiki **57**
Barboza, Anthony **10**
Barclay, Paris **37**
Barden, Don H. **9, 20**
Barker, Danny **32**
Barkley, Charles **5**
Barlow, Roosevelt **49**
Barnes, Roosevelt "Booba" **33**
Barnes, Steven **54**
Barnett, Amy Du Bois **46**
Barnett, Etta Moten **56**
Barnett, Marguerite **46**
Barney, Lem **26**
Barnhill, David **30**
Barrax, Gerald William **45**
Barrett, Andrew C. **12**
Barrett, Jacquelyn **28**
Barrino, Fantasia **53**
Barry, Marion S(hepilov, Jr.) **7, 44**
Barthe, Richmond **15**

Basie, Count **23**
Basquiat, Jean-Michel **5**
Bass, Charlotta Spears **40**
Bassett, Angela **6, 23**
Bates, Daisy **13**
Bates, Karen Grigsby **40**
Bates, Peg Leg **14**
Bath, Patricia E. **37**
Baugh, David **23**
Baylor, Don **6**
Baylor, Helen **36**
Beach, Michael **26**
Beal, Bernard B. **46**
Beals, Jennifer **12**
Beals, Melba Patillo **15**
Bearden, Romare **2, 50**
Beasley, Jamar **29**
Beasley, Phoebe **34**
Beatty, Talley **35**
Bechet, Sidney **18**
Beckford, Tyson **11**
Beckham, Barry **41**
Belafonte, Harry **4**
Bell, Derrick **6**
Bell, James "Cool Papa" **36**
Bell, James A. **50**
Bell, James Madison **40**
Bell, Michael **40**
Bell, Robert Mack **22**
Bellamy, Bill **12**
Bellamy, Terry **58**
Belle, Albert **10**
Belle, Regina **1, 51**
Belton, Sharon Sayles **9, 16**
Benét, Eric **28**
Ben-Israel, Ben Ami **11**
Benjamin, Andre **45**
Benjamin, Regina **20**
Benjamin, Tritobia Hayes **53**
Bennett, George Harold "Hal" **45**
Bennett, Gwendolyn B. **59**
Bennett, Lerone, Jr. **5**
Benson, Angela **34**
Bentley, Lamont **53**
Berry , Halle **4, 19, 57**
Berry, Bertice **8, 55**
Berry, Chuck **29**
Berry, Fred "Rerun" **48**
Berry, Mary Frances **7**
Berry, Theodore **31**
Berrysmith, Don Reginald **49**
Bethune, Mary McLeod **4**
Betsch, MaVynee **28**
Beverly, Frankie **25**

Lyttle, Hulda Margaret **14**
Mabley, Moms **15**
Mabrey, Vicki **26**
Mac, Bernie **29**
Madhubuti, Haki R. **7**
Madison, Joseph E. **17**
Madison, Paula **37**
Madison, Romell **45**
Mahal, Taj **39**
Mahorn, Rick **60**
Majette, Denise **41**
Major, Clarence **9**
Majors, Jeff **41**
Mallett, Conrad Jr. **16**
Malone Jones, Vivian **59**
Malone, Annie **13**
Malone, Karl **18**, **51**
Malone, Maurice **32**
Malveaux, Floyd **54**
Malveaux, Julianne **32**
Manigault, Earl "The Goat" **15**
Manley, Audrey Forbes **16**
Marable, Manning **10**
March, William Carrington **56**
Mariner, Jonathan **41**
Marino, Eugene Antonio **30**
Marrow, Queen Esther **24**
Marsalis, Branford **34**
Marsalis, Delfeayo **41**
Marsalis, Wynton **16**
Marsh, Henry, III **32**
Marshall, Bella **22**
Marshall, Kerry James **59**
Marshall, Paule **7**
Marshall, Thurgood **1**, **44**
Martin, Darnell **43**
Martin, Helen **31**
Martin, Jesse L. **31**
Martin, Louis E. **16**
Martin, Roberta **58**
Martin, Roland S. **49**
Martin, Ruby Grant **49**
Martin, Sara **38**
Mase **24**
Mason, Felicia **31**
Mason, Ronald **27**
Massaquoi, Hans J. **30**
Massenburg, Kedar **23**
Massey, Brandon **40**
Massey, Walter E. **5**, **45**
Massie, Samuel Proctor Jr. **29**
Master P **21**
Mathis, Greg **26**
Mathis, Johnny **20**
Matthews Shatteen, Westina **51**
Matthews, Mark **59**
Maxey, Randall **46**
Maxwell **20**
May, Derrick **41**
Mayfield, Curtis **2**, **43**
Mayhew, Richard **39**
Maynard, Robert C. **7**
Maynor, Dorothy **19**
Mayo, Whitman **32**
Mays, Benjamin E. **7**
Mays, Leslie A. **41**
Mays, William G. **34**
Mays, Willie **3**
Mayweather, Floyd, Jr. **57**
MC Lyte **34**
McBride, Bryant **18**
McBride, James C. **35**
McCabe, Jewell Jackson **10**

McCall, H. Carl **27**
McCall, Nathan **8**
McCann, Renetta **44**
McCarty, Osceola **16**
McClurkin, Donnie **25**
McCoo, Marilyn **53**
McCoy, Elijah **8**
McCray, Nikki **18**
McCullough, Geraldine **58**
McDaniel, Hattie **5**
McDonald, Audra **20**
McDonald, Erroll **1**
McDonald, Gabrielle Kirk **20**
McDougall, Gay J. **11**, **43**
McEwen, Mark **5**
McFadden, Bernice L. **39**
McFarlan, Tyron **60**
McFarland, Roland **49**
McGee, Charles **10**
McGee, James Madison **46**
McGriff, Fred **24**
McGruder, Aaron **28**, **56**
McGruder, Robert **22**, **35**
McGuire, Raymond J. **57**
McKay, Claude **6**
McKay, Nellie Yvonne **17**, **57**
Mckee, Lonette **12**
McKenzie, Vashti M. **29**
McKinney, Cynthia Ann **11**, **52**
McKinney, Nina Mae **40**
McKinney-Whetstone, Diane **27**
McKinnon, Isaiah **9**
McKissick, Floyd B. **3**
McKnight, Brian **18**, **34**
McLeod, Gus **27**
McMillan, Rosaylnn A. **36**
McMillan, Terry **4**, **17**, **53**
McMurray, Georgia L. **36**
McNabb, Donovan **29**
McNair, Ronald **3**, **58**
McNair, Steve **22**, **47**
McNeil, Lori **1**
McPhail, Sharon **2**
McPherson, David **32**
McQueen, Butterfly **6**, **54**
McWhorter, John **35**
Meadows, Tim **30**
Meek, Carrie **6**, **36**
Meek, Kendrick **41**
Meeks, Gregory **25**
Mell, Patricia **49**
Memphis Minnie **33**
Mercado-Valdes, Frank **43**
Meredith, James H. **11**
Merkerson, S. Epatha **47**
Metcalfe, Ralph **26**
Mfume, Kweisi **6**, **41**
Micheaux, Oscar **7**
Michele, Michael **31**
Mickelbury, Penny **28**
Millender-McDonald, Juanita **21**
Miller, Bebe **3**
Miller, Cheryl **10**
Miller, Dorie **29**
Miller, Reggie **33**
Miller, Warren F., Jr. **53**
Millines Dziko, Trish **28**
Mills, Florence **22**
Mills, Joseph C. **51**
Mills, Sam **33**
Mills, Stephanie **36**
Mills, Steve **47**
Milner, Ron **39**

Milton, DeLisha **31**
Mingo, Frank **32**
Mingus, Charles **15**
Minor, DeWayne **32**
Mitchell, Arthur **2**, **47**
Mitchell, Brian Stokes **21**
Mitchell, Corinne **8**
Mitchell, Leona **42**
Mitchell, Loften **31**
Mitchell, Parren J. **42**
Mitchell, Russ **21**
Mitchell, Stephanie **36**
Mo', Keb' **36**
Mo'Nique **35**
Mohammed, W. Deen **27**
Monica **21**
Monk, Art **38**
Monk, Thelonious **1**
Monroe, Mary **35**
Montgomery, Tim **41**
Moon, Warren **8**
Mooney, Paul **37**
Moore, Barbara C. **49**
Moore, Chante **26**
Moore, Dorothy Rudd **46**
Moore, Gwendolynne S. **55**
Moore, Harry T. **29**
Moore, Jessica Care **30**
Moore, Johnny B. **38**
Moore, Melba **21**
Moore, Minyon **45**
Moore, Shemar **21**
Moore, Undine Smith **28**
Moorer, Michael **19**
Moose, Charles **40**
Morgan, Garrett **1**
Morgan, Joe Leonard **9**
Morgan, Rose **11**
Morial, Ernest "Dutch" **26**
Morial, Marc H. **20**, **51**
Morris, Garrett **31**
Morris, Greg **28**
Morrison, Sam **50**
Morrison, Toni **2**, **15**
Morton, Azie Taylor **48**
Morton, Jelly Roll **29**
Morton, Joe **18**
Mos Def **30**
Moses, Edwin **8**
Moses, Gilbert **12**
Moses, Robert Parris **11**
Mosley, Shane **32**
Mosley, Walter **5**, **25**
Moss, Carlton **17**
Moss, Randy **23**
Mossell, Gertrude Bustill **40**
Moten, Etta **18**
Motley, Archibald Jr. **30**
Motley, Constance Baker **10**, **55**
Motley, Marion **26**
Mourning, Alonzo **17**, **44**
Moutoussamy-Ashe, Jeanne **7**
Mowry, Jess **7**
Moyo, Karega Kofi **36**
Moyo, Yvette Jackson **36**
Muhammad, Ava **35**
Muhammad, Elijah **4**
Muhammad, Khallid Abdul **10**, **31**
Mullen, Harryette **34**
Mullen, Nicole C. **45**
Murphy, Eddie **4**, **20**
Murphy, John H. **42**
Murphy, Laura M. **43**

Murray, Albert L. **33**
Murray, Cecil **12**, **47**
Murray, Eddie **12**
Murray, Lenda **10**
Murray, Pauli **38**
Murray, Tai **47**
Murrell, Sylvia Marilyn **49**
Muse, Clarence Edouard **21**
Musiq **37**
Mya **35**
Myers, Walter Dean **8**
Nabrit, Samuel Milton **47**
Nagin, C. Ray **42**, **57**
Nanula, Richard D. **20**
Napoleon, Benny N. **23**
Nas **33**
Nash, Joe **55**
Nash, Johnny **40**
Naylor, Gloria **10**, **42**
Ndegéocello, Me'Shell **15**
Neal, Elise **29**
Neal, Larry **38**
Neal, Raful **44**
Nelly **32**
Nelson Meigs, Andrea **48**
Nelson, Jill **6**, **54**
Neville, Aaron **21**
Neville, Arthel **53**
Newcombe, Don **24**
Newman, Lester C. **51**
Newsome, Ozzie **26**
Newton, Huey **2**
Nicholas, Fayard **20**, **57**
Nicholas, Harold **20**
Nichols, Nichelle **11**
Nissel, Angela **42**
Nix, Robert N.C., Jr. **51**
N'Namdi, George R. **17**
Noble, Ronald **46**
Norman, Christina **47**
Norman, Jessye **5**
Norman, Maidie **20**
Norman, Pat **10**
Norton, Eleanor Holmes **7**
Notorious B.I.G. **20**
Nugent, Richard Bruce **39**
Nunn, Annetta **43**
O'Leary, Hazel **6**
O'Neal, Ron **46**
O'Neal, Shaquille **8**, **30**
O'Neal, Stanley **38**
O'Neil, Buck **19**, **59**
Obama, Barack **49**
Odetta **37**
Oglesby, Zena **12**
Ogletree, Charles, Jr. **12**, **47**
Ol' Dirty Bastard **52**
Olden, Georg(e) **44**
Oliver, Jerry **37**
Oliver, Joe "King" **42**
Oliver, John J., Jr. **48**
Oliver, Kimberly **60**
Oliver, Pam **54**
Onyewu, Oguchi **60**
Orlandersmith, Dael **42**
Orman, Roscoe **55**
Osborne, Jeffrey **26**
Osborne, Na'taki **54**
Otis, Clarence, Jr. **55**
Owens, Helen **48**
Owens, Jack **38**
Owens, Jesse **2**
Owens, Major **6**

Cumulative Occupation Index

Volume numbers appear in **bold**

Art and design

Abele, Julian **55**
Adjaye, David **38**
Allen, Tina **22**
Alston, Charles **33**
Anderson, Ho Che **54**
Andrews, Benny **22, 59**
Andrews, Bert **13**
Armstrong, Robb **15**
Bailey, Radcliffe **19**
Bailey, Xenobia **11**
Barboza, Anthony **10**
Barnes, Ernie **16**
Barthe, Richmond **15**
Basquiat, Jean-Michel **5**
Bearden, Romare **2, 50**
Beasley, Phoebe **34**
Benjamin, Tritobia Hayes **53**
Biggers, John **20, 33**
Blacknurn, Robert **28**
Brandon, Barbara **3**
Brown, Donald **19**
Burke, Selma **16**
Burroughs, Margaret Taylor **9**
Camp, Kimberly **19**
Campbell, E. Simms **13**
Campbell, Mary Schmidt **43**
Catlett, Elizabeth **2**
Chase-Riboud, Barbara **20, 46**
Cortor, Eldzier **42**
Cowans, Adger W. **20**
Crite, Alan Rohan **29**
De Veaux, Alexis **44**
DeCarava, Roy **42**
Delaney, Beauford **19**
Delaney, Joseph **30**
Delsarte, Louis **34**
Donaldson, Jeff **46**
Douglas, Aaron **7**
Driskell, David C. **7**
Edwards, Melvin **22**
El Wilson, Barbara **35**
Ewing, Patrick A.**17**
Fax, Elton **48**
Feelings, Tom **11, 47**
Fine, Sam **60**
Freeman, Leonard **27**
Fuller, Meta Vaux Warrick **27**
Gantt, Harvey **1**
Gilliam, Sam **16**
Golden, Thelma **10, 55**
Goodnight, Paul **32**
Green, Jonathan **54**

Guyton, Tyree **9**
Harkless, Necia Desiree **19**
Harrington, Oliver W. **9**
Hathaway, Isaac Scott **33**
Hayden, Palmer **13**
Hayes, Cecil N. **46**
Honeywood, Varnette P. **54**
Hope, John **8**
Hudson, Cheryl **15**
Hudson, Wade **15**
Hunt, Richard **6**
Hunter, Clementine **45**
Hutson, Jean Blackwell **16**
Jackson, Earl **31**
Jackson, Vera **40**
John, Daymond **23**
Johnson, Jeh Vincent **44**
Johnson, William Henry **3**
Jones, Lois Mailou **13**
King, Robert Arthur **58**
Kitt, Sandra **23**
Knox, Simmie **49**
Lawrence, Jacob **4, 28**
Lee, Annie Francis **22**
Lee-Smith, Hughie **5, 22**
Lewis, Edmonia **10**
Lewis, Norman **39**
Lewis, Samella **25**
Loving, Alvin, Jr., **35, 53**
Manley, Edna **26**
Marshall, Kerry James **59**
Mayhew, Richard **39**
McCullough, Geraldine **58**
McGee, Charles **10**
McGruder, Aaron **28, 56**
Mitchell, Corinne **8**
Moody, Ronald **30**
Morrison, Keith **13**
Motley, Archibald Jr. **30**
Moutoussamy-Ashe, Jeanne **7**
Mutu, Wangechi **44**
N'Namdi, George R. **17**
Nugent, Richard Bruce **39**
Olden, Georg(e) **44**
Ouattara **43**
Perkins, Marion **38**
Pierre, Andre **17**
Pindell, Howardena **55**
Pinderhughes, John **47**
Pinkney, Jerry **15**
Pippin, Horace **9**
Porter, James A. **11**
Prophet, Nancy Elizabeth **42**
Puryear, Martin **42**

Reid, Senghor **55**
Ringgold, Faith **4**
Ruley, Ellis **38**
Saar, Alison **16**
Saint James, Synthia **12**
Sallee, Charles **38**
Sanders, Joseph R., Jr. **11**
Savage, Augusta **12**
Sebree, Charles **40**
Serrano, Andres **3**
Shabazz, Attallah **6**
Shonibare, Yinka **58**
Simmons, Gary **58**
Simpson, Lorna **4, 36**
Sims, Lowery Stokes **27**
Sklarek, Norma Merrick **25**
Sleet, Moneta, Jr. **5**
Smith, Bruce W. **53**
Smith, Marvin **46**
Smith, Morgan **46**
Smith, Vincent D. **48**
Steave-Dickerson, Kia **57**
Tanksley, Ann **37**
Tanner, Henry Ossawa **1**
Thomas, Alma **14**
Thrash, Dox **35**
Tolliver, Mose **60**
Tolliver, William **9**
VanDerZee, James **6**
Wainwright, Joscelyn **46**
Walker, A'lelia **14**
Walker, Kara **16**
Washington, Alonzo **29**
Washington, James, Jr. **38**
Wells, James Lesesne **10**
White, Charles **39**
White, Dondi **34**
White, John H. **27**
Williams, Billy Dee **8**
Williams, O. S. **13**
Williams, Paul R. **9**
Williams, William T. **11**
Wilson, Ellis **39**
Woodruff, Hale **9**

Business

Abbot, Robert Sengstacke **27**
Abdul-Jabbar, Kareem **8**
Adams, Eula L. **39**
Adams, Jenoyne **60**
Adkins, Rod **41**
Ailey, Alvin **8**
Akil, Mara Brock **60**
Al-Amin, Jamil Abdullah **6**

Alexander, Archie Alphonso **14**
Allen, Byron **24**
Allen-Buillard, Melba **55**
Ames, Wilmer **27**
Amos, Wally **9**
Auguste, Donna **29**
Avant, Clarence **19**
Baker, Dusty **8, 43**
Baker, Ella **5**
Baker, Gwendolyn Calvert **9**
Baker, Maxine **28**
Banks, Jeffrey **17**
Banks, William **11**
Barden, Don H. **9, 20**
Barrett, Andrew C. **12**
Beal, Bernard B. **46**
Beamon, Bob **30**
Beasley, Phoebe **34**
Bell, James A. **50**
Bennett, Lerone, Jr. **5**
Bing, Dave **3, 59**
Blackshear, Leonard **52**
Blackwell Sr., Robert D. **52**
Blayton, Jesse B., Sr. **55**
Bolden, Frank E. **44**
Borders, James **9**
Boston, Kelvin E. **25**
Boston, Lloyd **24**
Boyd, Gwendolyn **49**
Boyd, John W., Jr. **20**
Boyd, T. B., III **6**
Bradley, Jennette B. **40**
Bridges, Shelia **36**
Bridgforth, Glinda **36**
Brimmer, Andrew F. **2, 48**
Bronner, Nathaniel H., Sr. **32**
Brown, Eddie C. **35**
Brown, Les **5**
Brown, Marie Dutton **12**
Brunson, Dorothy **1**
Bryant, John **26**
Burgess, Marjorie L. **55**
Burns, Ursula **60**
Burrell, Tom **21, 51**
Burroughs, Margaret Taylor **9**
Burrus, William Henry "Bill" **45**
Burt-Murray, Angela **59**
Busby, Jheryl **3**
Cain, Herman **15**
Caldwell, Earl **60**
CasSelle, Malcolm **11**
Chamberlain, Wilt **18, 47**
Chapman, Nathan A. Jr. **21**
Chappell, Emma **18**

Cumulative Subject Index

Volume numbers appear in **bold**

Washington, Patrice Clarke 12

United Parcel Service Foundation
Cooper, Evern 40

United Somali Congress (USC)
Ali Mahdi Mohamed 5

United States Delegations
Shabazz, Ilyasah 36

United States Football (USFL)
White, Reggie 6, 50
Williams, Doug 22

United Way
Donald, Arnold Wayne 36
Steward, David L. 36

United Workers Union of South Africa (UWUSA)
Buthelezi, Mangosuthu Gatsha 9

Universal Foundation for Better Living (UFBL)
Colemon, Johnnie 11
Reese, Della 6, 20

University of Alabama
Davis, Mike 41
Lucy Foster, Autherine 35

University of California Berkeley
Drummond, William J. 40
Edley, Christopher F., Jr. 48

Univeristy of Cape Town
Ramphele, Maphela 29

University of Colorado administration
Berry, Mary Frances 7

University of Delaware's Center for Counseling and Student Development
Mitchell, Sharon 36

University of Florida
Haskins, James 36, 54

University of Michigan
Dillard, Godfrey J. 45
Goss, Tom 23
Gray, Ida 41
Imes, Elmer Samuel 39

University of Missouri
Floyd, Elson S. 41

University of Michigan
Fuller, A. Oveta 43

University of North Carolina
Floyd, Elson S. 41

University of Texas
Granville, Evelyn Boyd 36

University of the West Indies
Brathwaite, Kamau 36
Hill, Errol 40

University of Virginia
Littlepage, Craig 35

UniverSoul Circus
Walker, Cedric "Ricky" 19

Upscale magazine
Bronner, Nathaniel H., Sr. 32

Uptown Music Theater
Marsalis, Delfeayo 41

Urban Bush Women
Zollar, Jawole 28

Urbancrest, Ohio, government
Craig-Jones, Ellen Walker 44

Urban League (regional)
Adams, Sheila J. 25
Clayton, Xernona 3, 45
Jacob, John E. 2
Mays, Benjamin E. 7
Young, Whitney M., Jr. 4

Urban renewal
Archer, Dennis 7, 36
Barry, Marion S. 7, 44
Bosley, Freeman, Jr. 7
Collins, Barbara-Rose 7
Harris, Alice 7
Lane, Vincent 5
Waters, Maxine 3

Urban theater
Perry, Tyler 40, 54

US
Karenga, Maulana 10

U.S. Air Force
Anderson, Michael P. 40
Carter, Joye Maureen 41
Davis, Benjamin O., Jr. 2, 43
Gregory, Frederick 8, 51
Harris, Marcelite Jordan 16
James, Daniel, Jr. 16
Johnson, Lonnie 32
Jones, Wayne 53
Lyles, Lester 31

U.S. Armed Forces Nurse Corps
Staupers, Mabel K. 7

U.S. Army
Adams-Ender, Clara 40
Cadoria, Sherian Grace 14
Clemmons, Reginal G. 41
Davis, Benjamin O., Sr. 4
Delany, Martin R. 27
Flipper, Henry O. 3
Greenhouse, Bunnatine "Bunny" 57
Jackson, Fred James 25
Johnson, Hazel 22
Johnson, Shoshana 47
Matthews, Mark 59
Powell, Colin 1, 28
Stanford, John 20
Watkins, Perry 12
West, Togo D., Jr. 16

U.S. Army Air Corps
Anderson, Charles Edward 37

U.S. Atomic Energy Commission
Nabrit, Samuel Milton 47

U.S. Attorney's Office
Lafontant, Jewel Stradford 3, 51

U.S. Basketball League (USBL)
Lucas, John 7

USBL
See U.S. Basketball League

USC
See United Somali Congress

U.S. Cabinet
Brown, Ron 5
Elders, Joycelyn 6
Espy, Mike 6
Harris, Patricia Roberts 2
Herman, Alexis M. 15
O'Leary, Hazel 6
Powell, Colin 1, 28
Rice, Condoleezza 3, 28
Slater, Rodney E. 15
Sullivan, Louis 8
Weaver, Robert C. 8, 46

U.S. Circuit Court of Appeals
Hastie, William H. 8
Keith, Damon J. 16

U.S. Coast Guard
Brown, Erroll M. 23

U.S. Commission on Civil Rights
Berry, Mary Frances 7
Edley, Christopher 2, 48

U.S. Conference of Catholic Bishops
Gregory, Wilton D. 37

U.S. Court of Appeals
Higginbotham, A. Leon, Jr. 13, 25
Kearse, Amalya Lyle 12
Ogunlesi, Adebayo 37

USDA
See U.S. Department of Agriculture

U.S. Department of Agriculture (USDA)
Espy, Mike 6
Vaughn, Gladys Gary 47
Watkins, Shirley R. 17
Williams, Hosea Lorenzo 15, 31

U.S. Department of Commerce
Brown, Ron 5
Irving, Larry, Jr. 12
Person, Waverly 9, 51
Shavers, Cheryl 31
Wilkins, Roger 2

U.S. Department of Defense
Greenhouse, Bunnatine "Bunny" 57
Tribble, Israel, Jr. 8

U.S. Department of Education
Hill, Anita 5
Hill, Bonnie Guiton 20
Paige, Rod 29
Purnell, Silas 59
Thomas, Clarence 2, 39
Tribble, Israel, Jr. 8

Velez-Rodriguez, Argelia 56

U.S. Department of Energy
O'Leary, Hazel 6

U.S. Department of Health and Human Services (HHS)
See also U.S. Department of Health, Education, and Welfare
Gaston, Marilyn Hughes 60

U.S. Department of Health, Education, and Welfare (HEW)
Bell, Derrick 6
Berry, Mary Frances 7
Harris, Patricia Roberts 2
Johnson, Eddie Bernice 8
Randolph, Linda A. 52
Sullivan, Louis 8

U.S. Department of Housing and Urban Development (HUD)
Gaines, Brenda 41
Harris, Patricia Roberts 2
Jackson, Alphonso R. 48
Weaver, Robert C. 8, 46

U.S. Department of Justice
Bell, Derrick 6
Campbell, Bill 9
Days, Drew S., III 10
Guinier, Lani 7, 30
Holder, Eric H., Jr. 9
Lafontant, Jewel Stradford 3, 51
Lewis, Delano 7
Patrick, Deval 12
Payton, John 48
Thompson, Larry D. 39
Wilkins, Roger 2

U.S. Department of Labor
Crockett, George, Jr. 10
Herman, Alexis M. 15

U.S. Department of Social Services
Little, Robert L. 2

U.S. Department of State
Bethune, Mary McLeod 4
Bunche, Ralph J. 5
Keyes, Alan L. 11
Lafontant, Jewel Stradford 3, 51
Perkins, Edward 5
Powell, Colin 1, 28
Rice, Condoleezza 3, 28
Wharton, Clifton Reginald, Sr. 36
Wharton, Clifton R., Jr. 7

U.S. Department of the Interior
Person, Waverly 9, 51

U.S. Department of Transportation
Davis, Benjamin O., Jr. 2, 43

U.S. Department of Veterans Affairs
Brown, Jesse 6, 41

U.S. Diplomatic Corps
Garrett, Joyce Finley 59
Grimké, Archibald H. 9
Haley, George Williford Boyce 21
Harris, Patricia Roberts 2

Cumulative Name Index

Volume numbers appear in **bold**